THE EVOLUTION OF *HOMO ERECTUS*
COMPARATIVE ANATOMICAL STUDIES OF
AN EXTINCT HUMAN SPECIES

THE EVOLUTION
OF *HOMO ERECTUS*
COMPARATIVE ANATOMICAL STUDIES
OF AN EXTINCT
HUMAN SPECIES

G. Philip Rightmire

Department of Anthropology
State University of New York at Binghamton

CAMBRIDGE
UNIVERSITY PRESS

Published by the Press Syndicate of the University of Cambridge
The Pitt Building, Trumpington Street, Cambridge CB2 1RP
40 West 20th Street, New York NY 10011-4211, USA
10 Stamford Road, Oakleigh, Melbourne 3166, Australia

First published 1990
First paperback edition 1993

Printed in Great Britain at the University Press, Cambridge

British Library cataloguing in publication data
Rightmire, G. Philip
The evolution of *Homo erectus*.
1. Homo erectus
I. Title
573′.3

Library of Congress cataloguing in publication data
Rightmire, G. Philip.
The evolution of Homo erectus: comparative anatomical studies on
an extinct human species / G. Philip Rightmire.
p.   cm.
Includes bibliographical references.
ISBN 0 521 30880 1 (hbk)   ISBN 0 521 44998 7 (pbk)
1. Pithecanthropus erectus.   I. Title.
GN284.R54   1990
573.3—dc20   89-70814   CIP

ISBN 0 521 30880 1 hardback
ISBN 0 521 44998 7 paperback

EA

CONTENTS

PREFACE

My enthusiasm for *Homo erectus* dates from 1977, when I began the task of preparing anatomical descriptions for several of the crania from Olduvai Gorge. After working on the fine braincase from LLK in Bed II, I decided to review all of the Olduvai fossils that might be representative of the same species. Inevitably, this led to comparisons of the Olduvai crania and jaws with other East African specimens and later with the mandibles from Ternifine in northwest Africa. By 1980, it was clear that the project would go beyond Africa and grow into much more than a monograph on the Olduvai remains. After spending several months in Indonesia in 1981, I reorganized all of the notes that were accumulating, so as to make the Asian record a principal focus of research. Slowly, the book assumed its present outline, in which the famous Java finds are treated first, followed by a systematic survey of all the other fossils attributed to *Homo erectus*. The Middle Pleistocene material from Europe will be conspicuous by its absence. The complete cranium from Petralona and the Arago specimens are not included in my roster of *Homo erectus*, but I have brought them into a later part of my discussion, along with other Middle Pleistocene hominids from Africa. To this extent, the book tracks the transition from *Homo erectus* to a more advanced form of human. How this change occurred is certainly one of the more challenging questions facing paleoanthropologists.

A good deal of my text is devoted to anatomy, and there are many references to facial architecture, vault shape, and prominences or tori of the lower jaw. These parts of the *Homo erectus* skeleton have most often turned up as fossils, and they provide the basis for comparative study. Only by interpreting the bones can we learn enough about these extinct hominids to document their evolutionary history. An unavoidable consequence of this emphasis on details of form is that parts of the book will be heavy going. I have tried to make the material clear and concise, but readers will benefit from prior experience with basic human structure. This is not a text for introductory classes. Nevertheless, it should be useful to more advanced students and to others concerned with the hard evidence for human evolution.

Without the generous assistance of friends and colleagues, I would never have been able to complete this project. Many have helped, over the span of more than a decade. Mary Leakey encouraged me to undertake the initial studies of the Olduvai fossils. Richard Leakey gave me access to important specimens and provided laboratory facilities in the Kenya National Museums. I am grateful for this support in Nairobi and for opportunities to visit Koobi Fora and sites elsewhere in the Turkana basin. Emma Mbua and other members of the Museum staff also helped me in Nairobi, as did Andrew Hill, Louis Jacobs, Martin Pickford, Karen Bell and Hazel Potgeiter. The government of Kenya gave me clearance to carry out my research program.

In Dar es Salaam, Fidel Masao welcomed me at the National Museums of Tanzania. Officers of the Division of Antiquities and members of the faculty of the University of Dar es Salaam assisted me on several occasions, and I thank particularly A.A. Mturi, S. Waane and C.C. Magori. The government of Tanzania allowed me to study the Olduvai remains and the cranium from Lake Ndutu.

For access to the Swartkrans hominids and help at the Transvaal Museum, I am grateful to C.K. Brain, Alan Turner, and David Panagos. Permission to work on fossils from Ternifine and sites in Morocco was given by the Institut de Paléontologie of the Muséum National d'Histoire Naturelle, the Institut de Paléontologie Humaine, the Laboratoire de Paléontologie des Vertébrés et Paléontologie Humaine of the Université de Paris VI, and the Musée de l'Homme. Persons in Paris who offered me their time, professional expertise and hospitality include Herbert Thomas, the late J.P. Lehman, V. Eisenmann, Jean-Louis Heim, Jean-Jacques Hublin, Jean-Jacques Jaeger, Anne-Marie Tillier, Yves Coppens and M.

Sakka. Bernard Vandermeersch kindly supplied me with casts of the Ternifine jaws.

My visit to Indonesia was arranged with assistance from Teuku Jacob, who let me use his laboratory at Gadjah Mada University and took me to Sangiran. Robert Jones and Ellen Rafferty opened their home to me in Yogyakarta. In Bandung, I was able to examine more of the Sangiran material at the Geological Research and Development Centre, with the cooperation of H.M.S. Hartono and Darwin Kadar. For clearance to conduct this phase of my research on *Homo erectus*, I thank the Indonesian Institute of Sciences (LIPI) in Jakarta. The crania numbered Sangiran 2 and Sangiran 4, and several of the Sangiran mandibles, are housed in the Forschungsinstitut Senckenberg in Frankfurt-am-Main, and I am indebted to Jens Franzen for access to them. John de Vos allowed me to study the Trinil fossils at the Rijksmuseum van Natuurlijke Historie in Leiden.

Other persons who let me work on specimens in their care, or helped with anatomical matters or with questions about geological provenience of the fossils, are Chris Stringer of the British Museum (Natural History), John Melentis of the University of Thessaloniki, Ian Tattersall of the American Museum of Natural History, Ralph Holloway, Alan Walker and Richard Hay. Henry de Lumley and Marie-Antoinette de Lumley introduced me to Arago Cave and its contents, and to the wines of Tautavel. A.N. Poulianos showed me the site at Petralona.

Tom Webster devoted many hours to drawing crania and mandibles, and Stan Kauffman helped with other artwork. Herman Paikoff and Alice Hausman processed the photographs. Peg Roe prepared the typescript and never complained about my late changes to the text. Chris Stringer was able to serve as reader for the Cambridge University Press, and his comments enabled me to correct errors and strengthen my discussion at several points. I am grateful for this assistance and for all of the support that I received from Cambridge University Press during the editorial and production stages of this project.

Research requires funding, and I am pleased to acknowledge the several grants made to me by the National Science Foundation and the National Geographic Society. SUNY at Binghamton allowed me to take time away from other duties, and this helped to reduce the inevitable delay in preparing research results for publication.

Finally, I wish to express my thanks to two scholars who have not been involved directly with my work on *Homo erectus* but nevertheless have had an impact on my approach to paleoanthropology. They are William Howells and John Robinson, who guided me in the study of human evolution. This book is for them, and for my family.

I

Introduction

Following the discoveries of several Neanderthals in Europe, traces of a more archaic kind of human were uncovered in Asia, toward the close of the last century. These fossils were found at Trinil in Java by Eugene Dubois, who described them as *Pithecanthropus erectus*. Later in the 1920s, more human remains along with animal bones and stone artifacts were excavated from cave deposits at Zhoukoudian in China. On the strength of a few isolated teeth, this new hominid was named *Sinanthropus pekinensis*. Additional teeth, skulls and post-cranial pieces from Zhoukoudian were all lost during World War II, as is well known. It is most fortunate that this material had been described by the anatomist Franz Weidenreich, whose famous monographs were published between 1936 and 1943 by the Geological Survey of China.

The fossils from Java and China are now referred to the species *Homo erectus*. Since the war, many more specimens have come to light, in Africa as well as Asia. The hominids themselves have been studied in detail, and much effort has been put toward obtaining stratigraphic and paleoecological information from the more important sites. Better dates are becoming available. Lately, *Homo erectus* has become a topic of particular interest to paleoanthropologists, and new questions have been asked. Some of these concern the geographic distribution of the taxon and whether it should be recognized in Europe, or for that matter anywhere outside of the Far East. Others address continuity and change in the evolution of the species. How *Homo erectus* should be defined and how this extinct species evolved in relation to other groups of *Homo* is the subject of this book.

Approaches to the hominid record

Direct evidence for human evolution can be recovered only from the paleontological record. Traces of our own biological history are preserved as fossils, and it is important that these relics be subjected to close scrutiny, in order to extract from them as much information as possible. Fossil remains can now be studied in a number of different ways using modern techniques. Useful data about the internal structure of bone can be obtained either by standard radiography or by application of computerized x-ray tomography. Microscopic approaches are increasingly popular, and SEM examination of microwear patterns on teeth holds much promise for investigations of paleodiet. Chemical and isotopic analyses of bone constituents are also being explored. Where appropriate, I shall draw on this body of evidence as it bears on the story of *Homo erectus* and early *Homo sapiens*. However, the focus of this work is anatomical, and the methods employed are comparative, utilizing both non-metric characters and measurements. This sort of approach can succeed only where detailed anatomical descriptions of the fossils are available.

Describing a bone accurately and concisely is not an easy task. Where the item consists of a parietal bone, for example, or the shaft of a femur, one can proceed without too much difficulty. Even here, there is some risk of confusing a reader who is not familiar with the material. When the fossil is more complete, and it is necessary to provide a comprehensive account of facial structure or the anatomy of a cranial base, the job is much more demanding. Detail is important. But it is also necessary, without endless repetition or tedious reference to every groove and eminence, to convey an overall impression of the specimen. This should be done in such a way as to facilitate comparisons.

Descriptions provided in this book are based principally on observations of original fossils. At the invitation of Mary Leakey, I began systematic studies of the *Homo erectus* assemblage from Olduvai Gorge in 1977. This work was extended to include the Turkana hominids in 1978, and since 1980 I have examined fossils housed in Asia and in European collections. During this latter period, I have returned several times to Nairobi to take additional notes on the East

African specimens. By this process, I have been able to confirm or correct many of the earlier observations and to bring a degree of standardization to the entire project. In spite of such rechecking, a few errors are likely to be present, and some discussions may be judged as incomplete. To compensate for this and to illustrate the text as fully as possible, a number of photographs and drawings have been included. The latter have been executed from photographs and/ or casts by an illustrator trained in skeletal anatomy. The artist (Tom Webster) and I have inspected the results carefully, and I think that the drawings contain more information about the fossils than any but the best of photo prints.

Character selection and anatomical terminology

Since this project on *Homo erectus* was initiated in the late 1970s, I have kept close to hand Weidenreich's monographs on *Sinanthropus*. In many instances, these descriptions of Chinese *Homo erectus* serve as a bench mark, and it is still appropriate that Weidenreich's work be used to guide anatomical research on other mid-Pleistocene assemblages. It will be clear that I have borrowed heavily from his reports, and my debt extends both to matters of terminology and choice of characters to be emphasized. I have drawn extensively on Weidenreich (1943), where sections on the parietal and occipital bones, the temporal bone including the glenoid cavity and tympanic plate, other areas of the cranial base, and the interior of the braincase have been especially useful. For the most part, Weidenreich's terms as applied to these regions are retained here, although I have substituted English equivalents for the international Latin forms.

More recent paleontological studies have also influenced my research. Tobias' (1967) monograph on *Zinjanthropus* has helped with points concerning cranial morphology. Hublin's (1978a) investigations of the occipital squama and adjacent cranial base have prompted me to pay special attention to this part of the braincase. Other papers by Hublin (1978b) and Santa Luca (1978) on the morphology of European Neanderthal crania and by Santa Luca (1980) on the Ngandong hominids illustrate the importance of character selection in phylogenetic analysis. In any investigation of the relationships among species, the researcher must settle on a list of traits to be recorded. Similarities shared by (certain) groups provide the basis for reconstructing their phylogeny. Cladists, following Willi Hennig, insist that such similarities should be identified either as primitive or as derived for the groups in question. While I have not embraced all aspects of the cladist program, I do recognize that character analysis must be carried out. In my view, not shared by all cladists, a first step is to define anatomical traits carefully, in a way consistent with comparisons across closely related groups. Where possible, functional significance should be elucidated or an attempt made to relate bony features to development of muscles or other soft tissues. For some cranial and mandibular characters, this will be difficult. But to this extent at least, designation of characters is nonarbitrary.

Terminology applied to the mandible follows Weidenreich (1936), as well as several excellent reports by White (1977) on australopithecines from Laetoli, and by White & Johanson (1982) on the Hadar material. My comments on *Homo* jaws and other skeletal elements are guided also by papers from the Koobi Fora Research Project. Hominid fossils recovered from the Turkana localities are under study by M.H. Day, A.C. Walker, B.A. Wood and R.E. Leakey. Teeth are not emphasized in my treatment of *Homo erectus*, and discussions of crown or root structure are limited. Where dental anatomy is referred to, the terms are taken from Kraus, Jordan & Abrams (1969).

Measurements

A number of the skulls of earlier *Homo* are complete enough that some useful measurements can be taken. Only a few cran-ia approach the near perfect state of preservation exhibited by KNM-ER 3733 from Koobi Fora, Broken Hill and Petralona. For many other individuals the braincase is reasonably intact, and parts of the face or skull base may also be available. Cranial measurements are presented both in the text and in tabular form. Landmarks and techniques are mainly those discussed by Howells (1973) and Rightmire (1975). Here I have been selective, and measurements not readily taken on archaic specimens have been omitted.

Others have been added, to cover structures (eg., the supraorbital torus) not prominently developed in modern skulls or to insure that metric information will be recorded even from fragmentary material. Where these dimensions are not self-explanatory, references or definitions are provided. Where possible, I have taken measurements along the basicranial line, using landmarks described by Laitman,

Heimbuch & Crelin (1979). Widths related to bilateral structures of the cranial base are those of Dean & Wood (1981).

Measurements of the mandible are primarily those taken on the body, which is most frequently preserved. Standard dimensions of the lateral corpus and symphysis are provided, and in many cases I have followed the procedures of White & Johanson (1982). Buccolingual and mesiodistal diameters of tooth crowns are given. Measurements taken on several of the *Homo erectus* postcranial specimens are discussed in the appropriate text sections. Dimensions of the femur, which emphasize the head and shaft, are mostly those of Martin (1928), which have been in general use for a long time. Other metrics are designed specially to record aspects of iliac, acetabular and ischial proportions, as these structures are preserved on two of the innominate bones recovered in East Africa.

The hominid inventory

Fossils attributed to *Homo erectus* are known from a number of localities in the Far East, including the famous sites at Trinil, Sangiran and Zhoukoudian. Crania, jaws, teeth and a few postcranial parts are available for study. I have been able to examine a good deal of this material, although I have not had access to original fossils from China. In the case of the more recent Chinese discoveries, as of course with the Zhoukoudian specimens, I have worked from casts, photographs and published reports. Finds from Africa have also been referred to *Homo erectus* by earlier workers. Important localities include Ternifine (now Tighenif) in Algeria, Salé in Morocco, the Turkana basin in Kenya and Olduvai Gorge in Tanzania. All of this material should be assessed in an attempt to bring up to date our understanding of *Homo erectus*, and I have tried to study original specimens in every case.

Lists of the localities covered by this project are given in the tables. Table 1 provides an inventory of the hominids from Java and China, not in the form of a catalog but rather as a summary of skeletal parts represented at each site. Similar information is reported for Africa in Table 2. It should be noted that these lists are incomplete, as I have omitted a few sites which have yielded only very fragmentary material or isolated teeth. Such specimens, particularly where there are questions concerning provenience or dating, are of marginal interest. Hominids from Europe are not included in my survey of *Homo*

Table 1. *Listing of principal Indonesian and Chinese localities at which remains attributed to Homo erectus have been recovered. Fossils are inventoried by body part represented rather than as individual specimens*

	Trinil	Sangiran	Sambungmachan	Ngandong	Zhoukoudian	Hexian	Gongwangling
Whole crania							
Partial braincases	√	√	√	√	√	√	√
Mandibles		√			√	√	
Dentition		√			√	√	
Postcranial parts	√	?		√	√		

Table 2. *Localities in northwestern, eastern and southern Africa which have yielded remains comparable to Asian Homo erectus. Fossils are inventoried by body part represented rather than as individual specimens*

	Ternifine	Sidi Abderrahman	Thomas Quarries	Salé	Koobi Fora	Nariokotome	Baringo	Olduvai Gorge	Swartkrans
Whole crania						√			
Partial braincases	√		√	√	√			√	√
Mandibles	√	√	√		√	√	√	√	√
Dentition	√	√	√	√	√	√	√	√	
Postcranial parts	√			√	√	√		√	√

erectus. European fossils are not enumerated in the tables, although some are discussed in the final chapters of the book.

Plan of the study

The backbone of this work consists of descriptions of *Homo erectus* fossils, supplemented by measurements, photographs and drawings. The Asian hominids are dealt with first, in Chapter 2. This is appropriate, since the Indonesian and Chinese discoveries of *Homo erectus* were the earliest to be recorded. Dubois referred the Trinil fossils to *Pithecanthropus* (now *Homo*) in 1894, long before remains in Africa first came to light. For more than half a century, specimens from Javanese localities and from Zhoukoudian made up the hypodigm for the species. It would be technically correct to base all comparisons on these Asian assemblages, and to a degree I have done this. A primary aim of this project is to identify specimens which belong to *Homo erectus* and to formulate a definition of the species. Sorting of fossils or groups of individuals (phena) to *Homo erectus* must be carried out on the strength of similarities to the Asian hominids. Only by following this procedure can it be determined whether specimens from African or European localities should be lumped with the Far Eastern material in one species. However, the situation is complicated by several factors. Many of the Indonesian skulls are incomplete, and important parts such as the facial skeleton and the cranial base are not very well preserved. Almost all of the Zhoukoudian remains have been lost to science. At the same time, *Homo erectus* assemblages from Africa now include some fine specimens. Therefore I have elected to emphasize the African material in a number of my discussions where sorting is not an issue and where direct comparisons with Asian fossils would be less informative.

The Olduvai hominids are covered in Chapter 3. Because the Gorge has been so thoroughly studied from a geological perspective, and a secure chronological framework is established, I have devoted considerable space to the Olduvai remains. The famous cranium of OH 9 and the mandible of OH 22 are the more complete specimens, and their descriptions are presented in substantial detail. Other skull parts from Beds III, IV and the Masek Beds are fragmentary but do furnish information about variation in human populations of the Early and Middle Pleistocene. Postcranial remains from Bed IV are also important.

Other discoveries of *Homo erectus* from eastern Africa are covered in Chapter 4. Here an obvious focus is the Turkana area, where so many hominids have come to light. Advances in tuff correlation, along with studies of paleogeography and depositional history of the lake basin, now clarify the stratigraphic contexts in which the fossils occur. A number of the specimens have been described by members of the Koobi Fora Research Project, and more detailed anatomical work is in progress. Therefore my own accounts of the Turkana *Homo erectus* assemblages are limited, and I have emphasized comparisons with Olduvai. Much of my discussion centers on two good crania and several mandibles from the Koobi Fora region.

More material from localities in eastern and southern Africa is also treated in Chapter 4, while hominids from northwest Africa are covered in Chapter 5. Descriptions are detailed in cases where the fossils are judged to be especially important, or where reports of other workers do not provide all the information needed for this study. Where appropriate, I have referred to the more complete Olduvai hominids for comparative purposes. To the extent that this is done consistently, the comparisons are 'standardized', always using Olduvai as a yardstick. I make no claim that this procedure eliminates subjectivity, and I have not applied it in cases where other comparisons (within assemblages, for example) are clearly more useful. However, I have stressed the East African record even though it is of course Asian material (covered in Chapter 2) which constitutes the 'type' of *Homo erectus*.

Systematic comparisons of the Asian and African fossils are summarized in Chapter 6. Results show that there is a suite of features common to all *Homo erectus*, while some regional differences are also apparent. Cranial and mandibular characters which occur consistently in the assemblages are tabulated, in an attempt to reach a comprehensive description of the species. Such lists of traits have been compiled before, by Le Gros Clark (1964) for example, or more recently by Howell (1978). I have utilized these studies but have attempted to add new information, obtained through broad coverage of the material now available. Other changes from earlier descriptions reflect my own perspectives concerning the relevance of characters.

Several important questions are raised in the final sections of the book. One is whether *Homo erectus* should be defined (arbitrarily) as a grade within a gradually evolving lineage. An alternate view, which gains some support from the analysis of metric data provided in Chapter 6, is that *Homo erectus* is a stable species which can be characterized morphologically, without reference to chronology or gaps in the fossil record. Other questions concern the relationship of *Homo erectus* to *Homo sapiens*. Hominids widely assumed to be early members of our own species are discussed in Chapter 8. These specimens from Africa, Europe and Asia differ in significant ways from more archaic humans, but whether any (or all) of them represent transitional populations is disputed. Just how *Homo sapiens* first evolved is one of the major issues of paleoanthropology. Here the fossils and the stratigraphic record are limited, and many details may never be resolved. I have attempted simply to point toward some answers which are consistent with the evidence.

I have tried throughout the duration of this project to keep two broad goals in mind. One is to provide thorough and accurate accounts of the anatomy of the principal specimens. Such descriptions, prepared by one investigator familiar with the original fossils, can be used by any worker wishing to pursue the study of *Homo erectus* in new directions. A second aim is to make the book more than a catalog alone. I have not hesitated to advance my own interpretations of the material, and I have commented at length on the nature of paleospecies, rates of change in the skull and dentition of *Homo erectus*, and the evolution of brain size. Not all readers will agree with my assessment of *Homo erectus* as a geographically widespread but essentially conservative taxon, changing little through most of the Pleistocene. However, paleoanthropology is an endeavor in which progress comes slowly, as hypotheses are challenged and reformulated on the basis of evidence accumulating from diverse disciplines. If I have contributed to this process in a positive way, that is enough.

2

Homo erectus in the Far East

Much information about the evolution of earlier humans has come to light in Asia. A number of important Pleistocene sites are located in China and in Indonesia, and it was of course in Java that the first fossils of *Homo erectus* were discovered by Eugene Dubois late in the last century. Dubois, a young Dutch physician, went to Indonesia to find the missing link, and he was tremendously lucky. His first specimen, a mandibular fragment, turned up at Kedung Brubus in 1890, and the famous Trinil skullcap was excavated from the banks of the Solo River in central Java in 1891. Dubois' assistants continued to dig at Trinil for another decade, and large quantities of mammal bones were shipped back to Holland. Only a few more hominids were found, and some of the postcranial remains that did appear managed to escape notice for more than 30 years after they were returned to the museum in Leiden.

Later, in the 1920s, more fossils were recovered far to the north, from limestone cave deposits near Beijing in China. This site at Zhoukoudian proved to be immensely rich, and quite a number of well preserved skulls and other bones were eventually excavated from different levels in the cave. Although nearly all of this Chinese *Homo erectus* material was lost during World War II, descriptions of the crania, jaws, teeth and limb bones are on record (Weidenreich, 1936, 1937, 1941, 1943). After the war, exploration of the cave produced a few new fossil teeth, fragments of limb and a mandible found in 1959. In 1966, the frontal and occipital portions of a cranium were discovered and recognized as belonging to one of the individuals collected earlier in 1934. Excavations carried out more recently have yielded no further hominids but have addressed questions concerning the Zhoukoudian stone industry, paleoclimatic conditions and dating (Wu & Lin, 1983). Studies of the cave sediments suggest that most of the deposits were accumulated during the Middle Pleistocene. Dating evidence reviewed by Liu (1985) and Wu (1985) indicates that hominids were present at the site at least 0.5 million years ago. The cave was then occupied intermittently for several hundred thousand years.

Other important discoveries have also been made in China. A rather poorly preserved cranium from Gongwangling and a more complete lower jaw from Chenjiawo have been referred to *Homo erectus* (Woo, 1964, 1966). Assemblages of teeth are known from several localities, but perhaps the most significant find is a partial skull from Lontandong Cave, Hexian County, which came to light in 1980. This Hexian individual has been described briefly by Wu & Dong (1982), who feel that it is best compared to later specimens of *Homo erectus* from Zhoukoudian. None of these hominids has been dated very precisely. Faunal studies and paleomagnetic determinations suggest that most are Middle Pleistocene in age, and even the oldest sites such as Gongwangling may lie close to the Brunhes–Matuyama boundary (Pope, 1983, 1988; Wu, 1985).

In Indonesia, the tally of hominid discoveries has increased more dramatically. The Sangiran dome has proved to be the richest source of fossils. The famous B mandible was recovered there in 1936, and the first cranium turned up in 1937. This Sangiran 2 braincase is small, with an endocranial capacity of only a little more than 800 ml. This suggests that the individual may be female, despite obvious thickening of the section of supraorbital torus which can be measured. Many features of Sangiran 2, including the low contour of the vault, some sagittal keeling, and the strongly flexed occiput recall the morphology of the Trinil skullcap found by Dubois.

A maxilla with teeth, and the back portion of a thick-walled skull, were picked up at Sangiran in 1938 and 1939. This individual, numbered Sangiran 4, was referred first by Weidenreich to *Pithecanthropus robustus* and later by von Koenigswald to *Pithecanthropus modjokertensis*. On several subsequent occasions, the same species, now *Homo modjokertensis*, has been recognized from fragments thought to be derived from Pucangan horizons. Other material from Sangiran which may come from Pucangan levels includes mostly lower jaws. More fossils are known from the Kabuh sediments, and several of the crania are quite well preserved. The most complete is Sangiran 17, for which much of the facial skeleton is present. Altogether, more than 40 individuals have now been recovered at Sangiran.

Other localities in central and eastern Java have yielded fewer fossils. Apart from Kedung Brubus and Trinil, where the first discoveries were made, Modjokerto, Ngandong and Sambungmachan have produced interesting remains. The Modjokerto child, found in 1936, was the first specimen to be referred to *Homo modjokertensis*. Crania and postcranial parts recovered at Ngandong have been widely regarded as chronologically younger and anatomically less archaic than *Homo erectus*. However, both assumptions can be questioned. These crania also share many features with *Homo erectus*, as has been documented by Santa Luca (1980). At Sambungmachan, quite a well preserved braincase, unfortunately lacking the face, was discovered in 1973. This individual has been compared by Jacob (1975) to the Ngandong assemblage, but again it is apparent that there are resemblances to the *Homo erectus* crania from Sangiran.

It is the fossil material from Indonesia that I wish to emphasize in this chapter. Perhaps the best way to begin is by commenting on the sites themselves and recent attempts to tie them to a reliable time scale. I shall then discuss the hominid inventory and provide descriptive anatomical notes for a number of the more important specimens. Finally, it will be appropriate to raise the question of the number of different lineages or species that may be represented by the fossils.

Stratigraphy and dating of the Javanese localities

The principal hominid localities of Java are shown on the map (Fig. 1). Kedung Brubus and Trinil were investigated first, beginning in the last century, while discoveries at Ngandong and Sangiran began later in the 1930s. Local stratigraphic sequences have been developed by different workers, and there is still doubt concerning correlations between some of the important sites. The Sangiran area, which has been subject to considerable study, may be described as follows. Marine marls and limestones, deposited before Java was fully uplifted from the sea, occur under the earliest continental beds. Above these marine sediments, volcanic breccias (lahars) still contain marine diatoms and molluscs (Ninkovich & Burckle, 1978). Higher in the Pucangan Formation are the black clays, mostly of freshwater

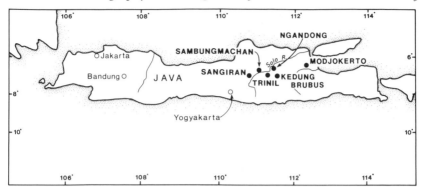

Fig. 1. Map of Java showing localities where discoveries of *Homo erectus* have been made. Fossils were picked up first at Kedung Brubus and at Trinil, late in the last century, but the dome at Sangiran has produced many of the more recent finds.

origin, which are approximately 100 m thick. Vertebrate assemblages collected from the middle and upper parts of the Pucangan sequence are said to comprise the Jetis fauna (von Koenigswald, 1934, 1935). Several of the Sangiran hominid fossils may also be derived from the uppermost Pucangan levels.

The overlying Kabuh Formation, composed mostly of sands and clays of fluviatile origin, is 6–60 m thick. These beds also contain fossils including fairly abundant remains of *Homo erectus*. The Kabuh mammals have been described as the Trinil fauna. However, these traditional associations of a (later) Trinil fauna with the Kabuh beds and an (earlier) Jetis fauna with the Pucangan Formation have been questioned. De Vos *et al.* (1982) and Sondaar (1984) have recently argued that the Trinil assemblage originally excavated by Dubois and his assistants is more archaic then the Jetis collection from Kedung Brubus. This suggests that the Trinil type locality may be older than sites containing Jetis fauna. This claim has been disputed by Bartstra (1983), but it is increasingly clear that the classic biostratigraphy established for central and eastern Java will have to be revised. Leinders *et al.* (1985) extend these discussions to include material from Sangiran. Fossils collected from the Grenzbank or boundary between the Pucangan and Kabuh beds are allocated to a Trinil fauna (as defined by De Vos *et al.*, 1982), while fauna from higher in the Kabuh is linked to a Kedung Brubus zone.

In the Sangiran area, the Kabuh Formation is followed by the Notopuro sands and volcanic breccias. Paleomagnetic studies show these sediments to be of normal polarity, as is also the case for nearly all of the samples obtained from the Kabuh levels (Semah, 1984). Hominids apparently are not known from the Notopuro beds of Sangiran, but human remains are of course on record at Ngandong, some distance to the east. The river terrace deposits at Ngandong are referred to the Notopuro Formation and are usually considered to be of later Pleistocene antiquity. Animal bones obtained during recent excavations of a remnant of the Solo high terrace give uranium-series disequilibrium ages that are in keeping with this interpretation (Bartstra, Soegondho & van der Wijk, 1988). However, the Ngandong crania show a good deal of surface abrasion, and it is quite possible that they have been transported by water. If some of the high terrace fossils, including the hominid remains, have had a complex history ending with redeposition in the Notopuro sands, they will be very difficult to date.

Absolute dating of the Javanese localities has in fact been problematical for a long time. Some claims have surely been exaggerated. Very old potassium–argon ages have been reported for Pucangan levels both at Kedung Brubus and at Modjokerto, and the Modjokerto figure of 1.9 ± 0.4 million years has been widely cited. However, because of questions about the provenience of this tuff sample, the date obtained from it cannot be considered to bear on the antiquity of any of the human fossils (Pope, 1983). More recent work has included better isotopic dating and construction of a paleomagnetic stratigraphy (Nishimura, Thio & Hehuwat, 1980; Semah, 1982, 1984; Shimizu *et al.*, 1985; Suzuki *et al.*, 1985). While it is apparent that some problems with potassium–argon and fission track ages remain to be resolved, magnetic polarity determinations confirm that at least the middle and upper Kabuh levels at Sangiran postdate the Brunhes—Matuyama boundary and therefore belong in the Middle Pleistocene. This evidence suggests that most of the Asian *Homo erectus* assemblages are less than 1.0 million years old.

The Trinil cranium

The skullcap recovered by Dubois is designated Trinil 2 in the *Catalogue of Fossil Hominids* (Oakley, Campbell & Molleson, 1975). This specimen is relatively incomplete. Much of the frontal squama is preserved, but there is damage to the brows. The supratoral surface has been thinned by erosion, and extensive sinus cavities are exposed on both sides of the midline. Only a little of the original contour of the supraorbital torus remains on the left, and the facial bones have all been lost. Both parietals are present, although their temporal margins are broken. On the right, a fragment of the anterior temporal squama is still attached to the vault. While the upper scale of the occipital bone is intact, most of the nuchal area and the rest of the cranial base are missing.

This fossil, like the other bones from Trinil, appears to be heavily mineralized. Because of weathering, sutural traces and other surface details are difficult to make out. Toward the rear of the cranium, near lambda, the surface is smooth and noticeably different from that of the rest of the vault. Here Dubois may have filled in a weathered area, as noted in his 1924 report. The parietal contours do not seem to have been altered. The endocranial surface, originally obscured by matrix but cleaned by Dubois, is better preserved. Patterns left by the meningeal vessels can be observed, and traces of the coronal suture are still present.

Because of damage to the supraorbital region, cranial length cannot be measured accurately. The distance from opisthocranion to the superior margin of the eroded torus is 182 mm, but this must be an underestimate. Length measured to glabella would be greater by several millimeters. Biparietal breadth is about 131 mm, so the Trinil cranium is comparable in size to Sangiran 10 and a little smaller than Sangiran 12. Endocranial capacity as determined by Holloway (1981a) is 940 ml.

The frontal bone is narrow anteriorly (least frontal breadth is 85 mm), so that postorbital constriction is pronounced. Behind the brows, the supratoral surface is only slightly hollowed. There is no appreciable development of a sulcus. Some blunt keeling is present in the midline, and this extends upward toward a prominent bregmatic eminence. Behind the vertex, the vault is flattened. Keeling does not continue for more than a few millimeters onto the parietals. Partly because of weathering, the temporal lines are very faint. On the left, the line is obscured almost completely. Preservation is a little better on the right, and here the line forms a low arc which can be followed toward asterion. This part of the specimen is damaged, so it is not clear whether the (broken) crest located near the parietal angle is actually the posterior aspect of an angular torus. This structure may instead mark the extension of the supramastoid crest onto the parietal surface.

In rear view, the Trinil cranium is strikingly low, and parasagittal flattening may be even more pronounced than in the smaller Sangiran individuals. A straight transverse torus is present on the occiput, but this is nowhere very prominent. Some surface detail has been lost, but a supratoral sulcus could not have been extensively developed. There is no sign of an external occipital protuberance. Damage near the midline has nearly obliterated the linear tubercle, and little of the morphology of the nuchal area can now be studied.

Trinil postcranial remains

Following discovery of the cranium, a complete femur was excavated at Trinil by Dubois in 1892. This famous specimen exhibits a large pathological excrescence toward its proximal end. Dubois claimed that this femur I, now designated Trinil 3, must be as ancient as the skullcap, but there is continuing doubt concerning contemporaneity of the two fossils. More femora turned up more than 30 years later in Holland, where they had rested in a box of Trinil bones stored at the museum in Leiden. Femur II, or Trinil 6, is less complete, as the head is badly eroded, most of the greater trochanter is missing, and there is no distal end. Three other specimens consist only of shafts, variously preserved and showing surface damage. For Trinil 6–9, no records specifying provenience have survived.

All the femora have been restudied by Day & Molleson (1973), who confirm that neither measurements nor details of microscopic anatomy distinguish these bones from those of modern humans. In several respects, the Trinil fossils do differ from femora found with the skulls of *Homo erectus* at Zhoukoudian in China. How this information should be interpreted is not clear, as long as the question of association of the postcranial bones with the Trinil cranium is unresolved. Results of bone chemistry microanalysis reported by Day (1984) do not yet provide a basis for regarding Trinil 3 as different in age from Trinil 2. Nevertheless, attribution of the femora to *Homo erectus* remains problematical, and the fossils are not considered further in this monograph.

The Sangiran crania

Several of the crania recovered since 1937 in the Sangiran area are reasonably complete. Descriptive notes are provided below for San-

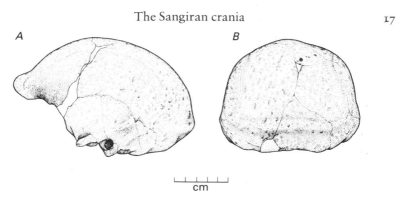

Fig. 2. Drawings of Sangiran 2, showing (A) left lateral and (B) posterior views of the braincase.

giran hominids 2, 4, 10, 12 and 17. A few of the less well preserved specimens (eg., Sangiran 3) are not covered by this work, and the most recently discovered fossils have still to be reconstructed and described by Indonesian scientists.

SANGIRAN 2 (Figs 2, 3, 4 & 21)

Fragments of this first Sangiran *Homo erectus* cranium were collected and reconstructed by von Koenigswald. The fossils are said to be from Kabuh levels, although Matsu'ura's (1982) analysis of

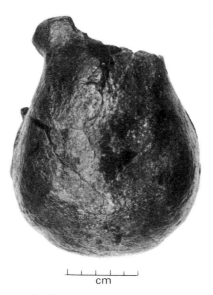

Fig. 3. Photograph of the Sangiran 2 braincase, in superior view.

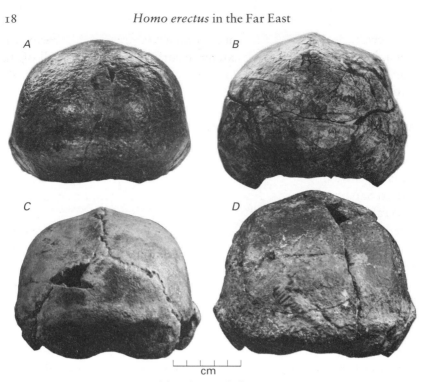

Fig. 4. Posterior views of four hominids from Sangiran. (A) Sangiran 2 and (B) Sangiran 4 are probably derived from Grenzbank or uppermost Pucangan levels, while (C) Sangiran 10 and (D) Sangiran 17 are thought to come from Kabuh sediments. Smaller individuals, such as Sangiran 2, are likely to be female, and the large Sangiran 17 specimen is probably a male.

fluorine content places this specimen in the Grenzbank, a layer of conglomerate taken as marking the Pucangan–Kabuh boundary. Sangiran 2, designated as *Pithecanthropus* II or as skull II in many earlier reports, is somewhat better preserved than either Trinil 2, Sangiran 10 or Sangiran 12. It is less complete than Sangiran 17. Part of the supraorbital rim and browridge are present on the left, although the torus is broken well short of the midline, and glabella has been lost. The parietals have been pieced together from a number of fragments, and several small gaps have been filled with plaster. Near bregma and elsewhere on the parietal vault, some surface bone has been worn away. The squamous portions of both temporal bones are intact. On the left side, the zygomatic process, glenoid cavity, tympanic plate and mastoid process are reasonably complete, although cracks and other damage obscure some morphological detail. The upper scale of the occiput and parts of the nuchal area are present. However, the nuchal plane exhibits rather extensive surface erosion, and all of the bone surrounding the foramen magnum has been broken. The remainder of the cranial base is missing, as is the facial skeleton.

Sangiran 2 is quite heavily mineralized. The bone is dark in color, and the major cranial sutures are almost completely obliterated. Locating some important landmarks is therefore difficult, but a number of measurements can be taken (see Table 23 in Chapter 6). This individual is a little smaller than Trinil 2 but is comparable in size to Sangiran 10. The endocranial volume estimated by Holloway (1981a) is 813 ml. Vault thicknesses (8 mm at bregma, up to 9 mm at asterion) are close to those measured for Trinil 2. The supraorbital torus is less heavily constructed than that of Sangiran 10, as are the supramastoid crests and the transverse torus of the occiput. Variation of this sort may be related to sex, although it is not possible to designate Sangiran 2 as female with any certainty.

The section of browridge remaining on the left side is about 12 mm thick near the center of the supraorbital margin. The torus is thinner laterally, and here the bone surface shows signs of weathering. The supratoral shelf is flattened. Erosion has blunted the temporal crests, but it is clear that postorbital constriction is as marked as in the Trinil cranium. Damage occurring along much of the frontal midline makes it difficult to ascertain whether some minor keeling was present, although there is a slight eminence near bregma. This swelling can be traced for several centimeters along the sagittal suture, and to either side the parietal surface is distinctly hollowed. Keeling does not extend toward the rear of the vault and is nowhere as pronounced as in Sangiran 10.

The course followed by the temporal line can be observed on the right side. The line and also the parietal surface confined within its arc are slightly raised. As it turns downward, the temporal line converges toward the superior nuchal line. The two merge near the parietal mastoid angle. A low but palpable ridge is produced which then splits anteriorly, giving rise to the weak mastoid crest and stronger supramastoid crest. On the left side, the anatomy of this supramastoid area is a little clearer. The supramastoid crest is separated from the bulge of the mastoid process by a very shallow sulcus, and the crest itself is expressed only on the temporal bone. It does not cross the squamosal suture, which is relatively straight and low in outline, as in other *Homo erectus*. Both mastoid processes are quite small and nipple-shaped, and their axes incline inward. Some surface damage is present, but there appears to be little flattening of the posterior aspect of either process.

In rear view, Sangiran 2 closely resembles the Trinil vault. The occipital torus is straight and mound-like and is slightly less projecting than the torus of Sangiran 10. Partly because of erosion, its upper and lower margins are not well defined, and no supratoral sulcus is apparent. Neither a linear tubercle nor an external occipital crest is preserved. Some rounded swellings are present on the nuchal surface, but individual muscle scars cannot be distinguished. Damage and weathering have affected other features, including the digastric incisures and associated crests. Some of the occipital bone medial to the mastoid process is still in place on both sides, but details can no longer be made out.

The glenoid cavity is best preserved on the left. Unfortunately, both the ectoglenoid and the entoglenoid processes are broken, so width of the joint surface cannot be measured satisfactorily. This must be substantially less than 30 mm. The long axis of the cavity is approximately perpendicular to the midline of the cranial base. The fossa is deep, and there is narrowing of its inner recess, which extends medially as a crevice between the (broken) entoglenoid pyramid and the tympanic plate. There is no bar-shaped articular tubercle. Despite damage to both sides, it is apparent that the postglenoid processes are small but distinct. The tympanic plate is very thick, both laterally where it encircles the auditory opening and inferiorly. This thickening of the lower tympanic margin is perhaps even more pronounced in Sangiran 2 than in the East African crania, described in Chapters 3 and 4. The petrosal crest is incomplete, but enough of the bone is left to suggest that a spine was prominently developed. The extent to which this petrosal spine was associated with a styloid groove or hollow can no longer be determined.

SANGIRAN 4 (Figs 4 & 5)

Sangiran 4, or skull IV, is a specimen about which there has been a good deal of controversy. When they were found in 1938 and 1939, the fossils were thought to be derived from the black clays of the Pucangan Formation. However, it is unlikely that an exact geological provenience could have been established at the time, as the remains were picked up by local collectors and not excavated *in situ*. It is now known that the mid-dome area of Sangiran has a more complicated

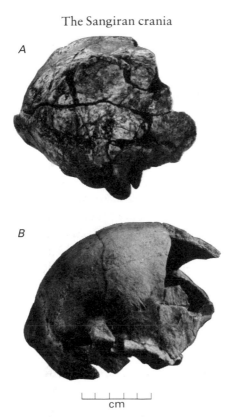

Fig. 5. Photographs of (A) Sangiran 4 and (B) Sangiran 10 in right lateral view.

stratigraphy than was recognized previously, and this adds additional uncertainty. Recent studies of the fluorine content of Sangiran fossils in fact suggest that skull IV could better be grouped with material from the Grenzbank or the uppermost Pucangan levels rather than with remains from lower in the stratigraphic sequence (Matsu'ura, 1982).

Both the famous palate, with teeth, and the rear portion of the cranium are preserved. The braincase has been reconstructed from numerous fragments and consists of two sections. One is comprised of parts of both parietal bones, united at the midline, together with the uppermost aspect of the occipital squama. This section has not been joined to the lower part of the vault made up of most of the rest of the occiput, the parietal angles and the temporal bones. The latter are damaged, but the glenoid cavities are preserved, and on one side the mastoid process is intact. The petrous bones are largely missing, but a little of the sphenoid is present on each side. Fairly extensive areas of bone damage and weathering are apparent, and some warping precludes a perfect fit between the two sections of the braincase. Although a liberal amount of filler has been used in reconstruction, there seems to be no serious distortion of the cranial base. Endocranial volume as measured by Holloway (1981a) is 908 ml.

Since all of the frontal is missing, and the parietal bone adjacent to the coronal suture is broken away on both sides, the position of bregma cannot be established. The sagittal suture is preserved along a chord only about 82 mm in length. A prominent feature of Sangiran 4 is the heaping up of bone that occurs along this midline, and a rounded 'keel' continues almost to lambda. Especially posteriorly, this structure is more massively developed than in Sangiran 10 or Sangiran 17. Such keeling does not characterize the Turkana *Homo erectus* crania, and in Olduvai Hominid 9 the relevant part of the vault is lost. Parasagittal flattening exhibited by Sangiran 4 and noted for other Indonesian specimens is also more pronounced than in the Turkana specimens, although some flattening is present in most early *Homo* crania.

Because of damage, the temporal lines are indistinct. On the right side, where the surface is too weathered to show much detail, there is a palpable bulge filling the parietal angle just above asterion. This angular torus must mark the passage of the superior line toward the mastoid crest. The crest itself is sharply defined and somewhat roughened as it approaches the apex of the mastoid process. A supramastoid crest is also prominent, particularly where it extends over the auditory opening as a strong shelf ending in the broken zygomatic root. Posteriorly, this crest is expanded to form a massive swelling. This thickening trends upward, at an angle to the zygomatic root, and subsides as it crosses the parietotemporal suture. It is separated from the lower mastoid crest by a broad sulcus, about 17 mm across. The floor of this supramastoid sulcus is smooth, and there are no tubercles. As a shallow angular sulcus, this hollow continues for a short distance onto the parietal bone.

The bone of the occiput is thick. The upper scale slopes forward and is quite short in comparison to the expanded nuchal surface below. This ratio of lower to upper scale lengths is higher for Sangiran 4 than for most other *Homo erectus* crania examined. As is not surprising in the case of a relatively large robust cranium, the occipital torus is strongly developed. Where it is most projecting near the midline, this structure is heavier than the torus of Sangiran 10 and comparable to that of Sangiran 17. Its superior aspect is shelf-like as in several of the Ngandong crania rather than rounded or simply roughened as in other Sangiran individuals. Height of this torus measured from the center of the linear tubercle is about 17 mm, and there is no distinct supratoral sulcus. Near the midline, there is some additional projection of bone above the linear tubercle, but this may be exaggerated as a consequence of weathering of the toral surface on the left side. A protuberance comparable to that found in Sangiran 12 is not apparent. On the right, where weathering is less severe, the torus can be followed laterally toward asterion, where there are traces of a blunt retromastoid tuberosity. On this side, the impression of the superior nuchal line is still clear, and below it the nuchal surface is slightly hollowed at the site of *m. semispinalis capitis* attachment. From the linear tubercle, an external occipital crest passes toward opisthion. This crest shows signs of damage but is prominent anteriorly. To either side, well defined depressions reach almost to the posterior border of the foramen magnum.

The mastoid process is quite large and cylindrical in form. The entire process is directed medially as well as obliquely downward, so that the distance between the mastoid tips (complete on the right, reconstructed on the left) is some 50 mm less than cranial breadth measured at the supramastoid crests. The posterior face of the mastoid, delineated from the more anterior aspect by a roughened crest, is flattened. This surface lies in approximately the same plane as does the nuchal area of the occiput. Here there is general resemblance to the condition seen in some African individuals, although the Sangiran 4 process is nipple-shaped rather than pyramidal in outline. Unfortunately, the course followed by the digastric incisure is partly obscured by reconstructive material. This groove does not appear to have been very wide. It is bounded medially by a massive (juxtamastoid) eminence, the surface of which has probably been weathered. Nothing resembling an arterial channel can be discerned, and there is no clear evidence to suggest division of this eminence into 'paramastoid' and/ or occipitomastoid crests, as occurs in some Ngandong specimens.

In depth and general proportions, the glenoid cavity is comparable to that of the large *Homo erectus* cranium from Bed II at Olduvai. What remains of the articular tubercle is hollowed, and the anterior wall turns smoothly onto the preglenoid planum. The ectoglenoid process is not preserved on either side. On the right, enough of the medial part of the cavity is present to show that the sphenotemporal suture passes just to the lateral side of the entoglenoid tubercle. This structure is thus wholly sphenoid in origin, but there is no projecting (sphenoid) spine of the sort normally occurring in modern human crania. The posterior wall of the glenoid cavity, formed by the tympanic plate, is oriented vertically. At its lateral extent, the plate is elongated and thickened, and the auditory porus is very deep and irregular in form, rather than circular. Computerized tomograms prepared for the Sangiran 4 temporal bone do not show any evidence of fracturing, so this shape is not due to crushing, as has sometimes been supposed (Wind, 1984). The inferior part of the plate is also heavily constructed, in comparison to the *Homo sapiens* condition. However, the tympanic is relatively short anteroposteriorly and may be described as less robust than that of other Asian specimens, eg., Sangiran 2. A distinct petrosal spine is no longer preserved. On the rear of the plate, there is a vertical groove, ending in a small pit containing no sign of a styloid process. More medially, the tympanic bone is greatly thickened. The rounded tubercle in which it terminates is larger in Sangiran 4 than in most other *Homo erectus* studied.

SANGIRAN 10 (Figs 4 & 5)

This rather fragmentary skullcap has been described by Jacob (1966). Pieces of braincase were found in 1963 by villagers at Tandjung in the Sangiran area. These were later recognized as representative of a single individual. As finally reconstructed, the cranium is composed from a small part of the right frontal carrying a section of the supraorbital torus, some of the left frontal squama, most of both parietal bones, the broken temporals, and the rear of the occiput. Nearly all of the cranial base is missing. The facial skeleton is represented only by the bit of upper orbital margin from the right side and by the left zygomatic bone. Neither of these fragments makes any contact with other parts of the reconstructed cranium. Fortunately, although the specimen is incomplete, the remaining bones are mostly in good condition. Both external and endocranial features are well preserved, and the bones have been carefully cleaned.

Sangiran 10 is not very different in size from Trinil 2 or Sangiran 2. An endocranial cast prepared by Holloway (1981a) has a volume of 855 ml. Despite its relatively small size, the cranium is remarkable for the thickness of its vault and for the development of both supraorbital and occipital tori. The remaining fragment of right frontal exhibits a browridge which is about 19 mm thick centrally. There are signs of some lateral thinning, but the fragment is broken short of the frontomalar suture. Above the torus, the frontal surface is slightly hollowed, but it is apparent that a deep sulcus was not present. The temporal crests are not preserved, and there is little indication of the shape of the temporal fossae. However, the configuration of the surviving frontal and sphenoid parts suggests that there was substantial postorbital constriction. The left zygomatic bone, adequately described by Jacob (1966), is small and more lightly built than that of Sangiran 17. Excavation of the masseter attachment on its inferior border is less pronounced than in the larger Sangiran hominid.

Keeling in the midline is a prominent feature of the parietal region. There is considerable heaping up of bone on either side of the sagittal suture, especially at and just posterior to the vertex of the vault. This keeling, which is stronger in Sangiran 10 than in Sangiran 17 or Sambungmachan, is accompanied by parasagittal flattening which extends outward to the temporal lines. The latter are only faintly marked and difficult to trace. No angular torus is developed, but on the right there is a massive, rounded supramastoid crest. This is continued anteriorly onto the shelf-like zygomatic process of the temporal. Since all of the tympanic is missing, the shape of the external auditory opening cannot be determined, but its outer margin must have been at least slightly recessed below the zygomatic root.

The tip of the mastoid process is missing, as is part of its posterior face. A mastoid crest is only weakly developed, and the supramastoid sulcus is narrow and restricted in extent. Further forward, the right glenoid fossa is quite incomplete. Neither the ectoglenoid nor the entoglenoid processes are preserved. The intervening anterior articular surface is strongly concave from side to side, and no true tubercle is present. The postglenoid process takes the form of a low ridge (termed by Jacob a postglenoid crest). Unfortunately, since both the tympanic bone and the petrous portion of the temporal are lacking, nothing can be said concerning either the medial aspect of the glenoid cavity or the nature of the adjacent cranial base.

In rear view, Sangiran 10 presents features which are generally characteristic of *Homo erectus*. The vault is low and flattened, and breadth across the supramastoid crests is greater than any breadth measurement taken higher on the inward sloping parietal walls. A straight transverse torus, rounded and most projecting near the midline, traverses most of the width of the occiput. Its upper border is more clearly defined than is usually the case, but there is no external occipital protuberance. There is little development of a supratoral sulcus. The upper scale of the occiput is inclined forward. The torus is limited below by the superior nuchal lines. These are not deeply incised, and the underside of the torus does not overhang the nuchal plane to the degree seen in some of the larger Javanese hominids. The area occupied by the nuchal muscles is gently curved, and there is no indication of either a strong linear tubercle or an external occipital crest. Jacob (1966) suggests that a roughened 'retromastoid tuberosity' is present, but in fact there is no distinct retromastoid process.

SANGIRAN 12

Found in 1965, this individual is even less complete than Sangiran 10. The heavily mineralized vault has been pieced together from a number of fragments, some of which show signs of weathering. Only the posterior part of the frontal squama is preserved. Both the parietal and the upper part of the temporal bone, including the mastoid process, are present on the left, but on the right side nearly all of the temporal is missing. The occiput is represented by most of the squama, which is complete to the rear margin of the foramen magnum. All of the cranial base as well as the facial skeleton have been lost. What remains of the vault is undeformed, and faint traces of the sagittal, lambdoid and occipitomastoid sutures can be observed in the outer table. Endocranial suture closure is complete, although some meningeal markings and other surface details are apparent.

Since all of the anterior part of the frontal bone is missing, glabella–occipital length cannot be compared to that of other specimens. Maximum breadth as measured at the supramastoid crests is approximately 146 mm, so Sangiran 12 is larger than Sangiran 10. This size difference is reflected also in the cranial capacity estimate, which is 1059 ml (Holloway, 1981a). The Sangiran 12 brain cast is in fact the largest measured for any of the Sangiran hominids.

Form of the supraorbital region and depth of the temporal fossae cannot be determined, but the overall shape of the remaining frontal squama suggests that there was at least a moderate degree of postorbital constriction. The frontal surface is flat, although there is a low eminence at bregma. The parietals are smooth, and only on the left, where weathering has been less severe, can the temporal line be discerned. Where this line curves downward toward the inferior angle of the parietal, there is a distinct bulge, restricted to the area just forward of asterion. This corresponds to the angular torus described by Weidenreich, but it is faintly marked in comparison to that in the Zhoukoudian specimens. As in Sangiran 10, there is also a heavy, rounded supramastoid crest. Posteriorly, this crest curves sharply upward, so that the rear border of the temporal bone forms a nearly vertical ridge in front of the deep parietal incisure. Here the Sangiran hominid resembles Sambungmachan and the Ngandong individuals and is less like the crania from eastern Africa. Unfortunately the anterior part of the supramastoid crest is broken, and all of the bone surrounding the auditory opening has been lost. The region behind the meatus is preserved, however, and the sulcus intervening between the supramastoid and mastoid crests is deep and relatively restricted in extent. The lower crest is rounded and shows no tubercles. The mastoid process itself is short and nipple-like, and its posterior face is markedly flattened.

In rear view, the Sangiran 12 braincase appears low and poorly filled. Behind the vertex, the raised sagittal keel which characterizes Sangiran 10 is missing, and the superior aspect of the vault is flat. As in the smaller Sangiran skull, these parasagittal depressions are extensive. The parietal is more evenly rounded at the temporal line, but the curve steepens rapidly, and the wall is again flattened as it falls toward the squamosal boundary. The supramastoid region is very prominent, while the axis of the small mastoid process is inclined medially.

On the right side, the exterior of the occipital squama has been weathered. This scouring has smoothed the nuchal region and has substantially softened the outline of the transverse torus, so that the occiput is now slightly asymmetrical. On the left, where less damage has occurred, it is clear that the torus is quite heavy. This shelf is most prominent centrally, and above it there is a shallow sulcus. Just at the midline, on the surface of the torus, there is a rounded tubercle, somewhat elongated transversely. This projection is some 18–20 mm across and is bounded inferiorly by a distinct groove. It does not represent the linear tubercle, which lies below the groove at the junction of the superior nuchal lines. It may instead mark the meeting of the highest nuchal lines, although these cannot be traced laterally for any distance. If this is the correct interpretation, then the swelling corresponds to an external occipital protuberance which overlies and almost masks the linear tubercle. Such a protuberance does not

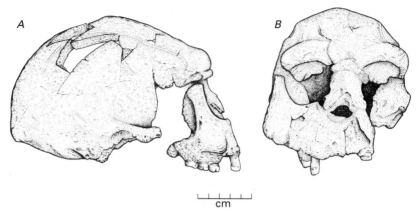

Fig. 6. Drawings of Sangiran 17, showing (A) right lateral and (B) facial
views of the cranium.

normally occur in *Homo erectus*. An alternate (less likely) possibility
is that the tubercle, which is slightly irregular in outline, is simply an
artifact left by erosion of the compact bone of the toral surface.

Immediately below the transverse torus, the nuchal plane is depressed at the sites of *m. semispinalis capitis* attachment. Narrower,
more restricted hollows are present on each side of the faint external
occipital crest, just behind the boundary of the (broken) foramen
magnum. More laterally, the nuchal surface is raised, and these
roughened bulges must coincide approximately with the attachments
of *m. rectus capitis posticus major*. Such swelling of the occipital
lower scale occurs in several of the other Asian crania and is
especially pronounced in the smaller East African individuals. On the
left, the digastric incisure is deep and wide, but all of the bone forward of the damaged mastoid tip is missing. Perhaps partly because
of weathering, a juxtamastoid eminence is not well defined. A low
ridge is present, but its surface is flattened. No division of this ridge
into separate crests can be discerned.

SANGIRAN 17 (Figs 4, 6, 9 & 13)

Sangiran 17 (skull VIII) has been described both by Jacob (1975) and
by Sartono (1975). It has been viewed as comparable morphologically
(and perhaps as drawn from a population ancestral) to the Ngandong
hominids. Much of the right side of the facial skeleton is preserved,
including both nasal bones, the zygomatic, and part of the maxilla

and hard palate with the crowns of (right) C, M^1, M^2 and M^3 in place. The face has been reconstructed, although some problems remain, especially with the positioning of the subnasal part of the maxilla. The floor of the nasal cavity is still partly obscured by matrix, but this opening is almost surely too low as presently restored. The join between the nasal root and the broken frontal is also suspect. The frontal itself has been pieced together from a number of fragments, and the right parietal is heavily damaged. The upper scale of the occiput has not been cleaned completely, and the nuchal area shows signs of weathering. Several of the basicranial structures including the left occipital condyle and tympanic plate, and both petrous bones, are either broken or missing altogether. Nearly all of the sphenoid has been lost. Otherwise the vault is in reasonable condition, and there is little indication that the bones have been plastically deformed.

Number 17 is one of the larger Sangiran crania and exceeds Sambungmachan in most linear dimensions. It is similar to several of the Ngandong crania and is also close in size to the braincase from Bed II at Olduvai (see Table 24 in Chapter 6). Glabella–occipital length is almost the same as in the African specimen, while the maximum breadth of Sangiran 17 is somewhat greater, mostly as a consequence of the exaggerated, shelf-like supramastoid crests. In breadth across the parietal bones, the skulls are similar, as they are in endocranial volume (measured as 1004 ml for skull VIII by Holloway).

The Sangiran 17 face is relatively narrow across the orbits but is broader below, with massive zygomatic arches. The nasal aperture is damaged, as is the maxillary alveolar process. All of the incisor teeth are missing, and their sockets have been resorbed or broken. The front of the maxilla appears to be short and not especially prognathic, but neither subnasal depth nor upper facial height can be measured with much accuracy. In its (moderate) degree of midfacial projection, Sangiran 17 may be comparable to KNM-ER 3733 from Koobi Fora. But the Asian hominid differs from the (African) specimen in that the rear of the alveolar process is very shallow. What remains of the hard palate is also shallow, and relatively long. Internal palate width at the level of M^1/M^2 cannot be much more than 45 mm. The occlusal plane defined by the three molar crowns slopes sharply (unnaturally) upward from front to back, and this may reflect the need for further reconstructive effort. The occlusal surface itself is helicoidal in form. The crown of M^1 shows more wear on its lingual aspect, while on M^2 the wear is more evenly distributed. At M^3, there

Table 3. *Measurements (mm) of the upper molar teeth of Sangiran 17*[a]

	M[1]	M[2]	M[3]
Mesiodistal diameter	11.0	11.4	9.2
Buccolingual diameter	12.8	12.6	13.0

[a] Mesiodistal and buccolingual diameters are taken parallel to the crown base as maximum readings. No corrections for interproximal attrition are included.

is clearly more loss of enamel on the buccal side. Dental measurements are given in Table 3.

The supraorbital torus is strongly developed, both centrally (17 mm) and at the lateral margin of the orbit (13 mm). The brow is similar in form to that of both Sambungmachan and the larger Solo skulls. There is also some resemblance to OH 9, although the torus is not quite so massively constructed as in the African individual. There is a slight depression of the supratoral surface near the midline, and glabella would protrude, if damage to the area just above the nasal root could be corrected. Behind the brows, the frontal is relatively broad and flat. There is some hollowing laterally, on each side, but there is no sagittal keeling. These features point generally in the direction of the Ngandong hominids, although the latter frontals are somewhat broader in every case.

In other respects, Sangiran 17 does not differ greatly from the braincase of Sangiran 12. There is a distinct eminence near bregma, but behind the vertex a faint sagittal ridge disappears before reaching lambda. On either side of the midline, the vault surface is depressed, to an extent not observed in any of the Ngandong specimens. Posteriorly, this parasagittal hollowing is less pronounced, but the lamboid borders of the parietals are still flattened. In side view, the temporal line describes a low curve which is raised only as it descends toward asterion. Details in this region are difficult to make out because of erosion and patches of matrix which still adhere to the bone surface. A strong angular torus is not present. There is a rounded, projecting supramastoid crest, more heavily built than that of the other Asian hominids examined. This crest is primarily horizontal in orientation. It does not slope steeply upward in the fashion characteristic of the Sambungmachan and Solo skulls. Anteriorly, the crest continues as a prominent shelf overhanging the external auditory meatus (which is blocked with matrix on both sides). The supramastoid sulcus is shallow. The small inturned mastoid process presents a lateral face which is rounded and not clearly divided into anterior or posterior portions.

The upper scale of the occipital is inclined forward, as in the other Sangiran individuals. This surface is covered almost entirely by a thin layer of hard deposit, so lambda cannot be located with much accuracy. The position of this landmark can be estimated, however, and the approximate length of the upper scale can be determined. The distance from lambda to inion (52 mm) is considerably less than the inion–opisthion length (57 mm), if inion is taken at the linear tubercle. The relatively short occipital plane is separated from the nuchal surface by a blunt transverse torus. This torus, slightly damaged at several points and still in need of cleaning, extends on each side toward a roughened retromastoid tuberosity but is nowhere as exaggerated in its development as that of some of the Ngandong crania. A shallow supratoral sulcus, if present, is obscured by matrix, and there is no external occipital protuberance.

The superior nuchal lines, limiting the torus inferiorly, converge at a linear tubercle which is partly eroded. The external occipital crest has also been weathered but can be followed to the rim of the foramen magnum. The broad nuchal plane, flattened on either side of the crest, is marked laterally by areas of swelling, less pronounced but otherwise comparable to the muscular impressions exhibited by Sangiran 12. Because of surface scouring, the sites of attachment of individual nuchal muscles can no longer be identified. The digastric notch is about 35 mm in length on the right and is deep and wide. As in Sangiran 12, the juxtamastoid eminence is low and not clearly set off from the more medial aspect of the occiput. No arterial groove can be discerned, and the position of the occipitomastoid suture cannot be located. The margin of the foramen magnum is damaged, but there appear to be no 'postcondyloid tuberosities' as described by Weidenreich for the Solo specimens.

The glenoid cavity is well preserved on the right side. There is no raised articular tubercle. As in the East African crania, the anterior articular surface is hollowed, and there is an even transition from this surface to the preglenoid planum. The cavity is relatively shallow and long in anteroposterior extent and is therefore more open than that typical of the Ngandong series. Laterally there is a well developed postglenoid tubercle, flattened on its inferior aspect. The entoglenoid process, partly eroded, is roughly pyramidal in form, and the spheno-temporal suture may (?) cross its apex. More medially, there is a small pointed spine, but this does not make any contribution to the wall of the mandibular fossa.

The tympanic plate, damaged on both sides, does not differ from that in most other *Homo erectus* crania examined. Its inferior border is thickened, especially near the stylomastoid opening. The spine which most probably arose from this part of the petrosal crest is broken, and the styloid pit is filled with matrix. At its medial ter-minus, the plate is again thickened, although a tubercle is not so prominent as that recorded for some other Asian and African indi-viduals.

The Sangiran mandibles

Parts of several lower jaws have been recovered from different levels in the Sangiran sediments. The famous B mandible was found first, in 1936. This was followed by the less complete Sangiran 5 specimen in 1939. Sangiran 6, a large jaw fragment referred to *Meganthropus*, was picked up in 1941. More remains have been collected since 1952, but there is little agreement about the significance of this assemblage. None of the mandibles has been found in direct association with a cranium, and as a consequence the fossils have been assigned to a variety of different taxa. This problem of the number of lineages represented by the Sangiran hominids deserves fuller treatment in a later section. Here only the original B mandible is described in some detail. This is still one of the best specimens, and there is (limited) agreement that it should be referred to *Homo erectus*.

SANGIRAN 1b

Stratigraphic provenience and dating of Sangiran 1b (the B mandible) are subject to some of the same uncertainties as in the case of San-giran 4. Said to be from the Pucangan Formation, this specimen con-sists of a right mandibular corpus, in which the crowns of P_4–M_3 are still in place. Dental measurements are given in Table 4. Sockets for I_2, C and P_3 are also preserved, but their anterior margins are eroded. The jaw is broken just short of the symphysis. The mandibular angle and nearly all of the ascending ramus are missing. The fossil is heavily mineralized and shows signs of weathering. It is likely that

Table 4. *Measurements (mm) of the teeth of Sangiran 1b (the B mandible)*[a]

	P_4	M_1	M_2	M_3
Mesiodistal diameter	8.9	12.9	13.2	14.4
Buccolingual diameter	10.8	12.9	13.4	12.5

[a] Mesiodistal and buccolingual diameters are taken parallel to the crown base as maximum readings. No corrections for interproximal attrition are included.

some surface features have been altered by this process or by rolling before burial, and the enamel on the buccal aspects of the tooth crowns has been eroded.

Measurements of the jaw are provided in Table 5. The Sangiran corpus is higher by several millimeters than that of Hominid 22 from Olduvai Gorge. It is closer in height to OH 51, but the latter is again thicker by a substantial margin. Sangiran 1b is less robust than either of the Olduvai specimens. The Javanese jaw also differs in its proportions from OH 13, which has been referred to *Homo habilis*. However, Sangiran 1b and OH 13 are similar in tooth row lengths and in some individual dental dimensions (Tobias & von Koenigswald, 1964). To approximately the level of P_4, the upper and lower borders of both bodies are parallel. Further forward, the lower margins curve upward, and probably the (damaged) anterior corpus of Sangiran 1b was slightly elevated relative to the occlusal plane of the cheek teeth,

Table 5. *Measurements (mm) of the corpus of Sangiran 1b (the B mandible)*

	I_2	$\bar{C}$	P_3	P_4	M_1	M_2	M_3
Breadth[a]	20	19	16.5	16	16	18	–
Minimum breadth[b]	16	16	16	15.8	16	17	–
Vertical height[c]	(31.5)	(31)	(31)	34	32.5	30	31
Minimum height[d]	–	–	–	33	34.2	32.2	33

[a] Taken with the shaft of the caliper held perpendicular to the long axis of the body and parallel to the occlusal plane.
[b] Caliper shaft is not necessarily held parallel to the occlusal plane.
[c] Taken on the internal aspect of the body. Where damage to the specimen is appreciable, ( ) indicates that only an estimate is possible.
[d] Taken from the base to the lateral alveolar margin.

as is true for OH 13. This shape contrasts with that of OH 22, where the base is quite straight all the way to the midline of the jaw.

The lateral prominence is rounded and is slightly better expressed than in OH 22, although it does not approach the size of the prominence exhibited by OH 13. This swelling subsides before reaching the base, and a marginal torus is either not developed or has been reduced by weathering. An anterior marginal tubercle is only faintly expressed. This lack of torus formation gives the mandibular base a gracile appearance, which changes only where the digastric fossa is impressed into the bone below the sockets for the anterior dentition. Higher on the external surface, the lateral prominence is continued forward as a superior torus, which ends below P_4. Several mental foramina are present, as noted in earlier descriptions. Below the sockets for P_3 and C, some minor damage has occurred, but the bone is otherwise smooth and gently rounded. No prominent canine jugum is developed. Toward the (broken) midline, the surface of the corpus is flat, and there is no evidence of chin formation.

Internally, an alveolar prominence is strong at the level of M_3 but is nowhere as projecting as that of OH 22. Both its upper border and lower margin exhibit signs of weathering, and there is no sharp division between the alveolar process and the posterior subalveolar fossa below. Anteriorly, the wall of the corpus is gently convex, and only near the base is there any indication of subalveolar hollowing. The alveolar planum shows little flattening and is less prominent than that of OH 22. Here there is strong contrast to the condition exhibited by OH 13, and among the Olduvai jaws, probably OH 51 provides the closest approach to the morphology of Sangiran 1b. The planum slopes rather steeply downward, and no superior transverse torus can be seen. Because of damage to the symphysis, details of genial anatomy are lost, and it is not possible even to confirm the presence of an inferior torus. Certainly the lower part of the symphysis is thickened, as in other archaic *Homo* specimens. However, since there is a great deal of variation among Pleistocene hominids in the expression of these transverse tori, the fact that they may be poorly developed in the Sangiran jaw should not be accorded special significance.

The Sambungmachan braincase (Fig. 7)

Sambungmachan 1 consists of the better part of a braincase discovered in 1973. The vault shows a number of deep cracks, some of

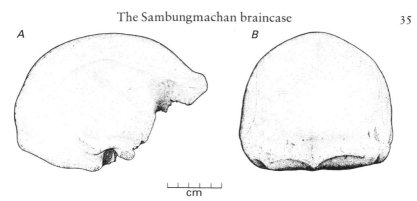

Fig. 7. Drawings of the Sambungmachan cranium, as viewed from (A)
the right side and (B) the posterior aspect.

which have spread slightly, but there is little serious distortion. All of
the facial skeleton is missing. The frontal is damaged anteriorly on
the left side, and the glabellar region is broken away. None of the
sphenoid is preserved, save for the uppermost part of the greater wing
on the right. The tympanic parts of both temporals are damaged, and
neither of the petrous pyramids remain. All of the basilar portion of
the occiput is also missing, as are the foramen magnum, condyles and
much of the more anterior aspect of the nuchal plane. Other parts of
the occipital squama, the right mastoid process, left glenoid cavity
and both parietal bones are in good condition, so quite a lot of
anatomical information can be obtained.

The Sambungmachan cranium is approximately 200 mm in length,
as measured from glabella to opisthocranion. It is a little shorter and
also a little less broad than Sangiran 17 (Table 24 in Chapter 6).
Cranial capacity is estimated by Jacob (1975) as 1035 ml, but this
figure must be regarded as tentative, pending final cleaning from the
specimen of the hard matrix which still partly fills the braincase. For
the present, it is clear that Sambungmachan is a better match to individuals such as Sangiran 12 and Sangiran 17 than to the smaller
Indonesian crania.

On the right, the supraorbital torus is preserved from a point some
15–20 mm short of the midline to approximately the position of the
frontomalar suture. The torus is thick and forms a straight shelf over
the orbit. There is little tendency for the brow to be reduced in thickness laterally. Postorbital constriction is less pronounced than in
Sangiran 17. This is a consequence partly of greater frontal width but

is also a result of decreased lateral flare of the supraorbital torus and accompanying temporal crests. The wall of the temporal fossa is flatter than in some of the other hominids examined.

The supratoral aspect of the frontal bone is flattened, although there is an indication of hollowing centrally, above glabella (which is missing). No groove-like sulcus is developed, but the squama rises somewhat more steeply and is less flattened from side to side than in Sangiran 17. This gives the frontal a more evenly rounded appearance, and there is just a trace of keeling in the midline. In all of these respects, Sambungmachan resembles several of the Ngandong hominids in frontal form.

In side view, the raised temporal line follows a low trajectory across the parietal. There is a broad, flattened expanse of bone above, between the uppermost temporal insertion and the midline of the vault. The distance between the two (superior) lines at their nearest approach is 98 mm, and there is some faint keeling along the sagittal suture. In front of asterion, the line curves down and forward, toward the mastoid crest. The supramastoid crest is very well developed, although it is less prominent than that of Sangiran 17. It arcs upward posteriorly for several centimeters, apparently as an unusually strong inferior temporal line and is continued forward over the external auditory meatus to produce a sharply defined shelf, which is continuous with the root of the zygoma. The recessed porus is rounded in outline, and behind it the supramastoid sulcus is deep and relatively narrow. There is no anterior mastoid tubercle. The external face of the mastoid process is blunt and roughened rather than strongly crested, and the process itself is short (20 mm). Its tip is incurved, as is usually the case for *Homo erectus* crania.

Much of the occipital squama is also preserved, and a transverse torus is quite prominent. Near the midline, the torus is rounded and not clearly delimited above, although a shallow supratoral sulcus can be discerned. There is no localized suprainiac depression. On the right side, where there is no damage, the torus is continued laterally at least to the limit of *m. semispinalis capitis* insertion. Its lower border is much more sharply marked by the superior nuchal line, and the areas of muscle attachment below are set deeply into the nuchal surface. This causes the torus and especially the associated linear tubercle to stand out in greater relief than in the East African *Homo erectus* crania, but there is some resemblance to the Ngandong specimens. No true external occipital protuberance is formed. Below the linear tubercle, some of the bone of the midline is missing, but an occipital crest is apparently not present.

The superior nuchal line arcs laterally from the linear tubercle, where it is clearly defined. It becomes less distinct and appears only as a slight surface roughening as it curves forward to approach the mastoid crest. There is no retromastoid process. The posterior aspect of the mastoid process is somewhat flattened. Since the mastoid crest is not prominent, this posterior face merges evenly with the more rounded lateral part of the process. There is some contrast here to the condition in East African *Homo erectus* crania, where the posterior aspect of the mastoid process may be more extensively flattened to form a plane limited by the stronger mastoid crest.

On the left, a digastric incisure can be traced for some 30 mm, and the stylomastoid foramen is preserved. The notch is about 5.5 mm across posteriorly, at its widest point. Its medial border is raised to produce a low ridge, corresponding to the 'paramastoid' crest (Weidenreich, 1951) or juxtamastoid eminence. More medially there is another groove, approximately parallel to the digastric notch and about as deep. This channel for the occipital artery is bounded in turn by the insertion of *m. obliquus capitis superior*. Since the course of the occipitomastoid suture is obliterated, it is difficult to determine whether all or only part of the juxtamastoid eminence lies on the temporal bone. Structures which should be located on the adjacent section of the occipital squama, below the inferior nuchal lines, are missing.

The glenoid cavity is best preserved on the left side of the Sambungmachan cranium, although the articular tubercle and medial wall are both damaged. The central part of the fossa appears to be relatively shallow and open from front to back. The anterior articular surface must have passed smoothly onto the preglenoid planum (most of which is missing), so a true articular tubercle is not present. Medially the fossa assumes a more restricted form, and it ends in a cleft between the broken entoglenoid process and the tympanic plate. Because the entoglenoid is so badly damaged, it is not possible to trace the sphenotemporal suture or to determine whether the sphenoid itself may have contributed to the medial wall of the cavity. Laterally, below the zygomatic root, the postglenoid process is small and flattened.

The tympanic plate, again least damaged on the left side, forms the front and lower border of the auditory porus. This part of the bone is thickened, but not to the extent seen in OH 9. Its inferior aspect is blunt rather than crested as in the African hominid. More medially, a petrosal crest is developed, and there are traces of a (damaged?) spine near the jugular opening. Unfortunately, the area where any pit or depression to receive the root of a styloid process would be located is obscured. It is not clear that either a styloid vagina or an actual process was present in the Sambungmachan specimen. Also, it cannot be determined whether the tympanic plate ends medially in a tubercle of the sort seen in African *Homo erectus* and in the Zhoukoudian crania. This region, anterior to the carotid canal and adjacent to the entoglenoid process, is broken.

The Ngandong crania

Cranial remains recovered between 1931 and 1933 at Ngandong in eastern Java are listed as Ngandong 1 through Ngandong 12 by Oakley *et al.* (1975). Two tibiae are also part of this assemblage. The first six crania were described by Oppenoorth (1932), and later 11 skulls and the tibiae were treated in an important monograph left unfinished by Weidenreich (1951). This material has been described most recently by Santa Luca (1980). New cranial remains recovered in 1976 are said to represent one or two additional individuals, but only brief comments concerning these fossils have been published. The more complete original braincases are touched on here. Measurements for Ngandong 1, Ngandong 7, Ngandong 11 and Ngandong 12 are listed in Table 24.

NGANDONG 1 (Fig. 8)

The first of the Ngandong individuals consists principally of the frontal, parietal and occipital portions of a vault. The face is missing, although the upper parts of both nasal bones are still in place below the brow. On the right, the squama and mastoid region of the temporal bone are present, but most of the rest of the cranial base is not preserved. As noted by Weidenreich, the specimen has undergone some plastic deformation. The occiput is slightly warped and skewed with respect to the long axis of the vault, and the frontal surface is no longer quite symmetrical. The bones also appear to have been polished. A good deal of surface detail has been worn away, and the meningeal patterns are very indistinct. Earlier application of a preser-

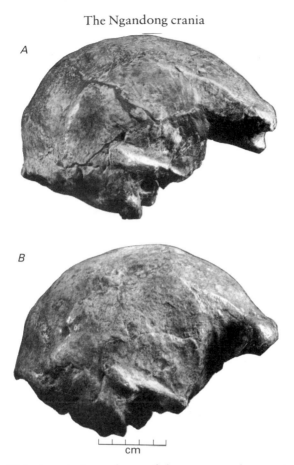

Fig. 8. Right lateral views of two of the more complete crania from Ngandong. (A) Ngandong 1 is described by Weidenreich (1951) as female, while (B) Ngandong 12 is claimed as male.

vative has probably contributed to the loss of definition of some external features.

The frontal is broad and flattened anteriorly, behind the brows. There is no hollowing of the surface of the squama above glabella, and no supratoral sulcus is developed. Although the bone is damaged on both sides, it is clear that postorbital constriction is not marked (least frontal breadth, about 106 mm, is greater than that of Sambungmachan). Very faint keeling in the midline extends over only a short distance and disappears several centimeters before reaching the vertex of the vault. The supraorbital torus, of even thickness throughout, is slightly less well developed than in Sambungmachan 1.

As compared to some other *Homo erectus* from Java, glabella is not prominent, resulting in only slight indentation of the nasal root. Weidenreich (1951) views this individual as female, while Santa Luca (1980) prefers to describe it as a male. Endocranial capacity as determined by Holloway (1980) is 1172 ml.

On the right, the broken temporal bone has been partly reconstructed, and there is a rounded (worn?) supramastoid crest. This is separated from the poorly defined and damaged mastoid crest below by a supramastoid sulcus which is extensive and flattened. Here there is some contrast to Sambungmachan, which exhibits stronger crests associated with a narrower sulcus, but in both individuals the supramastoid crest is continued posteriorly and upward, to follow the inferior temporal line. There is no connection with the descending arc of the superior line (or with the angular torus, which is not well defined in Ngandong 1). The mastoid process itself (>30 mm in length) is large by *Homo erectus* standards. Its tip is broken but was apparently inclined medially.

In occipital view, the cranium is similar to Sambungmachan and shows less parasagittal flattening than Sangiran 10. Slight keeling occurs along the sagittal suture. Maximum breadth of the vault cannot be measured satisfactorily, because of damage to the left side, but this must lie at or near the supramastoid crests. Biparietal breadth (149 mm) is somewhat less. The upper scale of the occiput, approximately vertical in orientation, is bounded below by a prominent transverse torus. An elongated supratoral sulcus is present, and this hollowing along its upper margin causes the torus to stand out in stronger relief than in the Sambungmachan individual, where the torus is more mound-like. The superior nuchal lines are also clearly marked, and the attachments of the *semispinalis* complex of muscles are deeply excavated. The transverse torus, linear tubercle, and an external occipital crest extending toward opisthion are therefore all sharply defined, and on the right there is a retromastoid process.

As a result of weathering, the anatomy of the mastoid region is indistinct. A digastric incisure, shallow and damaged anteriorly, is limited medially by a low ridge. In his general description of the Solo skulls, Weidenreich (1951, p. 280) refers to this structure as a 'paramastoid' crest, noting that an occipitomastoid crest may be located still more medially. However, in this individual only one ridge is present, and this seems to conform to what is elsewhere termed an occipitomastoid crest. In any case, it is not large. A more striking feature of the occiput is the rounded swelling of the right margin of the foramen magnum. This takes the form of an elongated tubercle, called by Weidenreich (p. 264) a 'postcondyloid tuberosity'.

Only the lateral part of the tympanic is preserved. This bone is thickened inferiorly, and a very prominent spine is developed from the petrosal crest. The posterior aspect of this spine shows a vertical furrow, at the base of which there is a circular pit. No styloid process is present. The tympanic plate falls steeply to the floor of the glenoid cavity, which is deep and short. The outer part of the cavity, including the ectoglenoid and postglenoid processes, is broken away, and only a part of the entoglenoid region is preserved.

NGANDONG 3

Ngandong 3 is quite incomplete, consisting only of two parietals, the posterior part of the frontal squama, the broken left temporal and fragments of the occiput. All of these parts are firmly united, and most sutural markings are obliterated. The bone is in good condition, showing no signs of warping. When this skull was first prepared, a piece of parietal found with the other bones was numbered as skull IIIA. Weidenreich (1951) originally concluded that both the parietal and the rest of the braincase represent the same individual. However, his view has been challenged, and Ngandong 4 (skull IIIA) is here treated as a separate specimen, not as a fragment of Ngandong 3.

There are clear parallels between this Solo individual and Sambungmachan. Ngandong 3 is a little less broad across the parietals, while the chord from bregma to lambda is slightly longer. The frontal exhibits only a trace of keeling, but this faint sagittal ridge is continued past bregma onto the parietal vault. In superior view, and again in the form of the parietal walls as seen from the rear, the two hominids are comparable. The bone of the Ngandong cranium is also very thick (17 mm at asterion). Partly because of this feature, Weidenreich has suggested that the skull is that of a male.

Ngandong 3 differs from Sambungmachan in that the temporal lines are less well defined, and there is no angular torus. A heavy, blunt supramastoid crest is present but is broken anteriorly, just after crossing the external auditory opening. This crest is also damaged behind, as it begins to swing upward in the same way as in Sambungmachan and Ngandong 1. The supramastoid sulcus is broad and only moderately deepened, while what remains of the mastoid process resembles the condition seen in Sambungmachan. Only the most posterior part of the mastoid notch is intact, and this appears to be quite deep and narrow.

On the occiput, a segment of the transverse torus is preserved on the left side. This is broken prior to reaching the midline and inion has been lost. The torus is low and rounded in form, and its upper margin is not well defined. Impressions left by *m. semispinalis capitis* attachments are much shallower than in Sambungmachan, and the torus is less prominent than in the other Solo hominids. It is largely on this account that Santa Luca (1980), who disagrees with Weidenreich concerning the sex of Ngandong 3, refers to the specimen as female.

NGANDONG 6 (Fig. 9)

This individual was excavated *in situ* by Oppenoorth in 1933. It had been crushed, and later attempts at restoration failed to correct completely for damage to the right side. Because of these breaks and also as a result of some plastic deformation of the bones, the braincase is asymmetrical. Warping has affected the right side and the occipit, and some measurements will not be reliable. Much of the cranial base is missing, but on the left, the glenoid cavity, tympanic bone and mastoid region of the temporal are still intact. As with the other Ngandong specimens, the facial skeleton has been destroyed.

The Ngandong 6 supraorbital torus, complete centrally and on the left side, curves downward slightly at glabella but is otherwise of approximately constant thickness. Only below the most lateral part of the brow, near the junction with the malar bone, is there any appreciable thinning. As with Ngandong 1, nasion is not depressed, and the supratoral surface of the frontal is flattened. Minimum breadth between the temporal crests is 104 mm, and postorbital constriction is relatively slight. There is little sign of keeling in the midline. In frontal characteristics and also in the overall proportions of its braincase, Ngandong 6 (or skull V) generally resembles Sambungmachan. However, skull V is larger, and glabella–occipital length is 221 mm. Its cranial capacity of 1251 ml (Holloway, 1980) makes Ngandong 6 one of the largest of the Solo hominids. The size and robust build of this individual originally prompted Weidenreich to label it a male.

On the left, the temporal line is lightly marked over most of its course but produces a low angular torus at its most posterior extent.

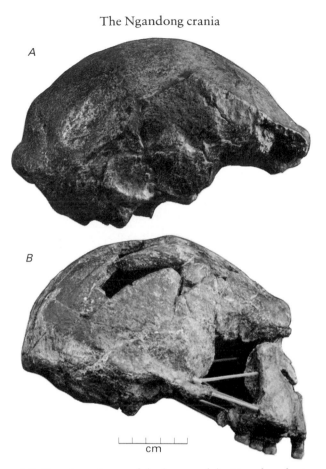

Fig. 9. (A) Ngandong 6, one of the largest of the Ngandong braincases said by Weidenreich (1951) to be that of a male, photographed in lateral view and compared to (B) the cranium of Sangiran 17.

In skull V, this torus conforms to the description provided by Weidenreich (1951) for all of the Solo specimens and is 'a distinct, elongated bulge, filling out the posterior part of the mastoid angle of the parietal bone' (p. 241). The supramastoid crest is angled upward, as in the other Ngandong and Sambungmachan crania. This crest is comparable in development to that of Sambungmachan. It forms a distinct shelf over the meatus and is continued forward into the root of the heavily built zygomatic process. On its superior surface, this process presents a concave channel which is quite broad. The recessed auditory porus is elliptical in form, and its long axis lies just a few degrees from the vertical. Behind this opening, the supramastoid sulcus is narrow and deep, although the mastoid crest is only faintly marked. The mastoid tip is broken, but the process apparently was large (> 30 mm in length), as in Ngandong 1. Its posterior face is broad, slightly roughened by muscle attachment, and flat. This somewhat resembles the condition seen in African *Homo erectus*, but in skull V, the mastoid surface is more laterally directed and does not merge evenly with the nuchal plane of the occiput.

A striking feature of the occipital is the transverse torus, which is more massive in Ngandong 6 than in either Sambungmachan or Sangiran 17. The torus is also large in comparison to that of the other Solo individuals and is much heavier than any developed in the African crania. An extensive supratoral sulcus is present, and this accentuates projection of the torus with respect to the upper scale of the occiput. No external protuberance is apparent. The torus is continued laterally and terminates on each side in a prominent, roughened retromastoid process. Impressions left by the nuchal muscles are very deep, and a linear tubercle, strongly defined, exends for some 10–12 mm downward below the torus in the midline. The external occipital crest is only slightly raised, but the lower margin of the torus itself is sharp and overhangs the nuchal surface in the same way as in Sambungmachan. Because of damage, the inferior nuchal lines are obscured in the center of the squama. But their posterosuperiorly-directed secondary branches form blunt ridges which arc upward to join the retromastoid tuberosities.

Enough of the temporal bone is preserved to show that the glenoid cavity is deep and more open than that of Ngandong 1. A postglenoid process is only slightly developed, as in other Ngandong specimens. The ectoglenoid process and the surface of the articular tubercle are worn and partly eroded, and the entoglenoid pyramid seems to be missing altogether. Whether there is any contribution by the sphenoid to the medial wall of the cavity can no longer be determined. The fossa does appear to be constricted medially, and probably there was a narrow fissure extending between the (damaged) entoglenoid process and the tympanic plate. The surface of the plate itself, forming the posterior boundary of the cavity, is slightly convex but is oriented vertically. The entire inferior margin is greatly thickened, and there is a large tubercle-like spine protruding from the petrosal crest. This is similar to the spine of Ngandong 1. Its posterior aspect is marked by a shallow groove which ends in a deep, elongated opening placed just to the medial side of the stylomastoid foramen. At its inner terminus,

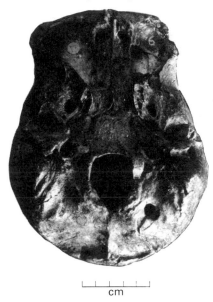

cm

Fig. 10. Photograph of Ngandong 7, in basal view.

the tympanic bone is damaged, but there are traces of another blunt projection, located forward of the carotid canal.

NGANDONG 7 (Fig. 10)

Ngandong 7 (or skull VI) is perhaps the best preserved of the Ngandong hominids. The braincase is complete except for some minor damage to the supraorbital region and to the temporal bones on both sides. Parts of the nasals, the ethmoid, the superior border of the vomer and sections of the sphenoid are intact, but the rest of the face is missing. This individual has not been subject to the plastic deformation which has affected Ngandong 1 and Ngandong 6, and there is no noticeable asymmetry. However, the vault surface shows a number of pits and irregular depressions, and there is an especially large area of damage on the left parietal. This oval-shaped lesion is interpreted by Weidenreich (1951, pp. 238–9) as evidence of a partly healed wound, perhaps inflicted by a blunt weapon.

Ngandong 7, with a cranial length of 192 mm, is appreciably smaller than Ngandong 6 and is viewed by Weidenreich and by Santa Luca (1980) as female. The frontal bone is not as flattened as in some of the other Ngandong hominids (skull V, for example) and is remarkably close in its breadth dimensions to that of Sambungmachan.

Postorbital constriction is also comparable to that of this latter skull, and in Ngandong 7, where the greater wing of the sphenoid is partly preserved on both sides, the wall of the temporal fossa is not deeply guttered. The browridge is straight and maximally thickened laterally, just at the corner of the orbit. As in skull V, the angular (zygomatic) process is then abruptly tapered as it drops downward to the frontomalar suture. The torus is interrupted centrally by a distinct depression at glabella, while the supratoral surface is gently hollowed as in Sambungmachan. There is slight keeling in the midline.

As in the other Solo crania, the upper (squamosal) border of the temporal bone is flattened, and the superior temporal line follows a low course across the parietal. This line is only faintly raised in Ngandong 7, and no angular torus is present. The supramastoid crest, occurring as a rounded swelling behind the external meatus, is bounded below by a shallow sulcus, more like that of Ngandong 3 than the groove-like sulcus of Ngandong 6. No anterior mastoid tubercle can be discerned. The mastoid process, said by Weidenreich to be 'relatively small', is nevertheless larger than that of Sambungmachan and quite well developed in comparison to other *Homo erectus* individuals. Its outer surface is roughened by muscle attachment but is not heavily crested. The auditory porus, preserved on both sides, is circular on the right but elliptical on the left. In each case, the thickened rim of the porus is overhung by the zygomatic root, which is moderately projecting.

In rear view, this individual exhibits characteristics seen in most of the other crania of the Ngandong series. Bone along the sagittal suture is heaped up to form a distinct ridge near the vertex, although this keel is not as pronounced as that of Sangiran 10. On either side of the midline, there is some parasagittal flattening. Below the temporal lines, the parietal walls are rounded, but there is no bossing, and greatest breadth of the vault falls near the base, at the supramastoid crests. The mastoid surfaces drop down and sharply inward, as is true also in the Chinese and African representatives of archaic *Homo*.

The upper scale of the occiput slopes slightly forward and is set almost at a right angle to the flattened nuchal plane below. The occiput is, therefore, strongly curved, as has been emphasized in most descriptions of *Homo erectus* crania. In Ngandong 7, the upper scale is actually somewhat longer than the lower, when inion is defined as the junction of the superior nuchal lines at the linear tubercle. However, these distances are affected by the choice of landmarks used, and if inion is taken instead on the most projecting part of the transverse torus (as by Weidenreich), the lengths of the two scales are more nearly equal. This is the technique also employed by Santa Luca, who notes that the occipital plane is slightly larger than the nuchal plane in some but not all of the Solo crania.

In the midline, above the occipital torus and impressed in part into its upper margin, there is a shallow depression. This is oval in form and approximately 30 mm across at its widest point. It resembles the suprainiac fossa seen in (some) European Neanderthal crania, although Santa Luca (1978) has argued that this distinctive Neanderthal feature does not occur in the Far Eastern hominids. Weidenreich (1951, p. 245) comments on the presence in the Ngandong skulls of an irregular furrow above the torus and notes that its central portion may appear to be eroded. However, in Ngandong 7 this depression is similar to several of the other pits and scars which mark the exterior of the vault, and it may well have resulted from damage inflicted before death. While a more elongated supratoral sulcus is frequently found in the Ngandong series, a localized suprainiac fossa of the sort described in European specimens does not occur in the other Solo skulls examined.

The transverse torus is as strongly developed as in Sambungmachan but is not so massive as the torus of Ngandong 6. The linear tubercle is continuous (below) with a rather delicate external occipital crest, and from the tubercle the superior nuchal lines curve laterally toward the retromastoid tuberosities. These tuberosities and also the inferior nuchal lines are much less prominent than in the larger Ngandong 6 individual. However, the attachments of the *semispinalis* complex are deeply imprinted into the nuchal surface, and the regions occupied by *m. obliquus capitis superior* insertions are outlined in strong relief. More medially, the area on either side of the foramen magnum is hollowed and irregular, as noted by Weidenreich (1951, p. 280). Just behind the occipital condyles, the rim of the foramen itself is greatly thickened. These 'postcondyloid tuberosities' are diffuse and roughened, rather than smooth and distinct as in Ngandong 1.

The digastric incisure is narrow and approximately 27 mm in length on the right. On the left it is deeper but is abruptly truncated at the rear of the mastoid process. The anatomy of this region is clearer on the right, where the incisure is bounded medially by a low ridge. Bordering this eminence there is another shallower groove (for the occipital artery?) which appears to bifurcate anteriorly to produce two faint channels which course forward toward the styloid recess.

The inner margin of this second groove is continuous with the line marking the more lateral extent of *m. obliquus capitis superior* insertion and is thus linked posteriorly with the nuchal line and with the retromastoid tuberosity. As is the case with Sambungmachan, the part of this complex which lies adjacent to the mastoid process can be regarded as a weak juxtamastoid eminence. The eminence is here partitioned into paramastoid and occipitomastoid crests, although the latter is only faintly expressed.

The tympanic bone is massive in construction, and its inferior border is rounded rather than sharp as in modern humans. From the margin of the auditory opening, this blunt petrosal 'crest' slopes in and downward, to give rise to a strong spine, as in Ngandong 6. No styloid process is preserved, but posteriorly this spine carries a vertical channel, which ends in a deep styloid pit. The more medial aspect of the petrosal crest is thinner but is drawn out at the end into a discrete tubercle. This is the process supratubarius of Weidenreich (1943), and it is prominently developed in other *Homo erectus* also. The petrous temporals are preserved on both sides. As in other Solo crania, the inferior surface of the pyramid is roughened but does not present the eroded appearance found in modern humans. The foramen lacerum is a relatively narrow crevice, interposed between the petrous apex and the basilar part of the occipital. The long axes of the pyramids seem to be inclined in an anteroposterior direction, so as to be angled more sharply relative to the tympanic axes than is characteristic of modern humans.

Unfortunately, the lateral parts of both glenoid cavities, including the ectoglenoid and postglenoid processes, are broken. Enough of this region remains to show that the cavity is deep. Its anterior face may be flatter and rise more steeply than that of Sambungmachan, and here there is more expression of an articular tubercle or ridge separating the fossa from the preglenoid planum. The entoglenoid processes are preserved, and on the left it is clear that this tubercle is made up of both squamous temporal and sphenoid contributions. The more medially located (sphenoid) portion projects slightly, as a low ridge applied to the adjacent tympanic bone, but a prominent sphenoid spine is not produced.

NGANDONG 10

In this individual (skull IX), most of the frontal is preserved, but the parietal bones and both temporals are heavily damaged. Most of the back of the occiput is intact, while other parts of the base and facial skeleton are missing. When it was discovered, the vault was shattered, and liberal amounts of plaster have been used in its reconstruction. These efforts have proven reasonably successful, although there are several areas where contacts between adjoining bone fragments are slightly misaligned. There is also some distortion of the remaining parts of the cranial base, and the biauricular axis is no longer quite perpendicular to the sagittal plane.

In many respects, Ngandong 10 resembles several of the smaller crania in the Solo series. It exceeds Ngandong 7 in both glabella–occipital length (approximately 202 mm) and maximum breadth (159 mm) but is close to Sambungmachan in these dimensions. Form of the rounded frontal squama and breadth across the temporal crests are comparable in all three crania, and in Ngandong 10 there is no frontal sagittal ridge or keel. The glabellar area is broken, but what remains of the supraorbital torus is a little thinner and more gracile in construction than in the other individuals. As in Ngandong 6 and 7, this torus is most thickened just at the corner of the orbit, while the surface of the frontal bounded in front by the brow and laterally by the temporal crest is flattened.

Morphology of the mastoid region is very robust. The supramastoid crest is as well developed as in any of the Ngandong crania but still does not match that of Sangiran 17. The rim of the auditory porus is damaged but must be quite deeply recessed below the sharply shelving zygomatic root. The area behind the external auditory opening is smooth and extends posteriorly and upward as a wide supramastoid sulcus. On the right, the distance between the mastoid and supramastoid crests is about 15 mm. The mastoid crest is also prominent, especially on the left side where it ends above as a roughened tubercle. This tubercle does not lie on the floor of the supramastoid sulcus or near its anterior end but instead is situated further back, well below and slightly behind the most posterior aspect of the upturned supramastoid crest. As in the other Solo crania, the mastoid processes are large, but the tips are broken on both sides.

Damage to the upper scale of the occipital is extensive, but it is apparent that the bone surface is hollowed above the projecting transverse torus. This torus is lightly constructed as in Ngandong 1 and is not as massive as the torus of the larger Ngandong 6 individual. The nuchal plane, which ends at the rear of the foramen magnum, is flattened but clearly shows the scars left by attachment of the major muscles. Although the retromastoid tuberosities are quite prominent, development of the superior nuchal lines, linear tubercle and external occipital crest is generally comparable to that described for Ngandong 7 or for Sambungmachan.

NGANDONG 11

This cranium has been rather heavily reconstructed, but shows no signs of plastic deformation. All of the facial skeleton is missing, as are the basal and lateral parts of the occiput, the petrous bones, and much of the sphenoid. The squamous temporals and mastoid processes are badly weathered, and there is extensive erosion over many areas of the vault surface. There are also several pits, which Weidenreich tentatively ascribes to blows or other injuries received at or before the time of death.

In the features that are well enough preserved to allow comparisons, Ngandong 11 falls well within the range of variation exhibited by the other Solo crania. It is thick-walled, and the frontal is very wide and flattened. The supraorbital torus is relatively thin, especially centrally, but other crests and prominences are heavily developed. The transverse torus of the occiput forms a rounded shelf, limited above by an extensive sulcus and below by the deep impressions left by the *semispinalis* muscle complex. There is no true external occipital protuberance, and the linear tubercle is small (by Ngandong standards). As with the other skulls, the occipital bone appears to be strongly flexed in side view, while the flattened nuchal plane reaches a level at or slightly above the Frankfurt Horizontal.

Of particular note are the proportions of the glenoid cavity. The fossa is damaged on both sides but is shorter in (anteroposterior) length and more constricted medially than is characteristic of the other fossils. The inner part of the cavity is crevice-like, and here Ngandong 11 closely resembles *Homo erectus* specimens from Zhoukoudian and Olduvai. The rim of the external auditory porus is very thick, and the tympanic plate is massive throughout. The remains of an eroded petrosal spine are present only on the right side.

NGANDONG 12 (Fig. 8)

Ngandong 12 is slightly less complete than Ngandong 7 but is still very well preserved. Only the facial parts are missing, although the zygomatic and mastoid portions of both temporal bones are damaged. The skull gives the appearance of having been flattened somewhat on the right side, but with the exception of certain vault breadth dimensions, measurements will not be seriously affected. All of the cranial base behind the spheno-occipital synchondrosis is in good condition.

This individual, rather thick-walled and heavily muscled, is claimed by Weidenreich as a male, although it is smaller than Ngandong 6. Holloway's (1980) estimate for cranial capacity is 1090 ml. In both facial and lateral views, the skull presents many of the characters common in other specimens of the Ngandong group. The frontal is relatively broad, especially anteriorly where there is little postorbital constriction. The shelf-like supraorbital torus is thickened laterally, while glabella lies in a slight hollow, restricted to the area just above the nasal root. The frontal squama is flattened, and there is no sagittal ridge or keel. Although the vault surface shows some signs of erosion, the temporal line is well marked on the left. There is a prominent angular torus, which swells to fill out all of the posterior inferior angle of the parietal. Neither the mastoid nor the supramastoid crests is as well developed as in some of the other crania (Ngandong 6 and 10, for example), and on the left the supramastoid sulcus forms a groove. There is no mastoid tubercle. In Ngandong 12, the sutures are still open, and it is clear that the superior border of the temporal bone is long, slopes downward toward the deep incisure, and is straight rather than arched as in more recent humans. Both of the external auditory openings are circular, and their rims are greatly thickened.

A striking feature of the occiput is the transverse torus, which bulges downward so as to overhang the hollowed nuchal plane. In this individual, the torus is most prominent centrally, where the linear tubercle stands out in strong relief. The curving superior nuchal line marks the inferior margin of the torus, which is thickened and carries several small bony exostoses. This margin is more rounded but still projecting laterally where it merges with the retromastoid tuberosity. As in several of the other Ngandong hominids, the occipital torus and its associated tubercles are more strongly developed than in the Sangiran (Kabuh) hominids, including Sangiran 17. The architecture of this part of the occiput, which is also more robust than in East African *Homo erectus* crania, suggests the presence of very heavy nuchal musculature.

The (broken) mastoid processes are also large, as might be expected in a male. On the left side, a deep and very narrow digastric notch covers a distance of 26 mm before reaching the stylomastoid foramen. Here the division of the juxtamastoid eminence into paramastoid and occipitomastoid crests, separated by a deep groove, is especially clear. The more medial occipitomastoid crest, which carries the occipitomastoid suture, is continuous with the superior oblique line and is joined thereby to the retromastoid process behind. This entire juxtamastoid complex is more strongly developed than in Ngandong 7. Unfortunately, the surface of the occiput lying between the stylomastoid foramen and the leading edge of the foramen magnum shows signs of (pathological?) damage on both sides. Deep pits containing small perforations occur behind the jugular openings, and the condyles are missing. Postcondyloid swellings are preserved, as described by Weidenreich (1951, p. 264).

The glenoid cavity is complete on the right and resembles that of Ngandong 7 in its general proportions. Breadth as measured from the ectoglenoid to the entoglenoid process is 32 mm. The cavity is deep and relatively short but is only moderately constricted medially, behind the entoglenoid process. The latter is small and is made up principally of squamous temporal. The course of the sphenotemporal suture is not quite clear, but there is certainly no prominent sphenoid spine. The anterior articular surface is slightly concave from side to side, and in this individual (as in Ngandong 7) there is a low ridge which separates the anterior margin of the cavity from the preglenoid planum. This ridge is oriented obliquely with respect to the transverse plane, so the rather flattened articular 'tubercle' which it delineates is triangular in form, with its apex facing forward. This tubercle is not prominent and bar-like as in many modern crania but is nevertheless better developed than in other *Homo erectus* specimens.

The anatomy of the massive tympanic bone is similar to that of the other Ngandong individuals, and there is a blunt petrosal spine. The most medial part of the plate seems to be damaged on the right, while on the left the process supratubarius is small and perhaps also incomplete. Both petrous temporals are intact and resemble those of Ngandong 7.

Sorting the fossils into lineages

Given this wealth of material from Java, and the likelihood that the fossils cover a lengthy span of time, it is important to determine how many distinct species may be present. Several answers to this question have been provided by different workers. Weidenreich was able to study all of the remains which were available before World War II. Although he expressed some distaste for taxonomy, he distinguished *Pithecanthropus robustus* from *Pithecanthropus erectus*. The former species, represented by Sangiran 4, was said to be primitive in several respects. The massive Sangiran 4 cranium with pronounced sagittal keeling and the wide maxilla showing a precanine diastema were regarded as evidence for gigantism in human evolution, and Weidenreich (1945) suggested that larger *Pithecanthropus robustus* had been transformed into smaller *Pithecanthropus erectus*. He also argued that these earlier forms were ancestral to the Solo people and ultimately to modern humans.

Von Koenigswald disagreed with Weidenreich and preferred to assign both the Sangiran 4 cranium and the B mandible, along with the child from Perning, to *Pithecanthropus modjokertensis* (von Koenigswald, 1950). He viewed this species as different from *Pithecanthropus dubius* and from *Meganthropus*, both at the time known only from fragmentary lower jaws and isolated teeth. In von Koenigswald's opinion, *Pithecanthropus modjokertensis* was ancestral to *Pithecanthropus erectus*, although links between this latter species and the Solo population were less clear. Von Koenigswald also doubted that the Ngandong hominids could be part of a single lineage evolving toward present day Australians. Instead, he referred to the Ngandong people as 'tropical Neanderthals' related to but still more primitive than the Neanderthals of Europe (von Koenigswald, 1958). Later he reaffirmed that 'no lineal development of mankind' could be established from the fossil evidence from the southeast Asian region (von Koenigswald, 1962).

Jacob, who has retained the nomen *Pithecanthropus* for the Indonesian hominids, also recognizes *Pithecanthropus modjokertensis* rather than *Meganthropus* as ancestral to Middle Pleistocene populations. However, he sorts the Kabuh age fossils into two taxa. One is *Pithecanthropus erectus*, as known from Trinil, Kedung Brubus and Sangiran. The other species is *Pithecanthropus soloensis*, recovered at Ngandong and Sambungmachan. In Jacob's (1975) view, at least one of the individuals from Sangiran also resembles the Ngandong hominids. The cranium of *Pithecanthropus soloensis* is described as broader and more voluminous than that of *Pithecanthropus erectus*, and the bones of the vault are thick. Form of the supraorbital torus is distinctive. An occipital torus is more prominent, and there are differences in the morphology of the mandibular fossa as well. Jacob (1981) thinks that these differences are so substantial as to rule out sex dimorphism within a single lineage as an explanation, and he suggests that only one species may have evolved further. *Pithecanthropus erectus* and not the more robust *Pithecanthropus soloensis* is identified as the ancestor of *Homo sapiens*.

These several scenarios agree in recognizing more than one morphologically distinct species from the Pucangan deposits. Also, differences between Pucangan and Kabuh assemblages are taken as clear evidence for species change within at least one of these Pleistocene lineages. Some workers have continued to support these points of view, while others have raised questions. Le Gros Clark (1964) noted more than 20 years ago that there is little real basis for distinguishing the Pucangan taxa. He argued that molar enamel wrinkling, a character used in von Koenigswald's (1950) description of *Pithecanthropus dubius*, does not justify separation of Sangiran 5 from *Homo* and that tooth and jaw size alone do not diagnose *Meganthropus* as a distinct species. New studies of isolated deciduous teeth collected at Sangiran by von Koenigswald seem to strengthen this conclusion. Grine (1984) has examined an upper canine and a lower first molar originally assigned to *Homo modjokertensis*, along with a lower second molar referred to *Meganthropus*. He finds that the canine cannot readily be distinguished from those of early *Homo* or species of *Australopithecus*. The dm$_1$ differs markedly from specimens of *Australopithecus* and appears most similar metrically and morphologically to *Homo erectus* homologues. The Sangiran dm$_2$ shows resemblances to species of *Australopithecus*, *Homo habilis* and *Homo erectus*. While the tooth exhibits buccolingual narrowing characteristic of *Homo habilis*, the crown index does in fact lie within the range of variation documented for *Homo erectus*. Dental evidence for the presence of two taxa in the Pucangan deposits is thus not by itself convincing.

Franzen (1985a) has also demonstrated that the Sangiran 5 and Sangiran 9 mandibles, both referred to *Pithecanthropus dubius*, share a number of features with other hominid taxa. In light of the very early date which he accepts for the fossils, Franzen interprets his results as supporting ties with African australopithecines. His analysis can also be read to demonstrate that there are few differences from later *Homo*. Although both the incomplete 1939 specimen and

the better preserved C mandible are robust, neither seems to fall outside of the range of variation exhibited by *Homo erectus*. Much the
same conclusion has been reached in regard to the *Meganthropus*
materials by Lovejoy (1970) and by Wolpoff (1980a), although Franzen (1985b) disagrees. Certainly the 1941 *Meganthropus* mandible is
large and the corpus is very deep. However, the lower jaws of *Homo*
show a great deal of size variation, and the 1941 and later mandibular
fragments do not by themselves provide convincing evidence that
Meganthropus should be identified as different from the other Sangiran hominids. More information bearing on this question should
become available when the badly crushed cranium of Sangiran 27 has
been fully reconstructed and described. This specimen has been attributed to *Meganthropus* by Jacob.

Le Gros Clark also saw no reason to refer the robust Sangiran 4
braincase and maxilla to any taxon other than *Homo erectus*, and he
was probably correct. Although Tobias & von Koenigswald (1964)
argued, mostly on the basis of tooth measurements, that the Sangiran
4 maxilla and the B mandible resemble Hominid 13 from Olduvai
Gorge, other comparisons do not suggest a close relationship
between the Pucangan population and African *Homo habilis*. The
robust, keeled and thick-walled but relatively voluminous cranium of
Sangiran 4 differs markedly from the smaller, thinner vault characteristic of early *Homo* in Africa. At the same time, there are many similarities linking Sangiran 4 with *Homo erectus*. In my own opinion,
there are no compelling reasons for recognizing more than one species of *Homo* at Sangiran, and the remains of this hominid apparently
are present both in upper Pucangan sediments and in the Kabuh
Formation. In the Kabuh levels, both small individuals (eg., Sangiran
2) and larger specimens (eg., Sangiran 17) have been recovered. These
discoveries may reflect a fair amount of sex dimorphism within the
species, but it is difficult to see that Jacob's (1981) claim for two
separate lineages is justified.

Questions about the hominids from Ngandong are perhaps more
difficult to answer. As already noted, there are doubts about the geological provenience of these specimens. They may have been re-
deposited in the high terrace at Ngandong, and the date of the
deposits themselves is still uncertain (see discussion in Bartstra *et al.*,
1988). The hominid assemblage may be later Pleistocene in age, but it
can also be as old as the material from Kabuh levels at Sangiran.
The broken crania have most often been regarded as intermediate in

morphology between *Homo erectus* and *Homo sapiens*, although Santa Luca (1980) finds unequivocally that the Ngandong people resemble other *Homo erectus* from Indonesia. I am inclined to accept this view but feel that some aspects of Ngandong cranial anatomy must be discussed further, in Chapter 6.

3

Homo erectus at Olduvai Gorge

Olduvai Gorge lies in the Serengeti Plain of northern Tanzania. The importance of the gorge and its fossils was recognized early in the century, and several expeditions carried out paleontological and stratigraphic fieldwork at the site before 1935. In that year, Louis and Mary Leakey spent three months at Olduvai, and shorter visits were made later. However, it was not until 1959 that *Zinjanthropus* was recovered from the deposits of Bed I. With funding from the National Geographic Society, the Leakeys began systematic excavations in 1960. These were continued until 1963. More intensive investigations followed between 1968 and 1972, and fieldwork has continued intermittently. The number of Olduvai fossil individuals attributed to *Australopithecus* and *Homo* now stands at 62.

Stratigraphy and dating of the Olduvai deposits

Deposits at Olduvai are up to 100 m thick and provide a relatively complete stratigraphic record for a period beginning over 2.0 million years ago and extending to the close of the Pleistocene. Early work undertaken by Hans Reck established that the sedimentary sequence overlying basaltic lavas at the bottom of the gorge could be divided into a series of units, of which Bed I is the oldest. Bed I is the thickest of the major subdivisions, consisting of lava flows and deposits associated with a shallow lake. This bed is well-dated and has yielded some of the most famous hominids, including *Zinjanthropus* and remains of *Homo habilis*.

Fossils referred to *Homo erectus* are known from Bed II and from deposits higher in the stratigraphic sequence. In contrast to the situation in Bed I, from which more than 50 potassium–argon dates are available, only one meaningful date has been obtained for a marker tuff in the lower part of Bed II. Age estimates are based instead on magnetic stratigraphy and sedimentation rates. Hay (1976), who has studied the geology of the Olduvai basin in great detail, notes that the top of the Olduvai (normal) event lies at or within the base of the Lemuta Member. The lowermost of these eolian deposits are thus about 1.67 million years of age. Rocks of variable but mainly reversed polarity occur through the Lemuta Member and extend into the middle of Bed IV, where the Brunhes–Matuyama boundary has been located. Extrapolation from relative stratal thicknesses between the top of the Lemuta Member and the reversal dated at 0.73 million years in Bed IV suggests an age of 1.2 million years for the Bed II–Bed III contact (Hay, 1976; M.D. Leakey & Hay, 1982). Below this disconformity, the upper part of Bed II is composed of fluvial and lacustrine deposits. The lake occupied a smaller area during these times and disappeared shortly before the close of Bed II deposition.

Beds III and IV are distinguishable lithologically only in the eastern regions of the Main and Side gorges. Here Bed III consists of reddish volcanic detritus, transported and deposited by streams. Bed IV is dominantly grey or brown in color. Elsewhere, to the west and northwest, the deposits of Bed III are less reddened and cannot be distinguished from Bed IV materials. In these areas the two units are combined as Beds III–IV (undivided). Ages of these two beds can be estimated using magnetic stratigraphy. Polarity studies show that the Brunhes–Matuyama reversal lies at Tuff IVB, near the middle of Bed IV. If this marker tuff is dated at 0.73 million years, relative stratal thicknesses measured from the Bed II–Bed III contact suggest ages of 0.83 million years for the top of Bed III and 0.62 million years for the top of Bed IV (M.D. Leakey & Hay, 1982).

Overlying Bed IV are the Masek, Ndutu and Naisiusiu Beds. The upper unit of the Ndutu Beds and the Naisiusiu deposits are of Late Pleistocene age, and need not be considered here. The older Masek Beds are made up of a lower section composed mainly of eolian tuffs and an upper section termed the Norkilili Member. Dating of these sediments can be established using several lines of evidence. The tuffs in question are derived from Kerimasi, a volcano to the east of the gorge which supplied large amounts of ash to the Olduvai region.

The age of Kerimasi is known from potassium–argon determinations to exceed 0.4 million years. An estimate of 0.62 million years for the top of Bed IV then suggests that the Masek Beds, which are of normal polarity, are between 0.62 and 0.4 million years in age. This assumption fits well with Hay's (1976) figure of about 200 000 years as the length of time needed for Masek sediment accumulation, given the same sedimentation rate as for Beds III and IV.

The Olduvai Hominid 9 braincase

Parts of the cranium designated Olduvai Hominid 9 (OH 9) were recovered by Louis Leakey in 1960. This discovery was made at site LLK, located in the Side Gorge at Olduvai. Although none of the pieces were found *in situ*, OH 9 can be placed in the upper part of Bed II and assigned an age of about 1.25 million years (M.D. Leakey, 1971a; M.D. Leakey & Hay, 1982). After the announcement of the discovery in 1961, brief comments on the specimen were published by Heberer (1963) and by Tobias (1968). A more detailed description, including some preliminary comparisons with other *Homo erectus*, has since been provided (Rightmire, 1979). This earlier study of my own is revised and expanded below.

PRESERVATION OF THE SPECIMEN

Olduvai Hominid 9 consists of a partially preserved braincase, including the supraorbital structures and the cranial base. The superior aspect and right side of the vault are missing, as is all of the facial skeleton below the broken nasal bones. Some plaster has been used in reconstructing the frontal and the parietals, and matrix still adheres to the underside of the specimen. However, much of the cranial base appears to be intact, and CT scans suggest no serious deformation (Maier & Nkini, 1984). Erosion of surface bone is minimal, and the many small cracks have been sealed. Some sutural patterns are obscured, but the anatomy of the exterior of the cranium can be studied in considerable detail. Rocky matrix fills parts of the cranial cavity, but many endocranial features are present. Cranial capacity is estimated as 1067 ml by Holloway (1973, 1975).

Individual bones are variably preserved. The frontal consists of two portions, separated by plaster reconstruction. One piece is made up of most of the supraorbital margin and orbital plate from the right side. The other (composite) part is complete anteriorly, from slightly beyond glabella in the midline to the zygomatic process on the left. The upper parts of both nasal bones are in place at nasion, and a little of the maxillary frontal process is preserved on both sides. Posteriorly, the frontal bone is broken away some distance in front of the coronal suture, and a gap in the left temporal surface removes most of the detail at pterion.

Only a small corner of the right parietal remains near asterion. The left parietal is more complete laterally, though both the frontal edge and the entire sagittal border are missing. The upper portion of the occipital squama is also broken, and the position of lambda cannot be determined. Some external bone is lost in the center of the occiput and along a crack which runs longitudinally toward the foramen magnum. The foramen itself is heavily damaged along its lateral borders and anteriorly, and both condyles are missing.

The left temporal is largely intact, though nearly all of the zygomatic process has been sheared away, and the tip of the mastoid process is broken. Most of the greater wing of the sphenoid is visible on this side, but the body of the bone is covered with matrix. The pterygoid process (both medial and lateral plates) is missing. On the right, the temporal squama is broken. The root of the zygomatic process remains, but the mastoid is again damaged. All of the greater wing of the sphenoid is gone, and this together with loss of the temporal surface of the frontal leaves a large gap in the side wall of the cranium. Some, but unfortunately not all, of the morphology of this region can be reconstructed by reference to the opposite side.

THE FRONTAL BONE AND NASAL REGION (Fig. 11)

The frontal is nearly complete anteriorly, and the supraorbital tori

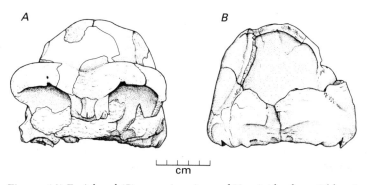

Fig. 11. (A) Facial and (B) posterior views of Hominid 9 from Olduvai Gorge.

are heavily constructed. These tori merge centrally with a massive glabellar eminence. The superior aspect of this prominence is depressed slightly, and glabella itself is indented relative to the tori which dip medially to follow the curve of the orbital margins. The supraorbital structures are vertically thickened (19 mm) over the middle of each orbit. The surface bone is vermiculate, and there is a large supraorbital notch (6.3 mm diameter) 31 mm to the left of the midline. On the right side, the notch (2.8 mm diameter) is in the same location and is accompanied by a small superior foramen. The rounded lateral margins of the orbits curve back as well as downward, and each torus tapers to a thickness of 14 mm at the fronto-zygomatic suture.

Nasion is set about 6 mm below and behind the glabellar point. The nasal bones are together 18 mm wide at the frontonasal suture but quickly contract to a width of 11 mm before beginning to fan out again below. Because of damage, the original length of the nasals cannot be determined. Breadth between the orbits is large (30 mm), reflecting the massive build of the interorbital pillar.

The supratoral surface is broad and shelf-like. There is some hollowing laterally, to form a shallow sulcus on each side. Behind this surface, the frontal squama rises evenly toward the (missing) coronal suture. The curve of the partly reconstructed forehead is rounded, and there is no indication of keeling in the midline. The temporal lines are well marked anteriorly and are slightly crested as they approach the broken posterior margin of the frontal bone. Minimum frontal breadth measured across these crests rather than lower on the walls of the temporal fossae is 88 mm. Additional vault measurements are given in Table 24.

LATERAL ASPECT OF THE CRANIUM (Figs 12 & 13)

The temporal line follows a flat arc as it passes posteriorly from the frontal onto the fragment of parietal remaining on the left side. Throughout most of its course, the line is raised slightly, especially in relation to the more superior aspect of the vault. The part of the parietal which is circumscribed by the line and which provides attachment for *m. temporalis* and its fascia is thus defined as a plateau-like surface, which stands out in considerable relief. The line itself is still prominent and thickened as it curves inferiorly across the mastoid angle of the bone, but an angular torus similar to that described by Weidenreich (1943) for several of the Zhoukoudian crania is not

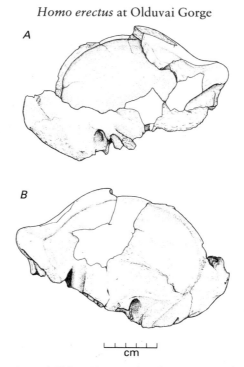

Fig. 12. Drawings of Olduvai Hominid 9, showing (*A*) right and (*B*) left
lateral views of the braincase.

developed. As it crosses the suture a few millimeters forward of
asterion, this line merges with the strong crest of the mastoid process.

A second (inferior) line is more lightly marked at the rear of the
parietal, where it can be followed for a short distance inside the curve
of the superior line. It fades out over the mastoid but reappears as a
weak suprameatal crest before merging with the posterior root of the
zygomatic process. The supramastoid sulcus, broad and slightly concave as it opens anteriorly toward the meatus, is sharply narrowed
posteriorly. There is no extension of this sulcus onto the parietal. The
zygomatic process is largely broken away on the left, but more of the
root is preserved on the right side. It is heavily built, with a broad
slightly concave superior surface that falls steeply downward into the
infratemporal fossa. This channel as measured from the temporal
wall to the point where the upper border of the broken process begins
to angle forward is estimated to be 16 mm in diameter. Anteriorly,
the greater wing of the sphenoid is deeply excavated to produce a
semicircular gutter for the converging fibers of *m. temporalis*.

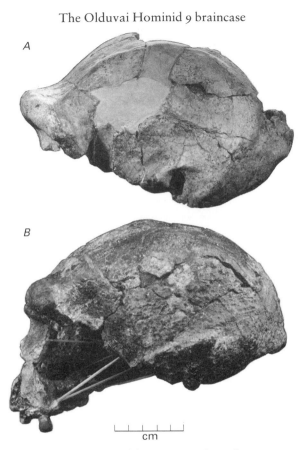

Fig. 13. Photographs of (A) Olduvai Hominid 9 and (B) Sangiran 17 in
left lateral view. The two crania from East Africa and Java resemble
one another in size and overall appearance, in so far as comparison is
possible. Olduvai Hominid 9 is also similar to other specimens from
Sangiran, Sambungmachan and Ngandong, and this observation
supports the contention that the Olduvai fossil should be assigned to
Homo erectus.

Air cells are exposed in the broken tips of both mastoid processes,
and mastoid length cannot be determined. Damage is least extensive
on the right side, and here the anterolateral face of the process is flattened. A shallow groove (for the posterior auricular artery and associated nerve?) cuts downward along this face just at its junction with
the posterior portion of the tympanic plate. The lateral margin of the
tympanic bone is thick inferiorly and curves forward and upward to
circumscribe much of the external auditory aperture. This rim is
overhung by the posterior root of the zygoma, which projects some

A   B

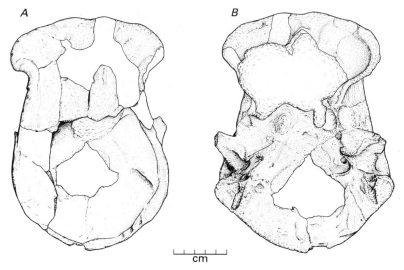

Fig. 14. Drawings of Olduvai Hominid 9, showing (*A*) superior and (*B*) basal views of the braincase. Since these illustrations were prepared, more of the matrix partly filling the right orbit and nasal cavity and obscuring the body of the sphenoid has been removed.

10 mm outward beyond the tympanic boundary. The meatus itself is elliptical in contour, and its long axis is nearly vertical. This aperture has a height of approximately 14 mm and a width of 6.5 mm on the right side, where it has been cleared of matrix.

THE OCCIPUT AND CRANIAL BASE (Figs 11, 14 & 15)

The upper occipital squama is broken, but the lateral segments of the lambdoid suture are visible on each side. On the left, the suture is preserved for 34 mm before reaching asterion. On the right side, two adjoining asterionic ossicles are present, and these are together about 23 mm in length by 16 mm in width. Some of the upper scale is still intact, but here and also in the more complete nuchal plane there are many hairline cracks, and areas of localized surface (weathering?) damage are present. Details of occipital torus formation are reasonably clear on the right side. On the left, a chip of bone approximately 18 mm across is missing, and this breakage extends just to the occipital midline. However, it is apparent that the transverse torus is rounded in form and maximally thickened in its central parts.

Following the procedure recommended by Hublin (1978c), inion

A   *B*

cm

Fig. 15. Posterior views of the two *Homo erectus* braincases from Olduvai Gorge. (*A*) Olduvai Hominid 12 is a small individual, likely to be female, while (*B*) Hominid 9 is probably male.

can be located on the roughened linear tubercle, corresponding to the junction of the superior nuchal lines. A 'true' external occipital protuberance is not well developed. There is little or no indication of supratoral sulcus formation, and the highest nuchal lines cannot be discerned. The torus itself can be followed laterally only to the limit of *m. semispinalis capitis* insertion, where it then fades out after covering about half the distance from the midline to the occipitomastoid suture. The superior nuchal line, lightly impressed into the lower margin of the torus, can still be traced along a course slightly below asterion and out onto the posterior face of the mastoid process. Here it merges with the prominent mastoid crest which sharply delimits the posterior face from the anterolateral surface of the process. Thus the nuchal area of the occiput is continuous with the broad, flattened back-facing portion of the mastoid, and the entire mastoid region is laterally expanded with respect to the sloping parietal walls above. Maximum cranial breadth is 150 mm measured between the mastoid crests, just where these begin to turn medially toward the incurved (broken) tips.

The nuchal surface is roughened, and there are remnants of a (strong?) external occipital crest passing from the linear tubercle toward the border of the foramen magnum. On either side of this broken crest, an oval depression presumably marks the position of *m. rectus capitis posticus minor*. The posterior borders of these hollows are not clearly defined, but the inferior nuchal line is more prominent laterally. Especially on the left, one of its branches is raised to separate the region occupied by *m. rectus capitis posticus major* from the insertion of *m. obliquus capitis superior*. This latter area is smooth and outlined in strong relief, and the muscle at its anterior extent seems to have reached right to and even slightly across the occipito-mastoid suture. Correct horizontal positioning of the Olduvai cranium is difficult because of damage to the orbits, but it is likely that the nuchal area rises to or exceeds the height of the Frankfurt plane at inion. Unfortunately, since both lambda and opisthion are missing, measurements of occipital length must be rough estimates.

The exact size of the foramen magnum cannot be determined. Bone is missing in the midline to a point well forward of the hypo-glossal canal openings, so that basion and the anterior rim of the foramen are lost. The jugular foramen and adjoining fossa are filled with matrix on both sides. A heavily indented jugular process is developed posteriorly on the right, and on this side the mastoid notch is deep and wide. This fossa for attachment of the posterior belly of *m. digastricus* is as much as 7.5 mm in width and narrows as it travels about 30 mm anteromedially toward the stylomastoid foramen.

Details of occipitomastoid anatomy are obscured by damage, but on the left side it is clear that the digastric incisure is bounded medially by a roughened ridge. The apex of this ridge is eroded, but on the surface remaining there is no sign of a groove for the occipital artery. As in the case of the Asian specimens described in Chapter 2, this structure is best termed a juxtamastoid eminence. To its medial side, there is a shallow depression, which was interpreted in my earlier report as a groove for the occipital artery (Rightmire, 1979). However, this hollow appears to extend across the occipitomastoid suture and probably represents the most lateral area of attachment for *m. obliquus capitis superior*. Whatever the course of the occipital artery, the juxtamastoid eminence itself must have been well developed. Since this process is continuous posteriorly with the superior oblique line, the term occipitomastoid crest as applied by Weiden-reich to the Zhoukoudian fossils is also justified.

Another interesting aspect of cranial base morphology concerns the vomer. The superior border of this bone, still partly obscured by matrix, rests on the sphenoid rostrum, between the (broken) medial pterygoid plates. This portion of the vomer is flattened, and there is no indication of a crest or nasal septum, which in *Homo sapiens* extends almost to the posterior margin of the border. This suggests that in OH 9 the septum has a more anterior origin from the superior border, as might be expected in an individual with a forwardly positioned facial skeleton. Further evidence bearing on the peculiar flatness of the cranial base is provided by Maier & Nkini (1984). Computed tomograms show the basioccipital to be horizontal, while the foramen magnum and shallow posterior cranial fossa are in a relatively high position. These observations, along with estimates for basioccipital length, indicate that kyphosis or bending of the cranial axis is much less pronounced than in a modern skull.

THE GLENOID CAVITY (Fig. 14)

The glenoid fossa is reasonably well preserved on the right, though its lateral extent is obscured by damage to the zygomatic process. The medial section of the tympanic plate is also broken. The cavity itself is very deep, and the articular surface seems to have extended far out onto the posteroinferiorly-directed root of the zygomatic process. The long axis of the articular tubercle is inclined slightly forward and is thus oblique to the sagittal plane. The surface of this tubercle is hollowed, deeply in its middle portion, and there is a smooth transition anteriorly into the infratemporal fossa. The morphology of this region is in fact quite distinct from that of modern *Homo sapiens*, in which a more prominent cylindrical articular eminence frequently forms the forward boundary of the glenoid cavity. In the Olduvai hominid, there is no true 'tubercle' at all, and a flattened expanse of preglenoid planum extends from the articular area for some distance toward the root of the broken lateral pterygoid plate. The anterior face of the cavity is also concave in the transverse plane, while the superoinferior curvature is slightly convex. The ectoglenoid (or tubercle of the zygomatic root) is missing, but a chord taken from the approximate position of this process to the entoglenoid is 32 mm in length. Depth to the floor of the fossa is difficult to measure but is about 15 mm from the midpoint of the articular tubercle. The entoglenoid process is pyramidal in form and strongly developed. Its posterior aspect is rounded and approaches to within a few millimeters of the tympanic plate. The intervening space is partly filled with matrix, but it is apparent that the glenoid fossa is extended medially along the line of the squamotympanic fissure to form a narrow recess. Details of the sphenotemporal suture are not clear in this region, but the entoglenoid process seems to be constituted mainly from squamous temporal. Its medial wall must overhang or actually incorporate the suture, and a sphenoid spine is not present. The large foramen ovale lies on the sphenoid, close to the boundary between the greater wing and the petrous temporal. A foramen spinosum, if present, is filled with matrix but must also be a sphenoid structure. Laterally, the postglenoid tubercle is also prominent and projects downward approximately 9 mm below the upper border of the external auditory meatus.

THE TYMPANIC PLATE AND PETROUS TEMPORAL (Fig. 14)

The tympanic plate constitutes the posterior wall of the glenoid fossa and is oriented nearly vertically. The bone is greatly thickened, not only laterally where it forms the border of the external auditory meatus (or porus) but also inferiorly, where the plate is much more heavily constructed than in modern humans. The inferior border slopes downward toward the midline to produce a strong spine, located in front of the stylomastoid foramen and to the side of the jugular opening. Apparently this corresponds to the spine of the crista petrosa identified by Weidenreich as a prominent feature of the Zhoukoudian crania. However, its posterior aspect is deeply grooved, and this vertical furrow ascends toward a circular depression. This in fact marks the location of the styloid process, as within the hollow the broken root of the styloid is clearly present. Between this tympanic sheath and the more laterally placed stylomastoid opening, a very small foramen is incompletely preserved.

The remaining tympanic border is somewhat damaged on the right but is prolonged medially to a position just anterior to the carotid canal, where a conical tubercle is formed. A similar structure occurs in at least one *Sinanthropus* individual, as Weidenreich (1943, p. 61) describes 'a small round tuber-like elevation which marks the medial anterior end of the tympanic plate' in skull III. This 'process supratubarius' is characteristic of Indonesian *Homo erectus*, as noted in Chapter 2. It is also found in some ape crania but is not usually developed in modern *Homo sapiens*.

The petrous temporal is preserved on both sides, and its inferior surface is roughened. Several good-sized pits are present on the apex (on the left, where detail is clearer), but the bone generally does not exhibit an eroded appearance. The pyramid fills almost all of the space between the basioccipital and the sphenoid greater wing, so that a foramen lacerum occurs only as a narrow crevice rather than as a much wider and more uneven opening characteristic of *Homo sapiens*. A first impression is that the petrous axis is aligned more nearly in an anteroposterior direction and therefore lies at a greater angle to the tympanic plate than would be expected for a modern cranium. Orientation of the pyramid is difficult to measure, but the angle formed by the petrous and tympanic axes is 145–147°, as assessed approximately on the specimen with a protractor. Weidenreich (1951) notes that this angle is about 140° for skull III from Zhoukoudian. Both results are just short of the range of 150–180° given by Weidenreich for modern humans. Similar findings are reported by Dean & Wood (1982). These authors measure inclination of the petrous pyramid relative to the transverse plane and obtain a value of 50° for OH 9. Here a range of 31–55° is recorded for recent *Homo sapiens*. This suggests that the Olduvai petrous temporal is not positioned very differently from that in modern populations.

THE INTERIOR OF THE BRAINCASE

The interior of the cranium has been partly reconstructed in plaster, and some areas are badly damaged. However, enough of the base remains so that limited description can be undertaken.

The anterior cranial fossa is partly preserved on the left side, although there is much damage on the right. A frontal crest is present but is broken off superiorly where it is about to merge with the surface of the squama. Unfortunately the bone is missing for several centimeters above this point, so it is not clear whether the crest has bifurcated to form a sagittal sulcus. There is no trace of such a sulcus higher on the frontal, where the bone is again intact. The region on either side of and immediately posterior to the crest is deeply depressed, so that this central part of the anterior fossa is much lower than its lateral floor. This hollowing is apparently also characteristic of Chinese *Homo erectus*, where the difference in depth from lateral to medial aspect amounts to approximately 15 mm (Weidenreich, 1943). Most of the crista galli is missing, and the small part which remains is largely obscured by matrix. Details of the cribriform plate are also lost, and presence of a foramen caecum cannot be confirmed.

The left middle cranial fossa is complete inferiorly, though not all of the foramina have been cleaned. The posterior border of the lesser wing of the sphenoid is broken, and no part of the anterior clinoid process remains. The sella turcica and hypophyseal fossa are also missing, and the sphenoidal sinus is filled with matrix. The floor and sides of the middle fossa are evenly rounded and free of strong relief, while the posterior wall slopes gently upward toward the blunt and flattened superior margin of the petrous pyramid.

The rear of the pyramid, forming the anterior wall of the posterior cranial fossa, is nearly vertical when the specimen is held approximately in the horizontal plane. The wall and the long axis of the pyramid lie at an oblique angle (approximately 65°) to the midline. The sigmoid sulcus is clearly defined as it climbs laterally but is lost medially as it approaches an area of extensive damage surrounding the foramen magnum. Behind this broken section, the internal occipital crest is thick and rounded as it ascends a short distance to the internal protuberance. The transverse arms (limbs) of the cruciate eminence are not so well developed in comparison, but the cerebellar impressions are deeply excavated. Relative size relationships of cerebellar fossae to cerebral fossae cannot accurately be ascertained, but the cerebellar impressions are small by modern standards. On the right, there is little trace of a sulcus for the transverse sinus. However, the area just to the left of and superior to the internal protuberance is depressed to form a channel, and the superior sagittal sinus may have swept past the protuberance on this side before passing laterally. There is no obvious connection with the left transverse sinus, which again is not clearly marked. In these respects, the Olduvai pattern differs from that more typical of modern humans, where the sagittal sinus normally deviates to the right rather than the left side of the occipital protuberance. But there is a great deal of variation.

Olduvai Hominid 12 (Fig. 15)

Remains of Olduvai Hominid 12 (OH 12) were found scattered on the surface at site VEK near the junction of the Main and Side gorges. Beds III and IV are lithologically distinguishable in this region, and gritty matrix adhering to one of the specimens makes it clear that the material is derived from Bed IV (M.D. Leakey, 1971a). The hominid consists mainly of the incomplete rear portion of a small braincase. In addition, there are pieces of both temporal bones, a frontoparietal fragment on which bregma lies, a section of orbital rim and part of the left maxilla containing tooth roots. A few other bits are too small and worn to warrant description. An indication of the size of this individual is conveyed by endocranial volume, estimated very approximately by Holloway (1973, 1975) as only 700–800 ml.

The back of the braincase has been pieced together from a number of fragments, some of which are badly weathered. The upper scale of the occiput is intact almost to lambda, and most of the lambdoid margin is preserved on the right side. Bone is missing on the left, and the occipital is broken transversely several centimeters below inion. Some 30 mm below the approximate location of lambda, a set of faint (highest nuchal?) impressions converge toward the midline. No external protuberance is formed, but below these lines there is an area of low swelling, which subsides laterally. This transverse torus reaches for more than 20 mm in sagittal extent but is nowhere prominent. The region is bounded inferiorly by the superior nuchal lines, which are best preserved on the right side. Here the more medial part of *m. semispinalis capitis* insertion is deeply excavated, while most of the remainder of the nuchal plane is missing. On the left, a short segment of the superior line survives, and a triangular eminence (linear tubercle) is present in the midline. All trace of an external occipital crest below the tubercle has been lost. Flexion of the occiput is apparent.

Part of the right parietal has been reconstructed to join the occiput, and the lambdoid suture can be traced posteroinferiorly to within a few millimeters of asterion. Segments of the sagittal suture are also present, and another, composite piece of parietal bone is attached on the left side. In rear view, the vault is rounded, and there is neither central keeling nor any pronounced degree of parasagittal flattening. Close to the midline, a long oval depression is present on the right parietal. This damage appears to have been inflicted before the skull was mineralized. The outer table has been pushed inward over an area of roughly 20 × 40 mm, while the endocranial surface remains intact. The temporal lines are very faintly marked. On the right, the line is preserved posteriorly over a considerable distance before it is lost near asterion. Here the mastoid angle of the parietal is flared outward, and it is probable that an angular torus was modestly developed. On the other side, the temporal line reaches upward to approach to within 65 mm of its fellow. Neither line can be followed very far anteriorly.

Another fragment comprises small bits of both parietals united with part of the frontal squama at bregma. Unfortunately this piece cannot reliably be joined to the rest of the parietal vault, and the bregma–lambda chord can therefore not be measured with any certainty. The frontal is preserved for only about 45 mm anteriorly and seems to be very gently keeled rather than evenly rounded across the midline. Traces of the sulcus for the sagittal sinus are present on the internal aspect of the bone, which is 10 mm thick at bregma.

More of the frontal is represented by a small quadrilateral piece from the central part of the upper rim of the right orbit. The rounded supraorbital torus is preserved along a length of 31 mm and presents a wide (7 mm) and shallow supraorbital notch near its broken medial margin. Part of the concave orbital plate is present on the underside of the fragment, and the internal surface of the bone can be discerned over a small area posteriorly. The torus itself is 10 mm thick and is thus much more lightly constructed than the brow of OH 9. The supratoral region is slightly concave anteroposteriorly, and the frontal squama appears to sweep upward more abruptly than that of the Bed II specimen.

A partly preserved petromastoid section of the left temporal bone incorporates the posterior wall of the acoustic meatus together with some of the overlying squamous bone. The external acoustic aperture seems to be circular in form, in so far as this can be judged from the remaining circumference. The lateral margin of the tympanic plate is thickened inferiorly, but all of its more medial part is missing. The root of the zygomatic process is also broken away, but the mastoid is undamaged, apart from minor weathering near its tip. This process is small and nipple-like. The lateral face is roughened but not drawn out to form a well developed mastoid crest. Orientation of the bone to conform to the Frankfurt Horizontal is difficult, but the mastoid length is approximately 25 mm. The posterior aspect of the process is flattened, and the mastoid notch is deep and narrow. This groove can be followed over a course of about 24 mm before it dips anteriorly toward the broken stylomastoid foramen. The medial lip of the digastric fossa is raised, but the nature of the occipitomastoid junction is unclear. The bone has fractured along the suture, and all of the adjacent occipital is missing. Internally, part of the deeply curved contour of the sigmoid sulcus has survived, and this is pierced posteriorly by the mastoid foramen. The petrous base is present, but nearly all of the apex has been lost.

From the right side, an additional piece of temporal squama is available. Only a small portion of the anterior wall of the acoustic aperture remains below the (broken) zygomatic root, and the mandibular fossa is heavily damaged. The postglenoid tubercle is strongly developed, but the original depth of the fossa is hard to ascertain.

The surface of the articular tubercle has been worn away, and the entire medial half of the cavity is missing.

There is finally a fragment of the left maxilla. The alveolar process is broken anteriorly to expose the length of the canine socket, while the damaged roots of P^3–M^2 are still in place. The anterior part of the alveolus for M^3 is present, but this tooth is missing. The buccal root of P^3 is clearly bifurcate, and the neck is heavily indented on its mesial side. The pulp cavity is exposed, and no part of the crown remains. Due to erosion of the alveolar surface, the buccal roots of P^4, M^1 and M^2 are partly revealed, but all the crowns are broken. The lingual root of M^1 is missing, and this part of the alveolus and its surrounding bone have been resorbed. It is not possible to take dental measurements. The palatine process is preserved anteriorly as far as the canine socket but is fractured well to the left of the midline. The left part of the floor and lateral wall of the nasal cavity are present, while the adjacent maxillary sinus has not been completely cleared of rocky matrix.

The Olduvai mandibles

Systematic excavations carried out at the gorge between 1968 and 1972 brought to light a number of important hominid specimens. Among these were the nearly complete right half of a mandible, containing the premolars and the first two molar teeth. This find, designated Olduvai Hominid 22 (OH 22), was coated with a hard reddish-brown matrix when it was picked up. Such material is characteristic of levels within Beds III and IV. These beds are not distinguishable at the site of OH 22 in the Side Gorge, but the fossil is probably not younger than 0.62 million years. Another more fragmentary jaw was recovered later from these same deposits, at site GTC. A third section of mandibular corpus, recorded as Olduvai Hominid 23 (OH 23), is known from the lower Masek Beds, which overlie Bed IV. Three teeth are preserved in this specimen, which was found *in situ* at FLK.

OLDUVAI HOMINID 22 (Figs 16, 26, 27 & 32)

OH 22, found on the surface at an unnamed locality between VEK and MNK in the Side Gorge, is the most complete of the Olduvai *Homo erectus* jaws. Nearly all of the right corpus is preserved, and traces of matrix still adhere to the fractured symphyseal surface. The

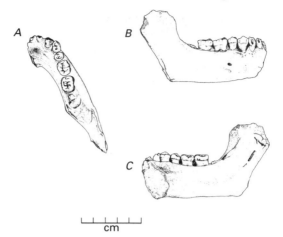

Fig. 16. Drawings of Olduvai Hominid 22, showing (*A*) occlusal, (*B*) lateral and (*C*) medial views of the mandible.

entire posterior border of the ramus has been sheared away so as to remove the mandibular angle, apparently just at its junction with the lower border of the body. The upper portion of the ramus is also damaged, and both the coronoid process and the condyle are missing. Just below this irregular zone of breakage, several flakes of bone have been lost, so that no part of the original contour of the sigmoid notch is left intact. What remains of the jaw is in good condition. A number of small cracks are present on the bone surfaces, but there is no noticeable distortion. The crowns of both of the right incisors are missing, and much of the enamel has been lost from the stump of the canine. The premolars and the first two molar teeth are well preserved, however, and a small distal contact facet on M_2 suggests that M_3 was fully erupted in this individual.

The mandibular body is thick relative to its height and is especially heavy anteriorly, in the region of the symphysis. At the level of M_1, the robusticity index as traditionally measured is 71.9. This figure exceeds that reported for most other *Homo erectus* jaws, including specimens from northwest Africa and the Far East. The upper and lower borders of the body are roughly parallel to a point forward of P_3, but height as measured vertically increases toward the symphysis. Minimum heights, taken laterally rather than internally on the corpus, show little change. Minimum dimensions of the mandibular body are given in Tables 6 and 7.

Table 6. *Measurements (mm) of minimum corpus breadth for the Olduvai jaws*[a]

	OH 22	OH 23	OH 51
I_1	19	–	–
I_2	19	–	–
$\bar{C}$	20	–	–
P_3	20.6	–	22
P_4	20.5	19.8	21.8
M_1	20.5	20	22
M_2	20.7	(19.5)	–

[a] Taken with the shaft of the caliper held perpendicular to the long axis of the body but not necessarily parallel to the occlusal plane. Where damage to the specimen is appreciable, ( ) indicates that only an estimate is possible.

Where the anterior border of the ramus joins the corpus, there is a slight lateral swelling which is continued inferiorly to merge into the marginal torus of the base. This lateral prominence is not well defined posteriorly but sends a superior branch toward the mental foramina, situated below P_4. This ridge stands out in more relief and is separated from the lower marginal torus by a shallow sulcus, which is clearly delineated only in a restricted area below M_1. Further

Table 7. *Measurements (mm) of minimum corpus height for the Olduvai jaws*[a]

	OH 22	OH 23	OH 51
I_1	(28.5)	–	–
I_2	28.5	–	–
$\bar{C}$	(29)[b]	–	–
P_3	(29)[b]	–	–
P_4	29.5	–	–
M_1	29.3	(30.5)	(36)
M_2	28	(31)[b]	–

[a] Taken from the base to the lateral alveolar margin at the center of each tooth crown. Where damage to the specimen is appreciable, ( ) indicates that only an estimate is possible.
[b] Denotes that a correction for resorption of the alveolar margin has been made.

forward, the lateral aspect of the body is smooth, and the rounded base shows no development of a strong anterior tubercle.

The two mental foramina, 5 mm apart, are located below P_4 and the interalveolar septum behind. The larger elongated foramen (4.1 mm in mesiodistal diameter) is about 12 mm from the upper margin and faces outward and posteriorly from a raised surface marking the anterior extent of the superior lateral torus. The smaller opening pierces the lower edge of this torus, about 10 mm above the base. The second foramen is directed inferiorly and back.

Near the symphysis, there is a faint depression, situated below the lateral incisor and bounded behind by the canine jugum. However, there is no real incurvation of the bone between the alveolar and basilar parts of the mandible, and the anterior profile is flattened and receding. Despite some loss of bone just at the midline, it is apparent that there is no basal eminence (no *mentum osseum* of Weidenreich), and other structures associated with the formation of a chin are lacking.

The internal surface of the symphyseal portion of the body is strongly shelved below the anterior dentition. This alveolar plane is hollowed slightly near the midline but is flattened and then more evenly convex as it curves laterally and back toward the level of M_1. The shelf is bounded below by a superior transverse torus, clearly visible in cross-section where the bone is broken. Below this torus, the profile drops steeply toward a small but well-defined posterior projection, situated within a few millimeters of the median plane. This swelling may be part of an inferior transverse torus, much restricted in its lateral extent. An alternate (and less likely) interpretation is that the projection represents a large mental tubercle or spine, sectioned by the break near the symphysis. Unfortunately the bone is incomplete just at the midline, and the morphology of the genial region is not clear. Below the projection, the symphyseal contour follows an unbroken curve forward to the base. On the base, a digastric fossa is faintly marked. This extends for only a short distance before fading out at the level of the lateral incisor. The fossa is narrow and faces almost directly downward, although it is situated on the posterior aspect of the basal margin.

The alveolar process of the mandible bulges medially to form an alveolar prominence which is strongest at the position of M_3. This prominence projects inward about 4 mm from the lingual rim of the molar alveolus and is slightly crested as it swings upward and back

onto the ramus. Inferiorly but still on this thickened ridge, the mylohyoid line can be traced for a short distance as it parallels the alveolar
margin. This line of attachment for *m. mylohyoideus* weakens after it
passes below the level of M_2. Below the line, the body wall slopes
downward into the subalveolar fossa, which is smooth as it opens
posteriorly toward the broken angle. Further forward, the medial
surface of the corpus is more evenly rounded, and the anterior subalveolar fossa is not clearly defined.

On the medial surface of the ramus, the alveolar prominence is
continuous with a heavy ridge termed the 'triangular torus' by
Weidenreich (1936). Between this torus and the anterior border of the
ramus, the bone is hollowed to form a deep buccinator gutter which
narrows as it passes along side the socket for M_3. Greatest width of
the extramolar sulcus is approximately 5 mm. Posteriorly, the division of the triangular torus into two segments is preserved. One
branch reaches sharply upward toward the (broken) coronoid process. The second and more prominent ridge is separated from the first
by a flattened surface. This endocondyloid crista continues in the
direction of the missing condyle. Just behind it the mandibular canal
opens downward into the thickened area of the ramus. The lower
border of this foramen lies about 50 mm above the mandibular base.
Its medial border is slightly damaged but is uninterrupted, and a
lingula is not recognizable as a separate plate-like structure. Morphology of the foramen corresponds approximately to what has been
termed a horizontal oval variant of canal opening (Smith, 1978),
although its long axis (8 mm) is oblique to the horizontal plane. The
deep mylohyoid groove emerges about 9 mm below the mandibular
foramen and is again bridged for a short distance as it travels downward toward the body.

The anterior border of the ramus is slightly thickened as it ascends
toward the missing coronoid, and behind this border the lateral surface is deeply excavated below the region of the notch. This hollow is
bordered posteriorly by a diffuse swelling which corresponds to the
ectocondyloid crista of Weidenreich. Relief on this remaining part of
the lateral surface is not strong, and a masseteric fossa is only faintly
marked near the lower border. There is a definite outcurving of the
base just where the posterior border is broken away, and this suggests
some eversion of the angle.

In occlusal view, the anterior teeth are set at the forward rim of the
mandibular contour, while the tooth row then passes obliquely

Table 8. *Measurements (mm) of the Olduvai Hominid 22 (OH 22) teeth*[a]

	P_3	P_4	M_1	M_2
Mesiodistal diameter	10.0	8.5	13.0	12.7
Buccolingual diameter	9.4	10.1	11.8	11.6

[a] Mesiodistal and buccolingual diameters are taken parallel to the crown base as maximum readings. No corrections for interproximal attrition are included.

across the axis of the body. The remaining premolar–molar row is straight, and M_2 and the socket for M_3 are placed close to the inner alveolar margin. Only the stumps of the anterior teeth are left. P_3 is well preserved, however, and the crown of this tooth is elongated mesiodistally and markedly asymmetrical. Measurements are given in Table 8. The large cusp is moderately worn, while the much smaller lingual cusp occupies a slightly more distal position on the occlusal surface. The anterior fovea is narrow and oriented mesiodistally. The posterior fovea is deeper and roughly triangular in outline. The symmetrical buccal face of the crown is gently convex above but is more projecting close to the cervical line. There is a strong mesiobuccal vertical groove and also a distal interstitial wear facet. The mesial root surface is very broad, and a deep indentation beginning just below the cervix suggests that the root is deeply grooved or double below the alveolar border.

The crown of P_4 is quadrilateral in outline. The buccal cusp is blunt and is linked by a narrow transverse ridge to the lower, more conical lingual cusp, located toward the mesial aspect of the crown. A deep distobuccal groove dominates the posterior fovea. Swelling of the buccal surface is less pronounced than in P_3, and there are two shallow grooves on this aspect of the crown. A distal contact facet is much larger than the mesial facet for P_3.

The crowns of M_1 and M_2 are well preserved, and M_1 is slightly longer in mesiodistal diameter. On the first molar the five principal cusps are moderately worn, but the fissure patterns are intact. The mesiobuccal and especially the distobuccal cusp encroaches onto the middle of the occlusal surface, and the central groove deviates lingually in this area. The mesiolingual cusp is high and conical. The distal slope of this cusp is smooth but is clearly transected by a groove

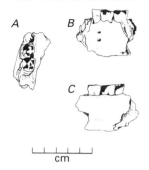

Fig. 17. Drawings of Olduvai Hominid 23, showing (A) occlusal, (B) lateral and (C) medial aspects of the broken left mandibular corpus. The teeth preserved are P_4, M_1 and M_2.

passing obliquely from the central fovea in a lingual direction. Between this fissure and the adjacent lingual groove, a small extra cusp (tuberculum intermedium) is outlined. The mesial enamel margin is wide and encloses a slit-like mesial fovea. No posterior fovea is formed, however, as the distal enamel extends from the distolingual to the distal cusp as a flattened shelf. Several small fissures pass posteriorly from the junction of the central and distobuccal grooves, but these are lost as they approach the periphery of the occlusal surface. Mesial and distal attrition facets are present, and the two buccal grooves are deeply incised. Both grooves end in narrow pits.

The second molar bears four cusps and is a little smaller than M_1. The occlusal surface is again moderately worn. The mesiobuccal cusp is large, and the two mesial cusps together occupy more than half of the crown surface. The principle grooves give off a number of small tributaries, and the lingual groove curves toward the apex of the mesiolingual cusp without reaching the inner margin of the tooth. A large mesial fovea is demarcated anteriorly by a low marginal ridge, but the posterior fovea is not well defined. As with M_1 there is a strong distal enamel margin, and tiny fissures radiating from the central groove do not clearly set this ridge apart from the two main distal cusps. The roots of this tooth incline steeply in a posterior direction, and there is a small distal contact facet for M_3.

OLDUVAI HOMINID 23 (Fig. 17)

This fragmentary jaw was recovered from the Masek Beds. Olduvai Hominid 23 (OH 23) is part of a left corpus which is broken anteriorly at the alveolus for the lateral incisor. The incisor itself is lost, and there is considerable damage to the bone below the roots of the anterior teeth. The base is preserved for a length of only about 25 mm, below M_1 and M_2. The alveolar process is in better condition. A small section of root fills the bottom of the canine socket, and more of the root of P_3 is intact, without the crown. The lingual half of the P_4 crown is broken, and this tooth is heavily worn. The first two molars are also worn, and cusp and fissure patterns are obscured. Nearly all of the enamel has been broken away from the buccal faces of the crowns. Posteriorly, the bone is fractured and eroded at the socket for M_3 and no part of the ramus remains. A distal wear facet on the crown of M_2 shows that M_3 was fully erupted before the time of death, and this specimen is clearly adult.

Height of the body is marginally greater than that of OH 22, while thickness at the level of M_1 is approximately the same (see Tables 6 and 7). The upper and lower borders are parallel in so far as can be determined from the fragmentary evidence available. The superior and middle portion of the lateral surface is evenly convex, and two mental foramina are placed below the septum separating P_4 from M_1. The smaller opens posteriorly and is 11 mm below the alveolar border. The second foramen is longer (2.7 mm in diameter), faces superiorly, and is approximately 5 mm below the first. A shallow intertoral sulcus traverses this surface above the lower border, but a marginal torus is not well developed. The base itself is narrower and rather more delicately defined than that of OH 22, while OH 51 is substantially heavier in this region.

Details of the symphysis are lost, and the internal surface is broken unevenly to the left of the midline. However, enough of this surface remains behind the canine and anterior premolar roots to confirm the presence of a sloping planum alveolare, probably bounded inferiorly by a superior transverse torus. All of the genial region is missing, as is the anterior portion of the base. In medial aspect, the wall of the body below M_2 is expanded inward to form the forward extension of an alveolar prominence. At this level the prominence is not pronounced, and the subalveolar fossa is shallow. No trace of a mylohyoid line is visible on the surviving bone surface.

OLDUVAI HOMINID 51 (Fig. 18)

This fragment from Beds III–IV (undivided) consists of part of a left mandibular corpus. The specimen is broken through the alveoli for

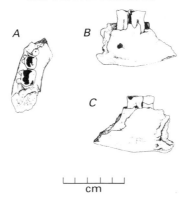

Fig. 18. Drawings of Olduvai Hominid 51, showing (A) occlusal, (B) lateral and (C) medial views of the left mandibular corpus. The crowns of P_4 and M_1 are both heavily worn, and dentin is exposed.

the canine and lateral incisor, but the base is intact below these teeth and for a short distance anteriorly. All of the incisor and canine roots are missing, as is most of the root of P_3. The crown of P_4 is heavily worn, and details of the cusp and fissure pattern are obscure. The lower parts of mesial and distal contact facets are visible, and the roots are exposed within the broken alveolus. M_1 is also badly worn, and the buccal and distal cusps are lost. The dentin is deeply eroded over this surface, and enamel is preserved only at the crown periphery. Dentin is also exposed in the center of the mesiolingual cusp, and the enamel of the distolingual margin and posterior face of the crown has been cracked and broken. Only the mesial wall of the M_2 socket remains. Here also the alveolar process has been severely eroded, while the base is preserved approximately to the level of M_3, which is missing. The lateral surface and lower border of the corpus are cracked and weathered, but the bone of the medial surface is in better condition.

The body is slightly deeper than that of OH 22 but is still heavily built (see Tables 6 and 7). Some bone has been lost through resorption of the inner alveolar margin, so the estimate of 36 mm for body height at M_1 is subject to error. Thickness at this level is measured as 22 mm. On the lateral surface, an incurving of the bone at the septum between M_1 and the broken socket for M_2 marks the anterior extent of the extramolar sulcus. Below this sulcus, the wall swells outward to form the lateral prominence. Weathering obscures some details of ridge formation, but the prominence does not appear to reach as far forward as the mental foramen in the form of a superior lateral torus. Instead the bone surrounding the foramen is gently convex and becomes flattened inferiorly, although an intertoral sulcus is not well defined. Posteriorly the prominence extends downward, nearly to the marginal torus in the region where the body has been sectioned. The marginal torus is blunt and indistinct as it passes below M_1, and the base is rounded in its exposed cross-section. Anteriorly, the torus ends in an exaggerated flange-like tubercle. This laterally-projecting anterior tubercle is 21 mm in length and subsides back into the contour of the base at the level of P_3.

The single mental foramen is placed roughly 15 mm below the septum between the P_3 alveolus and P_4. It is circular in outline, 3.8 mm in diameter and opens upward. Other features of the lateral surface and symphysis are lost, as the cortical bone has been fractured in a curve downward from the first premolar root toward the chin. The base does not quite reach the midline, and its underside is cracked and eroded so as to obscure the area of anterior digastric attachment.

A definite alveolar plane is present on the posterior aspect of the jaw. Its upper part is faintly concave and seems inclined less steeply than the plane of OH 22. A superior transverse torus is not developed, however, and this surface slopes evenly downward until it is interrupted by a groove. This transverse groove deepens anteriorly and is apparently all that remains of a large genial foramen. No genial spines are preserved. Because the jaw is damaged just at the approach to the symphysis, the presence of an inferior transverse torus cannot be verified. What is left of the inner aspect of the more lateral part of the body is smooth. There is no division between the anterior and posterior subalveolar fossae.

Size differences and sexual dimorphism

Anatomical descriptions and measurements show that there is considerable variation in size among the crania and mandibles from Olduvai. Size differences are especially apparent when the two braincases are compared, and OH 9 is one of the larger *Homo erectus* skulls on record. It is quite possible that these differences are at least partly determined by sex and that the thick brows and heavily constructed vault of OH 9 mark this individual as male. However, this hypothesis is complicated by several factors. One obvious problem is that the Olduvai *Homo erectus* assemblage is made up of individuals which are very incomplete. Crania and lower jaws are not associated, and none is found with postcranial material. When only fragmentary skull parts are available, identification of sex is difficult. Analysis is also hampered by small sample size, which obscures the range of variation present. Unfortunately this is nearly always the case in paleoanthropological work, as noted in a review by Armelagos & van Gerven (1980). Chronology presents another complication. The Olduvai fossils span a period of perhaps 750 000 years, and populations of both Early and Middle Pleistocene antiquity are represented. Under such circumstances, differences due to evolutionary change may be confused with variation to be expected in any population of contemporaneous individuals.

It is not possible to assign the Olduvai specimens to one sex or the other with much certainty. Nevertheless, the overall size of the OH 9 braincase, together with the degree of supraorbital development and glabellar prominence, elevation of the temporal lines and associated crests, and size of the mastoid process, are in keeping with male status. The cranium of OH 12 is smaller, with an endocranial volume some 300 ml below that of OH 9. This difference has led Holloway (1973) to question whether the Bed IV individual should be referred to a taxon distinct from *Homo erectus*. In my view, OH 12 exhibits morphological features (occipital curvature, probably occipital proportions, thickened vault bones) which justify its assignment to *Homo erectus*, and this specimen may well be female. Tobias (1975) rightly argues that cranial capacity alone is not a good guide to sex determination, but in this case the thin supraorbital torus and lack of strong muscle marking on the vault also suggest OH 12 to be female, even if the mastoid process and mastoid crest are well developed.

Sex differences in the mandibles are less clear. Hominid 22 from Beds III–IV (undivided) is the most robust individual, where corpus robusticity is measured as breadth/height at the position of M_1. This may be a sign that OH 22 is male, but the jaw is not especially large in cross section. The mandibular cross section can be treated as a solid ellipse, even if this procedure ignores internal structural features of mechanical significance (Smith, R.J., 1983). Calculating the area below M_1 in this way gives a figure of about 460 mm² for OH 22. Size of the corpus is here close to the average for *Homo erectus*, and this information does not warrant attribution to either sex. The OH 23 fragment is less robust (62.8) but has a slightly larger cross section (505 mm²) at M_1. As with OH 22, this jaw should be regarded as unsexed. The third Olduvai individual is larger. Cross-sectional area of the OH 51 corpus is about 625 mm² at M_1, which places this hominid toward the upper extreme of the *Homo* range. This mandible is probably male, although its robusticity index is 61.4. Such an assignment is supported by the development of a strong anterior marginal tubercle.

Postcranial bones from Bed IV

The shaft of a left femur and part of a left innominate bone were recovered *in situ* at WK in upper Bed IV in 1970 (M.D. Leakey, 1971b). These two specimens are designated as OH 28 and are referred to *Homo erectus* by Day (1971). At the proximal end of the femur, some of the neck and lesser trochanter are preserved. The shaft is largely complete, but all of the distal extremity is missing. The hip is also incomplete, although the lower part of the ilium and some of the ischium are present. A wide sciatic notch suggests that this individual is female. Day (1971) notes also that the Bed IV hip displays several features which set it apart from the bones of modern humans. Some of these differences are quite striking.

All of the crest of the ilium is missing, and cracking has caused some slight lateral displacement of the anterior part of the iliac blade. The anterior inferior iliac spine is preserved and serves as a landmark for measuring. The iliac pillar is extremely robust in comparison to that of any modern human. A prominent vertical ridge marks the region of maximum thickening, and this must have extended toward a large (missing) tubercle. The lower margin of the iliac fossa is also thickened, to produce what Day (1971) describes as a horizontal iliac bar. This bar terminates at the auricular surface. The sacral articulation is relatively small, and its inferior part faces downward, so as to lie at an angle to the rest of the auricular plane. The tuberosity of the ilium is very prominent and roughened.

The acetabulum is large in vertical diameter and deep, with a thickened rim. This rim is well preserved in the iliac region but has been thinned by weathering below. Much of the lunate surface is present, and this is widest superiorly as in modern bipeds. The center of the acetabulum can be located at the approximate point of union of the three pelvic elements. Biomechanical length of the ischium, as measured from this landmark within the acetabulum to the midpoint of the transverse ridge on the ischial tuberosity, is 83 mm. Maximum length of the part of the ischium which is preserved is 89 mm. The tuberosity is separated from the acetabular rim by a deep notch. This portion of the ischium is said by Day (1971) to be rotated medially, but in fact the orientation of the bone does not appear to differ much from that in *Homo sapiens*.

Both the femur and the hip provide a basis for estimating body size of OH 28. Transverse and anteroposterior diameters of the femur, taken at mid-shaft, can be used to calculate a cross-sectional area, and this area can be treated as a predictor of body weight. When entered in a regression relating femoral size to body size, the cross-sectional area of the Olduvai femur predicts a weight of approximately 50 kg (Rightmire, 1986a). Measurements taken on the innominate produce similar results. Both iliac breadth and acetabular diameter can be employed as independent variables in regression analysis, and the weights estimated for OH 28 are between 49 and 52 kg. These figures, which are of course subject to uncertainty, suggest that the Bed IV female (?) weighed less than the average recorded for many groups of living people.

4

Discoveries from the Turkana basin and other localities in sub-Saharan Africa

Apart from the Olduvai remains, fossils referred to *Homo erectus* are known from several localities in sub-Saharan Africa. Some of the most important discoveries have come from the East Turkana sites in northern Kenya (see Fig. 19). Plio-Pleistocene sediments are exposed over a large region on the east side of the Turkana basin, and these deposits contain a wealth of bones and artifacts. Skulls and postcranial parts of *Homo erectus* have been found in several areas near Koobi Fora. The earliest of the fossils must be older than 1.6 million and perhaps as old as 2.0 million years, so these remains are more ancient than those from Olduvai. Other important material has been recovered from the western side of the lake basin at Narioko-tome. Fossils from Lake Baringo, which lies to the south of Turkana, may also represent *Homo erectus*. In Ethiopia, the species is known so far only from isolated teeth or fragmentary specimens, mostly from excavations at Melka Kunturé. Affinities of the more complete cranium from Bodo in the Middle Awash Valley are still unsettled, but this hominid is probably best referred to another taxon.

In southern Africa, localities containing Acheulian stone artifacts do occur in some abundance, although many of the assemblages are surface scatters rather than sealed sites. Dating is frequently un-certain. It is likely that the earlier tools were made by *Homo erectus*, but traces of the people themselves are quite scarce. Only at Swart-krans are there fossils which seem definitely to represent this species. Located in the Transvaal in South Africa, Swartkrans is best known for discoveries of *Australopithecus*, but several finds have been

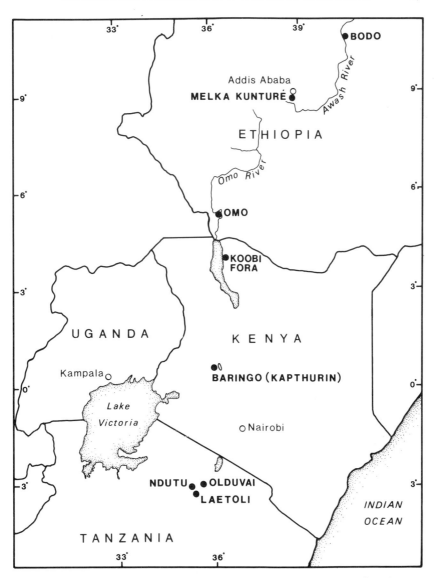

Fig. 19. Map of eastern Africa showing localities where fossils referred to *Homo erectus* and early representatives of *Homo sapiens* have been recovered.

referred to the genus *Homo*. A small cranium, very incomplete, may best be assigned to *Homo habilis*, but a mandible from a younger section of the breccia deposits is clearly similar to *Homo erectus* jaws. Unfortunately this individual is poorly preserved and is not particularly informative.

Localities east of Lake Turkana

Reconnaissance of the Koobi Fora region began in 1967, and a longer survey of the more promising exposures was organized in 1968. Only three weathered hominid jaws were discovered during the 1968 season, but more systematic paleontological collecting in subsequent years has greatly increased the fossil inventory. Assemblages now include quantities of invertebrate (mostly molluscan) remains as well as the bones of mammals and other vertebrates. A number of hominid specimens are well preserved, and both *Australopithecus* and *Homo* are represented. Archeological as well as paleontological field research has been carried out at the Turkana localities, and laboratory analyses are continuing. A preliminary account, covering discoveries made through the mid-1970s, has been published by M.G. Leakey & R.E. Leakey (1978), and other monographs are in preparation. Geological interpretations, which have been substantially revised since 1980, are discussed in more detail below.

GEOLOGICAL SETTING

Plio-Pleistocene deposits which have accumulated on the eastern side of the Turkana basin are now thought to span about the same time interval as those to the north, in the well studied Lower Omo Valley. Although there are discontinuities in the section, the total thickness of deposits in the Koobi Fora region is at least 500 m. Sedimentation is associated with streams and deltas, and with the lake itself, which has expanded and shrunk at intervals during the last several million years. Of particular importance are the numerous, mostly waterlaid volcanic tuffs, which may be horizontally extensive. The same tuff can often be located in different areas. Such marker horizons allow correlation of sedimentary sequences for different localities within the Koobi Fora region and also help to tie these sections to others in the basin. Tuff correlations are now based on chemical characterization of glass separates. Using x-ray fluorescence techniques, Brown & Cerling (1982) and Cerling & Brown (1982) have been able to recognize more than 40 tuffs which are chemically distinct. A number of the marker beds present in the Koobi Fora sequence can also be identified in the Shungura Formation in the Lower Omo Valley. Work of this sort, coupled with detailed biostratigraphic investigations (White & Harris, 1977; Williamson, 1982), is contributing to a more complete understanding of the history of the entire Turkana basin.

One tuff in particular has been much discussed. Identified as the KBS Tuff at Koobi Fora and as Tuff H2 of the Shungura Formation, this bed is important because of the stratigraphic proximity to it of fossils and stone tools. Dates for the KBS Tuff are now firm, and an age of about 1.88 million years has been obtained using both the potassium-argon (Drake *et al.*, 1980; McDougall *et al.*, 1980; McDougall, 1985) and the argon-argon dating methods (McDougall, 1981). This part of the Koobi Fora sequence is thus about as old as lower Bed I at Olduvai Gorge. Remains of *Homo erectus* occur mostly in levels above the KBS horizon. A few postcranial bones which may belong to this species have been located in lower sediments, but crania, mandibles and teeth are known from localities which lie stratigraphically in the upper part of the Koobi Fora Formation.

An example is the well preserved cranium of KNM-ER 3733, which was found in collection area 104, below the level of the Koobi Fora Tuff Complex. These tuffs are chemically similar to the Ileret and Okote Tuff Complexes (Cerling & Brown, 1982), and all three must be approximately the same age (Brown & Feibel, 1985). A date of 1.6 million years has been reported for the Okote Tuff Complex by McDougall *et al.* (1985). The KNM-ER 730 mandible and other skull fragments, from an area nearer to the present lakeshore, are also derived from sediments below the Koobi Fora Tuff Complex. More fossils occur above the Koobi Fora/Ileret/Okote Tuff Complexes, but *Homo erectus* is not definitely known from levels higher than the Chari Tuff, dated to approximately 1.39 million years (McDougall, 1985).

The East Turkana crania

Of the crania found in the Koobi Fora region, KNM-ER 3733 is the most complete. Collected in 1975, this specimen possesses facial parts, although the lower jaw is missing. KNM-ER 3883 is most of another braincase, to which the upper portion of the face is still

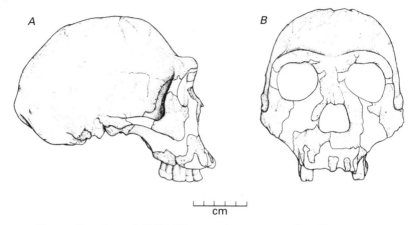

A   B

cm

Fig. 20. Drawings of KNM-ER 3733, the most complete *Homo erectus* cranium from Koobi Fora. Both (A) right lateral and (B) facial views are illustrated.

attached. These individuals display some deformation but are nevertheless better preserved than OH 9 and many of the Asian hominids. Other cranial remains have been recovered but provide less information.

THE KNM-ER 3733 CRANIUM (Figs 20 & 21)

This specimen has been described by R.E. Leakey & Walker (1976, 1985). There are many cracks in the vault, some of which have spread and filled with matrix. Several cm² of the outer table are missing at bregma, and there is more damage to the frontal squama to the right of the midline. The occiput has been deformed slightly, and the base is asymmetrical. The braincase is otherwise in good condition, and these small defects do not seriously affect the integrity of the reconstruction. Measurements are provided in Table 23.

KNM-ER 3733 exhibits prominent keeling in the frontal midline, while to either side of this elevation the squama is flattened. The temporal lines are strongly crested anteriorly, and there is marked postorbital constriction. The shelving supraorbital torus is thinner than that of OH 9. This torus is a little heavier laterally (9 mm) than at the center of the orbit (8 mm), but it is fairly uniform in thickness. Glabella is much less massive than in OH 9, and the nasal root is only moderately recessed. Above glabella there is some hollowing of the frontal surface. This shallow sulcus extends laterally behind the brows but is not pronounced or groove-like.

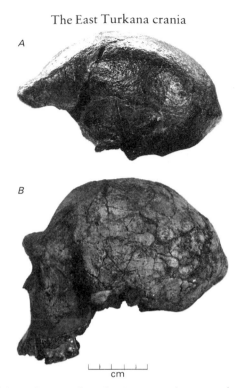

Fig. 21. Left lateral views of (A) the Sangiran 2 braincase from Java and (B) the KNM-ER 3733 cranium. The two hominids are similar in size and overall appearance.

The facial skeleton is not so well preserved. Most of the frontal process of the maxilla is missing on the right, and there is damage to both zygomatic processes. The maxillary alveolar process is severely eroded, but the contour of the bone below the nasal opening can be reconstructed reasonably accurately. There is little definition of a nasal sill, and an anterior nasal spine has been largely worn away. The floor of the nasal opening now appears to grade evenly onto the subnasal portion of the maxilla, and this lower part of the face is relatively short and projecting. The bony palate is narrow and deep. The size of the (empty) alveoli suggests that the anterior teeth were large. The canine socket is broken along most of its length on the left, while on the right a prominent jugum is partially preserved. This extends upward alongside the nasal opening to give the maxilla a 'square' appearance.

From the side, KNM-ER 3733 shows the low cranial profile characteristic of *Homo erectus*. Mostly because of midline keeling, the frontal seems to rise more steeply behind the brows than is the case for OH 9. There is no sagittal keeling on the parietals. The temporal line is slightly raised as it passes from the frontal onto the parietal vault. This line becomes more prominent as it traverses the length of the parietal to arc downward before approaching the lambdoid margin. There is some cracking at the mastoid angle, and the temporal line cannot be discerned clearly in this region. Certainly no strong angular torus is developed, but on the right side a faint ridge above asterion may mark the passage of the temporal line forward toward the mastoid crest. In relation to the size of the small (but broken) mastoid process, the crest itself is prominent. Above it, there is a shallow (not grooved) supramastoid sulcus, containing no tubercles or other relief behind the ear. Especially on the right side, the supramastoid crest is sharply defined. It does not appear to extend onto the parietal bone, and no angular sulcus is formed. Anteriorly, the supramastoid crest merges with the shelving root of the zygomatic process.

The KNM-ER 3733 occipital is quite complete, although this part of the cranium has been subject to some plastic deformation. It is apparent that the entire nuchal region has been skewed to the left, and on this side of the midline the occiput is higher and more flattened. On the right, there is slightly more protrusion of the region covered by the deeper nuchal musculature. The foramen magnum is also distorted, and both condyles are broken. Especially on the left, there is severe damage to the lateral part of the occipital and to the adjacent petrous temporal. However, much anatomical detail is still present, and some measurements can be taken.

Form and proportions of the KNM-ER 3733 occiput seem comparable to those of OH 9. The bone is flexed, and there is a rounded transverse torus which is most projecting near the midline. Above the torus, the occipital squama slopes forward. Because of cracks and subsequent displacement of numerous small plates of the outer table, it is difficult to assess the extent of supratoral sulcus formation, but there is some definite hollowing immediately above the center of the torus. The upper margin of the torus is also distinct laterally for some distance on each side, though it is impossible to be certain that this boundary corresponds to the course of the highest nuchal line. The lower border is more clearly set off by the superior nuchal lines, which converge at the midline to produce a triangular eminence. This is best interpreted as a linear tubercle rather than as an external occipital protuberance, and its downward facing apex is continuous with a raised external occipital crest, well defined from inion to the posterior rim of the foramen magnum. From inion, the superior line passes on each side in a shallow arc towards another strong tubercle, located posterior to the insertion of *m. obliquus capitis superior*. This retromastoid process is most prominent on the left, and from it the nuchal line then curves gently forward to join the mastoid crest.

The nuchal plane exhibits considerable relief. Depressed areas extend underneath the torus on either side of the occipital crest to mark the sites of *m. semispinalis capitis* attachment, and there is a pair of narrower hollows closer to the midline, between the inferior nuchal line and the foramen magnum. Laterally, the nuchal surface is raised and rounded, particularly toward the occipitomastoid boundary. Because of damage, it is difficult to locate precisely the regions occupied by individual muscles, but much of the occipital swelling seems to be related to insertion of *m. rectus capitis posticus major* and *m. obliquus capitis superior*. On the left, a substantial amount of surface bone is missing in this area, and only the most posterior part of the digastric fossa is preserved. Breakage has also affected the right side, but here more of the mastoid wall and incisure are intact. Between the notch and the occipitomastoid suture, the temporal is drawn into a ridge or juxtamastoid eminence which is broad and flattened. Unfortunately the anterior part of this ridge is missing. Its posterior aspect is not clearly associated with a superior oblique line, so it apparently does not qualify as an occipitomastoid crest in the sense of Weidenreich. Surface detail is partially obscured, but there is no trace of a groove for the occipital artery, either crossing the juxtamastoid eminence or more medially in line with the occipitomastoid suture. A final point worth emphasizing is that the entire posterolateral face of the mastoid process as well as the bone behind the digastric notch forms a distinctive, flattened surface. As in OH 9, this temporal portion of the nuchal plane is continuous with that of the adjacent occiput, so that an unbroken expanse of backward facing nuchal area sweeps far out onto the most laterally projecting part of the cranial base.

The glenoid fossa and surrounding structures are best preserved on the right side. Both ectoglenoid and entoglenoid processes are well defined, and the width of the articular surface enclosed between them is approximately 33 mm (32 mm on the left). As in OH 9, the long axis of the fossa is oblique rather than perpendicular to the basicranial line. There is no true articular tubercle, and the anterior wall of the cavity is deeply concave from side to side. This causes the fossa to appear shallower than that of OH 9, and the middle articular surface is so depressed as to contribute as much to the floor of the cavity as to its forward boundary. Anteriorly, there is a smooth transition from the joint onto a flattened, upward sloping preglenoid planum. Laterally, a small but definite postglenoid tubercle is present, while at its inner extent, the fossa is very constricted. Its form is similar to that of OH 9 in that a deep recess is produced between the entoglenoid pyramid and the vertical tympanic plate. Sutural details are not entirely clear in the entoglenoid region, but the sphenotemporal junction appears to pass directly across the apex of the process rather than along its medial wall. There is no appreciable development of a sphenoid spine.

The most lateral part of the tympanic bone is broken, and there is slight damage to other sections of the plate as well. This plate is oriented vertically and is similar in structure to that of OH 9. The tympanic is thickened in comparison to that of modern humans, and in the region where the styloid should be located, there is a strong spine corresponding to Weidenreich's spine of the crista petrosa. The posterior slope of this process shows a faint vertical groove, ending (above) in a circular hollow. This hollow is best interpreted as a styloid vagina. More medially and just anterior to the carotid and jugular canals, there is a prominent, spine-like projection of the tympanic bone. Perhaps because of deformation, this process is more closely applied to the sphenoid portion of the entoglenoid than is the case for OH 9, but its location and appearance is otherwise quite comparable in the two East African specimens.

Unfortunately, the petrous temporal is badly damaged on both sides. Very little surface detail has survived on the left, and on the right it is not possible to make out much more than the outlines of the carotid and jugular canals. Whether the surface of the pyramid is smooth or pitted and eroded cannot be determined. The long axis of the pyramid also seems to have been shifted slightly, so that angular relationships cannot be determined with much accuracy. The petrous axis appears to be more sagittally oriented than is usual for modern humans.

In other respects, the base of KNM-ER 3733 more closely resembles the *Homo sapiens* condition. Measurements taken by Dean & Wood (1982) show that the anterior rim of the foramen magnum

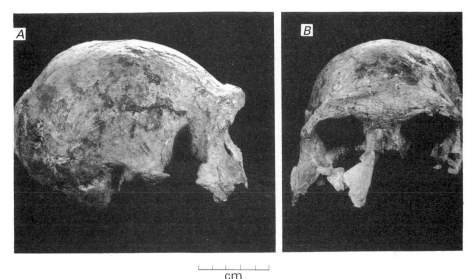

Fig. 22. The KNM-ER 3883 cranium from Koobi Fora, photographed in (A) right lateral and (B) facial views.

lies in line with the lateral ends of the tympanic plates. In pongids and in gracile australopithecines, the foramen is located more posteriorly. Also, the body of the sphenoid is broadened, so that a chord connecting the infratemporal crests is longer than the biforamen ovale and bicarotid canal widths. These proportions distinguish KNM-ER 3733 and other *Homo* crania from robust australopithecines, where the base is especially wide at the level of the tympanic bones.

THE KNM-ER 3883 CRANIUM (Fig. 22)

A second cranium, from the Ileret area, is of slightly more recent geological age than KNM-ER 3733. Numbered KNM-ER 3883, this less complete Ileret individual has been described by R.E. Leakey & Walker (1985). Much of the vault is intact, though there are numerous cracks, and some of the bone has been plastically deformed. The cranial base is affected most, and relationships across the midline are no longer quite symmetrical. Especially serious is the crushing and upthrusting of the region surrounding the foramen magnum. Some of the nuchal plane as well as lateral parts of the occiput have been displaced upward into the endocranial cavity, with the result that measurements of occipital curvature may no longer be reliable. The left temporal is also damaged, and on this side the zygomatic process, the glenoid cavity and the auditory meatus are badly broken.

Although the supraorbital region and most of the right zygomatic bone are preserved, much of the rest of the facial skeleton is missing. Both nasal bones are broken about 15 mm below the nasal root, and the frontal process of the maxilla is complete enough only to outline the right orbit. Other parts of the maxilla, the palatines, and the pterygoid processes of the sphenoid are lost. Nearly all of the vomer is also broken away, but enough of the superior border remains to delimit the zone of contact with the sphenoid rostrum. On the left side of the face, only a little of the zygomatic bone still adheres to the orbital margin.

In size and general appearance, KNM-ER 3883 is quite similar to KNM-ER 3733. The two crania are identical in glabella–occipital length. Frontal measurements are also comparable, although the Ileret frontal bone is a little narrower (Table 23). In this individual, the supraorbital torus is extensively cracked, and traces of matrix remain between small bone fragments which have been sealed in place. Thickness of the torus at the center of the orbital margin is not much affected, however, and the brow is certainly heavier than that of KNM-ER 3733. Maximum thickening on the left, where the bone is most complete, amounts to 13 mm. Above glabella, there is a slight depression. The supratoral surface is otherwise flat and shelving, and a sulcus is not developed. Postorbital constriction is more marked than in KNM-ER 3733, and the frontal profile seems to rise less steeply. There is no trace of keeling in the midline, and in anterior view the frontal contour is evenly rounded between the temporal crests. The relatively heavy brow ridges, inflated glabellar region, and extent of supratoral flattening all recall the morphology of OH 9, although the latter frontal is larger and more heavily built.

Apart from the lower frontal profile of KNM-ER 3883, the two Turkana hominids are alike in lateral view. On the right side, a thin layer of surface bone has spalled away from much of the Ileret parietal, so the course of the temporal line is indistinct. On the left, the line is not well marked, and there is no sign of an angular torus above asterion. On the temporal bone, there is little expression of a distinct mastoid crest. The supramastoid crest also is weaker than that of KNM-ER 3733 and does not appear to extend onto the parietal behind. In between these crests there is a shallow supramastoid sulcus. The zygomatic process of the temporal is still in place but damaged, and its broad superior surface is slightly concave from side to side. Although there is little actual projection of the posterior root of the zygoma, the external auditory meatus is recessed, and on the right, where the tympanic is complete, the rim of the meatus is 6–7 mm medial to the auricular point. The porus itself (17 mm by 10 mm) is elliptical and oriented vertically. Behind it, the antero-lateral face of the mastoid is inflated (but not heavily crested), and the mastoid process is large in comparison to that of the Koobi Fora cranium. As in KNM-ER 3733, the surface of the sphenoid greater wing is deeply guttered to accommodate the converging fibers of *m. temporalis*, and the area enclosed within the temporal fossa is extensive. Form of the upper (squamous) border of the Ileret temporal bone is like that of other *Homo erectus* and is long and straight rather than arched. There is little indentation of a parietal notch.

Damage to the nearly vertical upper scale of the occipital is extensive, and plates of compact bone are missing from the left side and from the midline. Enough of the surface remains on the right to demonstrate that an occipital torus is not as prominent as in KNM-ER 3733, although there is a mound-like swelling toward the center of the bone. The shape of the linear tubercle cannot be ascertained (but most probably no external occipital protuberance is present). From the region of the tubercle, the superior line can be followed along an irregular course toward asterion, where there is no clear indication of retromastoid swelling. Only a faint superior nuchal impression curves from this point forward onto the mastoid process.

Despite crushing of the lower aspect of the nuchal plane, it is apparent that the regions occupied by several of the deeper nuchal muscles are raised and rounded, much as in the Koobi Fora specimen. The remains of an external occipital crest are preserved only toward the foramen magnum. Unfortunately, although the right mastoid process is intact, the insertion for *m. digastricus* is eroded, and it is no longer possible to reconstruct details of the occipitomastoid junction. A juxtamastoid eminence could not have been strongly developed, however, and the bone adjacent to the occipitomastoid suture is now flattened. As in KNM-ER 3733, the back of the mastoid is coplanar with the nuchal occiput, and the tip of the process is inclined medially.

Many cracks run through the right glenoid cavity, but its dimensions and morphology are clearly similar to those of KNM-ER 3733. The articular tubercle is a little less concave, so that the anterior joint surface is steeper and passes more abruptly onto the preglenoid planum. The tympanic plate is somewhat more horizontally aligned, and the postglenoid process is very prominent. But ectoglenoid to entoglenoid distances are about the same in the two crania, and the Ileret entoglenoid pyramid is entirely of temporal origin. As in KNM-ER 3733, the medial aspect of the cavity is deeply recessed, between the entoglenoid and the tympanic bone behind.

The inferior portion of the tympanic plate is thick, but the bone is slightly damaged just where a spine of the crista petrosa should be present. There is little doubt that a spine-like structure did exist, and its stump is strongly grooved to form a styloid sheath. Medially, the tympanic is even more thickened, where it terminates in a blunt process. This part of the plate may be incomplete, but a conical tubercle comparable to that produced in the Koobi Fora hominid is not developed. Orientation of the petrous temporal is more nearly parallel to the cranial midline than in KNM-ER 3733, as noted by Dean & Wood (1982). The long axes of the pyramid and of the tympanic plate must come together at an angle as large or larger than that measured for OH 9.

THE KNM-ER 730 CRANIAL FRAGMENTS

Pieces of the KNM-ER 730 cranium were recovered in 1980, a decade after the mandible of this individual had been discovered in collection area 103. The cranial parts have been described by R.E. Leakey & Walker (1985). They consist of the squamous portion of an occipital bone, part of the left parietal articulating with the occiput, and some of the frontal on which a section of the left supraorbital area is preserved. In addition, there is a small fragment from the left maxilla containing tooth roots. There are no dental crowns from the left side, but the entire root and very worn crown of the right upper canine are present.

Both the parietal and the frontal squama are quite thick. Glabella is not present, but on the left the browridge is intact over a length of some 40 mm of the supraorbital margin. Centrally, this torus attains a height of 12.5 mm. There is some supratoral hollowing, but this is less pronounced than in KNM-ER 3733. Morphology of the frontal is perhaps more like that of KNM-ER 3883, although there is little cresting of the temporal line. Well behind the brow, this line is expressed for a short distance as a roughened ridge, blunted by weathering. Still on the left side, the temporal line can be picked up again posteriorly on the parietal. There is damage to the surface, but it is apparent that the bone along and below the line is raised and slightly thickened.

Much of the occipital squama is preserved. In its width and height measurements, this bone is a little smaller than that of KNM-ER 3733 but is similar to the occiput of KNM-ER 3883. Although the specimen cannot be oriented in any standard plane, the upper scale probably slopes forward. The height of this scale is 47 mm. Only a remnant of the lateral margin of the foramen magnum is present, but this curved rim can be extended posteriorly to provide an approximate location for opisthion. Length of the nuchal plane measured to this landmark is 41 mm. As in other Turkana *Homo erectus*, this lower scale of the occipital is relatively short. The bone is strongly flexed. A mound-like torus is most prominent centrally and is bounded below by the superior nuchal lines. These lines span the width of the squama and meet at the midline to form a linear tubercle. Both the tubercle and the external occipital crest have lost definition as a consequence of weathering.

ADDITIONAL CRANIAL REMAINS

Other specimens from the Koobi Fora region have been attributed to *Homo erectus* by Howell (1978), but several of these individuals are very fragmentary. KNM-ER 1466 and KNM-ER 1821 are pieces of frontal and parietal bone, too small to convey much information. KNM-ER 807, described by R.E. Leakey & Wood (1973), consists of two fragments of maxilla from the right side. One is a portion of the alveolar process bearing the exposed roots and nearly complete crown of M^1. The second piece completes the posterior part of the alveolar process. A roughened maxillary tuberosity extends for some distance behind the M^3 alveolus. A small section of the adjacent palatal floor is also preserved, and this carries a clear vascular groove, leading forward from the greater palatine foramen. The foramen itself is incomplete, and only a trace of the palatomaxillary suture may be present near its medial margin. The crown of M^2 has been sectioned to leave only the distal half in place, and the broken buccal roots are exposed at the damaged alveolar margin. All of M^3 is preserved. These teeth are large (Table 9), and the palate must have been quite deep. While identification of such an incomplete specimen is difficult, KNM-ER 807 does seem to resemble KNM-ER 3733, and assignment as *Homo* sp. (cf. *erectus*) is appropriate.

Table 9. *Measurements (mm) of the upper molar teeth of KNM-ER 807*[a]

	M[1]	M[2]	M[3]
Mesiodistal diameter	(13.2)	–	11.0
Buccolingual diameter	13.8	(14.2)	12.5

[a]Mesiodistal and buccolingual diameters are taken parallel to the crown base as maximum readings. No corrections for interproximal attrition are included. Where crown damage is appreciable, (   ) indicates that only an estimate is possible.

KNM-ER 2598 is a fragment of thick occipital squama, rather heavily weathered. Parts of the lambdoid suture are preserved on either side of the midline. On the endocranial surface, fossae for the cerebral occipital lobes are indistinct, but the internal protuberance is lower than external inion. Externally, there is a very prominent, rounded occipital torus. Where the bone is broken to provide a cross-section, it is clear that in the region of the torus the outer table rather than the diploe is most thickened. Below this torus, faint superior nuchal markings are present. There is neither a raised linear tubercle nor more than a trace of external crest on the lower scale. Most of the nuchal plane is missing, but enough remains to show that occipital curvature is comparable to that of KNM-ER 3733. Given this morphology, the individual from Ileret area 15 should be regarded as similar to *Homo erectus*.

The East Turkana mandibles

Of the many lower jaws recovered in the Koobi Fora region, several have been referred to the genus *Homo*. One is KNM-ER 730, which is associated with cranial remains described as similar to *Homo erectus*. Another is KNM-ER 992, which is more complete and carries nearly a full set of teeth. Additional mandibles, either juvenile or badly broken, are described only briefly in this section.

THE KNM-ER 730 MANDIBLE (Figs 23, 26 & 27)

This specimen has been described by Day & R.E. Leakey (1973) and compared to *Homo erectus* by Wood (1976). The mandible is rather poorly preserved. The symphysis and anterior portion of the corpus are complete, although there is damage to the front of the alveolar

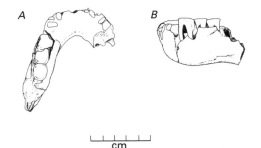

Fig. 23. Drawings of KNM-ER 730, showing (A) occlusal and (B) lateral views of the mandibular corpus. Crowns of the left molar teeth are in place but show heavy wear.

margin. The sockets for the central incisors are badly eroded, while the left lateral incisor alveolus has been resorbed. Crowns of all of the anterior teeth are missing. On the right, the body has been sectioned just behind the P_4 roots, while on the left the bone extends past the level of M_3 to end in an irregular break which has removed all of the ramus. The heavily worn crowns of only the three left molar teeth remain.

Measurements of the jaw are given in Tables 10 and 11. The KNM-ER 730 corpus is nearly as thick as that of OH 22. Resorptive

Table 10. *Measurements (mm) of minimum corpus breadth for the Turkana jaws*[a]

	KNM-ER 730	KNM-ER 992A
Midline	17.7	—
I_1	17.5	—
I_2	—	19
C	19	20
P_3	20	20.8
P_4	19	20
M_1	(19)	19.8
M_2	18.5	20.5
M_3	18	24

[a]Taken with the shaft of the caliper held perpendicular to the long axis of the body but not necessarily parallel to the occlusal plane. Where damage to the specimen is appreciable, ( ) indicates that only an estimate is possible.

Table 11. *Measurements (mm) of minimum corpus height for the Turkana jaws*[a]

	KNM-ER 730	KNM-ER 992A
Midline	(33)	38
I_1	–	–
I_2	–	–
$\bar{C}$	–	$(33)^b$
P_3	–	$(32.8)^b$
P_4	–	–
M_1	–	–
M_2	(33.8)	33.2
M_3	(31.8)	34.5

[a]Taken from the base to the lateral alveolar margin at the center of each tooth crown. Where damage to the specimen is appreciable, ( ) indicates that only an estimate is possible.
[b]Denotes that a correction for resorption of the alveolar margin has been made.

damage to the alveolar margin near the molar roots makes measurement difficult, but corpus height must be slightly greater than that for the Olduvai jaw at the level at M_1. Upper and lower borders of the body are approximately parallel, although the base is not uniformly straight. There is some upturning of the lower border near the symphysis, and posteriorly the bone of the base begins to flare out and downward toward the (missing) angle. The lateral prominence and marginal torus are no more strongly developed than in OH 22. Only a weak superior lateral torus is present, while there is more swelling of the bone which sheaths the buccal root of P_3. This coupled with flattening of the symphyseal surface gives the jaw a blunt or square appearance, from the front.

What remains of the symphyseal profile is nearly vertical but must have receded noticeably when the alveolar margin was still intact. There is a faint incurvation in the midline, and the *mentum osseum* is expanded below into a rounded swelling which merges on each side with the marginal torus of the base. Distinct lateral (mental) tubercles are not developed, so there is no real trigone (*contra* Day & R.E. Leakey, 1973). Internally there is a sloping alveolar planum which is a little less exaggerated than that of OH 22 but quite comparable to that preserved in OH 23. Shallow depressions occur in the planum on

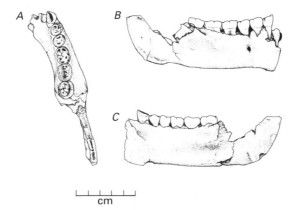

Fig. 24. Drawings of KNM-ER 992A, showing (A) occlusal, (B) lateral and (C) medial views of the right corpus and broken angle of the mandible.

either side of the midline, and there is a rounded superior torus. Below the torus, a genioglossal hollow is divided into two fossae by a roughened vertical spine, and in the floor of each pit an additional smaller tubercle is apparent. Just above the central spine, there is a small foramen, while the genial fossae are bounded below by the converging and strongly marked mylohyoid lines. The thickened contour of the mandibular base is very similar to what is observed in the most complete Olduvai jaw. However, in KNM-ER 730, the digastric impressions are much more deeply excavated, and there is a prominent interdigastric tubercle.

THE KNM-ER 992 MANDIBLE (Figs 24, 25, 26, 27 & 32)

This mandible from Ileret is much more completely preserved than KNM-ER 730 and constitutes a valuable addition to the collection of earlier *Homo* jaws from East Africa. As described in a preliminary report by R.E. Leakey & Wood (1973), the fossil consists of two broken hemimandibles, a fragment of right ramus including the lingula, and the detached crown of the left central incisor tooth. The right half of the jaw (KNM-ER 992A) is complete to the symphysis and carries all of the teeth from C to M_3. Both incisors are missing, and the lower part of the socket for I_1 shows signs of pathological deformation. The corpus is broken behind M_3, and except for part of the angle and the separate ramal fragment (KNM-ER 992D), all of the ramus has been lost. The left hemimandible (KNM-ER 992B) has been damaged anteriorly, and several plates of bone below the canine

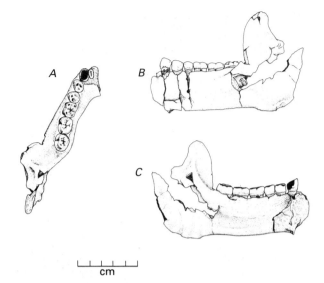

cm

Fig. 25. Drawings of KNM-ER 992B, showing (A) occlusal, (B) lateral
and (C) medial aspects of the left half of the mandible.

and premolars have been displaced. Crushing has also affected the internal symphyseal contour, and it is primarily for this reason that the
left and right bodies can no longer be joined together satisfactorily.
The canine crown is broken, but all of the premolar and molar teeth
are still intact. On this side, more of the ramus is preserved, although
sections including the internal and external condyloid buttresses, and
the condyle itself, are missing.

The superior and inferior borders of the corpus are parallel, and
the Ileret jaw is comparable to KNM-ER 730 in height. However, the
KNM-ER 992 body is thicker, especially below the last two molars,
where a lateral prominence is maximally developed (see Tables 10
and 11). This prominence takes the form of a rounded bulge, centered
below M_2 and extending down and forward to merge with the thickened base. It is limited behind by the concavity of the masseteric fossa
and above by the buccinator gutter, which is broad and slightly hollowed. Width of the extramolar sulcus is 8.5 mm on the left, opposite
the septum between M_2 and M_3. Anteriorly, the surface of the corpus
is smooth, as there is little or no expression of a superior lateral torus.
Only a faint sulcus sets off the marginal torus, and there are no well
defined marginal tubercles.

The alveolar margin is damaged at the symphysis, but enough of

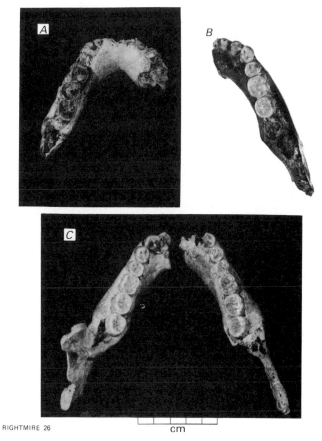

RIGHTMIRE 26
cm

Fig. 26. Photographs of (A) KNM-ER 730, (B) Olduvai Hominid 22 and (C) KNM-ER 992. These three lower jaws from East Africa, all shown in occlusal view, are similar to mandibles from Asia attributed to *Homo erectus*.

the midline remains to show that the chin region is gently rounded and receding. There is neither incurvation of the bone below the incisor roots nor swelling or formation of mental tubercles below to mark the presence of a trigone. In this respect the jaw differs somewhat from KNM-ER 730 but is similar to the mandible from Bed IV at Olduvai. Another resemblance to OH 22 is apparent in the form of the alveolar planum, which is extensive and flattened. This sloping mandibular shelf is bounded by a strong superior transverse torus, which can be followed laterally to about the level of the first molar. Even here, the torus does not subside entirely into the internal con-

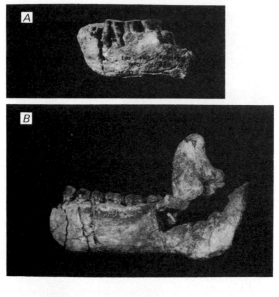

Fig. 27. Photographs of (A) KNM-ER 730, (B) KNM-ER 992B and (C)
Olduvai Hominid 22, all shown in lateral view.

tour of the body but instead merges with the projecting alveolar prominence. As a result, the anterior and posterior subalveolar fossae are
continuous, although the latter is more deeply excavated below the
faint mylohyoid impression. Unfortunately, crushing near the midline has distorted the profile below the superior torus, so the anatomy
of the geniglossal region is not clear. Small plates of cortical bone
have been deformed and pushed forward, and this has exaggerated
the depth of the genial fossa. At least a shallow fossa must be present,
and this seems to be perforated by a small foramen, as noted by R.E.
Leakey & Wood (1973). Inferiorly, traces of a second transverse torus
are preserved on the left hemimandible, and this lower torus bears
several small (genial) spines, rather eroded and indistinct.

The base of the Ileret jaw is heavy and rounded. As in KNM-ER

730, the digastric fossae are strongly imprinted and face perceptibly to the rear as well as downward. A triangular interdigastric eminence is present but not marked. Posteriorly, the base is thinned as it approaches the angle, which is slightly everted and has a roughened border limiting the masseteric insertion. The internal aspect of the angle exhibits a series of radially oriented corrugations, which mark the attachment of *m. pterygoideus medialis*. On the left, where the ramus is more complete, some of the triangular torus is preserved, and this extends upward as a sharply defined endocoronoid crest. Just at the level of the sigmoid notch, the posterior face of this endocoronoid buttress shows a deep pit-like indentation, while on its anterior surface there is a vertical groove which widens below to produce the buccinator gutter. Both pit and groove may be associated with insertion of *m. temporalis* fibers, as suggested by R.E. Leakey & Wood (1973). Apparently the retromolar space is short, although this region is affected by damage which has exposed the broken roots of the third molar tooth. The leading edge of the ascending ramus is also incomplete, but this rises from the body in such a way as to obscure the rearmost part of the M_3 crown, when the jaw is viewed from the side.

ADDITIONAL MANDIBULAR REMAINS

Other mandibles tentatively referred to *Homo erectus* are either juvenile or very incomplete. The KNM-ER 820 jaw is nicely preserved, although all of the right ramus and much of the left ramus are missing. This individual has been described by R.E. Leakey & Wood (1973), but because it is so immature, comparison with adult mandibles is difficult. The KNM-ER 1506 jaw fragment is comparable in geological age to the KNM-ER 3733 cranium. Only a portion of the right corpus is preserved, containing the crowns and roots of M_1 and M_2 (Table 12). Two upper premolars of this individual have also been recovered. Height of the body is about 33 mm at M_1 and 31 mm at the position of M_2. Because of damage to the internal surface, thickness cannot be measured accurately. The lateral prominence is maximally expanded at the level of M_2 and subsides anteriorly. Part of a faint sulcus can be seen in this region, just above the rounded base. Assignment to a taxon is difficult, but probably KNM-ER 1506 is best matched by other jaws attributed to *Homo erectus*.

Table 12. *Measurements (mm) of the KNM-ER 1506 teeth*[a]

	M_1	M_2
Mesiodistal diameter	$(13.2)^b$	14.0
Buccolingual diameter	(12.7)	13.2

[a]Mesiodistal and buccolingual diameters are taken parallel to the crown base as maximum readings. Except where indicated, corrections for interproximal attrition are not included. Where damage to the crown is appreciable, ( ) indicates that only an estimate is possible.
[b]M_1 displays a large mesial contact facet and a smaller distal one. Correction for this wear gives a length of 13.6 mm.

The East Turkana postcranial bones

Of the postcranial bones uncovered on the eastern shore of Lake Turkana, only a few are associated with crania or jaws. An example is KNM-ER 1808, which consists of fragments representing much of an adult individual. Pieces of the pelvis are similar to the corresponding parts of OH 28, and KNM-ER 1808 is also likely to be female (R.E. Leakey & Walker, 1985). Unfortunately this skeleton is affected by disease, and most of the postcranial elements are encrusted with pathological bone. These deposits of coarse woven tissue are up to 7.0 mm thick and may stem from a case of hypervitaminosis (Walker, Zimmerman & R.E. Leakey, 1982). The presence of such severe pathology makes comparative study and measurement of the specimen difficult at best.

KNM-ER 737 is the shaft and a little of the proximal end of a left femur. This individual is referred to *Homo* sp. by Day (1976) and to *Homo erectus* by Howell (1978). Other finds which may represent *Homo erectus* include KNM-ER 803, consisting of fragments of limbs and extremities, among which is the shaft of a femur. KNM-ER 1809 is part of the shaft of a small right femur. This bone, which is cylindrical in section rather than flattened anteroposteriorly, is less like OH 28 or the Zhoukoudian femora than is KNM-ER 737. Still another, more complete, femur is KNM-ER 1481. This specimen is said by Kennedy (1983) to share features with *Homo erectus*, but her assessment is challenged by Trinkaus (1984). Although measurements for all four Turkana femora are reported in Table 13, it must be recognized that attribution of either KNM-ER 1481 or KNM-ER 1809 to

Table 13. *Measurements (mm) of femora from Lake Turkana and Olduvai Gorge*[a]

	KNM-ER 737	KNM-ER 803	KNM-ER 1481	KNM-ER 1809	OH 28
Measurements taken below the lesser trochanter:					
Anteroposterior diameter	26.5	(26)	21.8	(21)	24
Transverse diameter	38	(33.5)	29.5	(27)	37.4
Shaft circumference	102	(94)	81	(76)	100
Measurements taken approximately at midshaft:					
Anteroposterior diameter	27	28	22.6	24	24.8
Transverse diameter	32.8	31.9	25.4	23.5	32
Shaft circumference	92	93	75	75	90

[a]Where extensive weathering has occurred, ( ) indicates that the measurement is subject to uncertainty.

Homo erectus is questionable. Cross-sectional areas of the shaft can be used in regression to estimate body weights of about 54 kg for KNM-ER 737 and also for KNM-ER 803 (Rightmire, 1986a).

Another of the Koobi Fora postcranial fossils which cannot unequivocally be assigned to a taxon is KNM-ER 3228. This is a right innominate bone, found in deposits underlying the KBS Tuff which must be about 1.9 million years in age. As described by Rose (1984), the Turkana hip is more complete than that from Olduvai. All of the ilium is well preserved, although there is some damage anteriorly to the crest and to the superior iliac spine. High in the iliac fossa, where the bone below the crest is very thin, there is a small perforation. Otherwise, there are few cracks, and no deformation is apparent. Most of the pubis and ischiopubic ramus are broken away, but more of the acetabulum is present than in the Olduvai specimen. Measurements are given in Table 14.

KNM-ER 3228 is remarkably similar to the Olduvai innominate. Both bones are very robust, and the iliac pillar is again prominent in the Turkana individual. Here the tubercle is preserved, and its superior aspect is broad and flattened. Width of this tubercle is about 25 mm. In this region, the lateral margin of the crest presents several irregular projections. The anterior iliac spine is blunt and thickened. The pelvic surface of the ilium is buttressed horizontally as in OH 28,

Table 14. *Measurements (mm) of hip bones from Lake Turkana and Olduvai Gorge*[a]

	KNM-ER 3228	OH 28
Vertical diameter of acetabulum, measured internally	53.4	55.3
Minimum distance from acetabular rim to superior aspect of ischial tuberosity	12.5	14.1
Ischial shank length, measured from center of acetabulum to nearest point on hamstring surface	53	`59
Hamstring moment arm, measured from center of acetabulum to intersection of vertical/transverse ridges on ischial tuberosity	79	(83)
Iliac breadth, measured from anterior inferior iliac spine to nearest point within sciatic notch	70	71
Distance from anterior inferior iliac spine to nearest point on auricular surface	75.5	81.5
Maximum height of auricular surface	(53)	(46)

[a]Where there is damage to the specimen, ( ) indicates that only an estimate is possible.

but definition of the arcuate line is sharper. The margins of the auricular surface are indistinct. The inferior aspect of this surface again faces downward as well as medially. The iliac tuberosity is roughened, and the greater sciatic notch is narrow. This suggests that KNM-ER 3228 may be a male. However, there is a pit-like sulcus on the preauricular surface.

The acetabulum is nearly as large as that of OH 28, and its rim is more uniformly thickened. The cavity is deep, and the floor of the acetabular fossa is relatively thin. The lunate surface is expanded superiorly. Between the acetabular rim and the ischial tuberosity, there is a narrow notch. The upper part of the tuberosity is intact, and the hamstring attachments, separated by an oblique line, are clearly outlined. Orientation of this surface is comparable to that seen in OH 28. Below the level of the transverse ridge, the bone of the ischium is eroded, and no details are preserved. The distance measured from the center of the acetabulum to the approximate mid-point of the transverse ridge is 79 mm, while the maximum length of the surviving ischial shank is 91 mm. Measurements of KNM-ER 3228 suggest a body weight of 48 or 49 kg for this Turkana individual.

Discoveries west of Lake Turkana

Searches for fossils have been conducted on the west side of the Turkana basin as well as in the Koobi Fora region. Among the most exciting recent finds is a *Homo erectus* skeleton, discovered in 1984 on the south bank of the Nariokotome River (Brown *et al.*, 1985). Excavations at this site have produced few other mammalian bones, but an age for the deposits can be obtained through tuff chemistry. The hominid fossils occur in hardened silts within a stratigraphic sequence also containing several ash layers. One of these tuffs, which immediately underlies the *Homo erectus* remains, is similar in composition to tuffs sampled elsewhere in the basin. Correlations worked out by Brown & Feibel (1985) suggest a date of about 1.6 million years for this horizon. Thus the new skeleton (KNM-WT 15000) is a little younger than KNM-ER 3733 from Koobi Fora.

Nearly the entire skeleton of this individual is well preserved. KNM-WT 15000 is subadult, and the dentition suggests an age of close to 12 years. Postcranial characters are consistent with an identification as male. All of the epiphyses are unfused, so the boy would certainly have grown further. Stature as estimated by regression relationships applicable to modern humans is already surprisingly great. The lower jaw has been recovered, and the cranium has been reconstructed from a number of pieces. Because KNM-WT 15000 is juvenile, direct comparisons to other adult *Homo erectus* individuals must be undertaken cautiously. Heavy tori and crests are not yet developed on the skull, but the brows are thicker than those of KNM-ER 3733. Endocranial volume as measured by A.C. Walker is greater than that of either KNM-ER 3733 or KNM-ER 3883. After some additional growth, this boy would likely have resembled other Turkana *Homo erectus*, although the cranium would most probably have been more massively constructed. More detailed comments concerning this valuable skeleton will be published by R.E. Leakey and his colleagues.

Questions concerning sorting of the Turkana hominids

Since both *Homo* and *Australopithecus* are known to occur at the Turkana localities in deposits above the KBS Tuff, the question of identification of individual specimens is important. The cranial and mandibular remains considered here are all quite distinct from any belonging to robust species of *Australopithecus*, and most workers would refer this material to the genus *Homo*. In many cases there is consensus that *Homo erectus* is the species represented. However, there is some disagreement about a few of the fossils, and their taxonomic status should be discussed. The larger issue of how *Homo erectus* is to be defined and/or diagnosed is addressed in detail in later chapters.

Doubt centers especially on certain well preserved lower jaws, including KNM-ER 992 from Ileret. Walker & R.E. Leakey (1978) note that these jaws resemble one of the hominids from Olduvai Gorge. KNM-ER 992 is similar to OH 13 in general appearance and in dimensions of the tooth row. It is also evident that the Ileret mandible differs from specimens such as KNM-ER 730 and OH 22 in some of the same ways as does OH 13. The lateral prominence is very strong and is maximally developed as a rounded bulge below M_2. Because of damage, shape of the dental arcade cannot be reconstructed precisely, but this seems to be rounded at the front. Such anterior curvature of the arcade also characterizes OH 13. This small jaw from middle Bed II exhibits similarities to *Homo erectus* but has been referred to *Homo habilis* by L.S.B. Leakey, Tobias & Napier (1964).

Other parts of OH 13, including the upper teeth, palate and some of the cranial base, resemble another of the Turkana hominids, numbered KNM-ER 1813. The KNM-ER 1813 cranium is more complete and has an endocranial capacity of only about 500 ml. Walker & R.E. Leakey (1978) interpret this evidence to indicate that both OH 13 and KNM-ER 1813 may be assigned to early *Homo* sp. or even to a gracile species of *Australopithecus*. A continuation of this argument suggests that, since jaws such as KNM-ER 992 are similar to OH 13, these Turkana mandibles may belong with small-brained, thin-walled crania such as KNM-ER 1813 rather than with *Homo erectus*. KNM-ER 992 has also been regarded as distinct from *Homo erectus* by Groves and Mazák (1975). These authors place the Ileret specimen in another species of *Homo* said to be contemporaneous with *Homo habilis*, but their suggestion has not received very much support.

It should be noted, however, that KNM-ER 992 is certainly not identical to OH 13. Height of the corpus is greater in the Ileret jaw, and the body is straight rather than curved in lateral view. Development of an alveolar planum is extensive in both individuals, but in KNM-ER 992 this shelf is flatter and more sloping at the level of the premolar teeth. Unlike the Olduvai mandible, KNM-ER 992 does not provide a particularly good fit to the KNM-ER 1813 braincase. The jaw is long, and the ramus is broad enough to place the (missing) condyle well behind the KNM-ER 1813 glenoid cavity when the teeth of the two hominids are aligned. In these and other features, KNM-ER 992 is in fact indistinguishable from *Homo erectus*. This is recognized by Wood (1976), who uses both corpus robusticity and dental proportions to place the jaw with later *Homo*. Howell (1978) also assigns KNM-ER 992 to *Homo erectus*, and this seems most appropriate, given the evidence available.

The nearly complete KNM-ER 3733 cranium from Koobi Fora has been accepted as *Homo erectus* since its discovery (R.E. Leakey & Walker, 1976). The second skull from Ileret is also considered to be *Homo erectus* by Howell (1978), and both individuals are said by Walker (1981) to be similar to material from Java and from China. My own studies of KNM-ER 3733 and KNM-ER 3883 lead me to agree with these assessments. At the same time, it is clear that the Turkana individuals are lightly built and exhibit some differences from larger African *Homo erectus* crania such as OH 9 (Rightmire, 1979). Wood (1984) has recently suggested that the Turkana specimens also lack some features of frontal form and vault thickening that are characteristic of the Indonesian and Chinese populations, and he raises the question of whether the African hominids should be grouped with *Homo erectus* as presently defined. Wood's comments deserve careful consideration, but it is significant that KNM-ER 730 does exhibit relatively strong supraorbital development and thickened vault bones. Although the cranial remains of this individual are fragmentary, they provide more evidence that (some) Turkana people are similar to later Asian *Homo erectus*. Further comparisons of the African and Far Eastern *Homo* assemblages are presented in Chapter 6.

The mandibles from Lake Baringo

Sites near Lake Baringo, Kenya, have produced both fossils and stone artifacts. The discovery west of Baringo of a nearly complete human mandible associated with postcranial remains and Acheulian tools has been reported by M. Leakey *et al.* (1969). Deposits containing this assemblage are known as the middle silts and gravels of the Kapthurin Formation. The sediments show normal magnetic polarity

(Dagley, Mussett & Palmer, 1978) and are overlain by a tuff tentatively dated as 0.24 million years in age (Tallon, 1978). Dates for tuffs lower in the section are still not certain, but some or all of the middle silts and gravels must be of Middle Pleistocene age.

The first Kapthurin mandible, designated KNM-BK 67, is somewhat less robust than other jaws from East Africa that have been referred to *Homo erectus*. This is apparent from comparisons with the Olduvai material, and there are other differences as well. It is evident, for example, that the superior transverse torus, which buttresses the symphysis internally, is less prominent in KNM-BK 67 than in OH 22. Although surface bone has been lost from the chin region, and the sockets for the anterior teeth have been eroded, the Baringo jaw may also exhibit a more vertical symphyseal profile. What these differences signify and whether the mandible should be identified as *Homo erectus* or as archaic *Homo sapiens* has not been settled.

THE KNM-BK 8518 JAW

More recent explorations of the Kapthurin sediments have produced a second mandible, numbered KNM-BK 8518. This fossil, said to be from the middle silts and gravels, was found with other animal bones and stone tools (van Noten, 1983). The site yielding KNM-BK 8518 lies some distance from the area where the first jaw was discovered, but the two hominids may be of approximately the same age. The 1982 mandible, which has suffered some damage but is not warped in the manner of KNM-BK 67, has been described by Wood & van Noten (1986). Measurements are given in Table 15.

This new jaw seems less heavily built than Hominid 22 (OH 22) from Olduvai Gorge and is less thickened at the symphysis. Upper and lower borders of the KNM-BK 8518 body are roughly parallel, but the corpus is curved in lateral view. Anteriorly, there is slight hollowing of the basal contour to either side of the midline, which is expressed independently from the sculpting caused by digastric attachment. Such a feature is not pronounced in OH 22, but here there is a resemblance to the contour of OH 13 from Bed II. The lateral prominence, which is very strongly developed, shows maximum swelling below M_2, again as in OH 13. This prominence is continued as a superior lateral torus, which can be followed forward to the mental foramen. On the left (less so on the right), this torus is separated by a shallow sulcus from the thickened basal margin. There

Table 15. *Measurements (mm) of the corpus of KNM-BK 8518*

	Midline	I₁/I₂	C̄	P₃	P₄	M₁	M₂	M₃
Minimum breadth[a]	17.5	17	17.5	18.3	19	20	21	21
Vertical height[b]	30	29.5	(28)	28	27.5	29.5	30	–
Minimum height[c]	(29.5)	(30.5)	(29)	(28)	(27)	29	29.5	31

[a]Caliper shaft is held perpendicular to the long axis of the body but not necessarily parallel to the occlusal plane.
[b]Taken on the internal aspect of the body. Where damage to the specimen is appreciable, ( ) indicates that only an estimate is possible.
[c]Taken from the base to the lateral aspect of the alveolar margin or inter-proximal contact zone.

are no marginal tubercles. On the right, there is localized swelling below P₃, as a consequence of cracking and some anterior displacement of the tooth row (see Wood & van Noten, 1986). On the side that is less damaged, there is no development of a jugum either at P₃ or below the canine alveolus.

The anterior symphyseal profile is rounded and receding. There is no incurvation between the alveolar margin and the base, so no true chin is present. Wood & van Noten (1986) do make reference to a 'mental trigone'. Here the bone is cracked, and some bits of surface are missing near the midline. It is possible to detect a small median crest reaching inferiorly toward the base, but other components of a trigone do not seem evident. In comparison to OH 22, the digastric fossae are deeply incised. These hollows face posteroinferiorly and extend to the level of P₄.

Behind the incisors, the alveolar plane is slightly concave and slopes posteriorly toward a rounded transverse torus. The plane itself is less extensive than that of OH 22 and is more comparable to the internal shelf exhibited by the OH 13 mandible. Below the superior torus, there is a deep, nearly circular genial pit. In the floor of this cavity, in line with the symphysis, there is a vertical ridge, very faintly marked. Such prominent genial hollowing does not occur at the symphysis of OH 22. In the case of OH 13, the area immediately below the torus is damaged, but it is not likely that deep genial fossae are developed. The Baringo jaw displays a very strong inferior transverse torus, on the surface of which there are several tiny spines. To either side, this rounded torus merges evenly with the internal contour of the corpus. Alveolar prominences are moderately projecting. Here and also in the morphology of the mandibular base, KNM-BK 8518 is closely similar to Hominid 13 from Olduvai.

Homo erectus in South Africa

In South Africa, fossils which represent an ancient species of *Homo* are known from sites in the Sterkfontein Valley. A pair of broken mandibles, a maxillary fragment and other bones found during earlier excavations at Swartkrans were originally placed in a new genus, called *Telanthropus* by Broom & Robinson (1949, 1950). At the time, there was some doubt about the date of the breccia containing these remains, although Robinson subsequently argued that all of the *Telanthropus* specimens were as old as the Swartkrans australopithecines. This genus has since been sunk into *Homo*, and more recent fieldwork carried out at the site by C.K. Brain has confirmed that some (not all) of the material is indeed contemporary with an early australopithecine assemblage. The maxillary fragment (SK 80) has been joined to other parts of a braincase, to produce an incomplete composite cranium known as SK 847 (Clarke, Howell & Brain, 1970). This cranium together with the SK 45 mandible and one or two additional fossils provides convincing evidence for the presence in the hanging remnant deposit of Member 1 of hominids anatomically distinct from *Australopithecus*.

There is enough of the frontal of the reconstructed skull to show that the supraorbital torus is rounded and thicker than expected for a robust australopithecine of comparable size. Behind the torus, there is a definite depression or sulcus, and the forehead then appears to rise rather steeply upward. Unfortunately, most of the rest of the frontal squama and temporal fossa are missing, though it is evident that postorbital constriction is only moderately developed. Other features of the face and cranial base are also cited by Clarke & Howell (1972) to support their referral of this material to the genus *Homo*, and Olson (1978) has dealt with nasal, palatal and mastoid characteristics in considerable detail. That there are definite resemblances to *Homo erectus* has recently been suggested by Clarke (1985), who calls attention to features shared by SK 847 and KNM-ER 3733 from Koobi Fora. However, this Swartkrans hominid is very incomplete. Endocranial volume cannot be determined, though it has been argued that the high frontal profile is in keeping with an expanded brain.

The skull is not that of *Australopithecus* and must represent *Homo*, but it may be best to leave the question of species identification open, as Clarke & Howell (1972) have recommended.

THE SK 15 JAW

One other specimen may more certainly be linked with *Homo erectus*. The SK 15 mandible, considered at first to be part of the *Telanthropus* collection, is now thought to be derived from deposits of Member 2 (called the 'brown member' by Brain, 1985). This section of the breccias is likely to be substantially younger than Member 1. Faunal comparisons presently being carried out should provide more information about dating and the nature of the Member 2 paleo-environment. Unfortunately, although the jaw is rather complete, it has been crushed and is therefore not particularly informative.

Much of the body is preserved, but the bone is cracked in a number of places, and some of the parts are no longer properly aligned. Damage is especially severe on the right side, where all of the lateral prominence has been lost. The alveolar process is eroded, and sockets for the anterior teeth are either crushed or partly filled with matrix. On the right, M_2 and M_3 are in place, while on the left all three molar crowns are present. Dimensions of the teeth are given in Table 16. The angles of the jaw are plastically deformed, and the superior portions of the rami are missing.

Corpus height can be estimated on the left side, and results are comparable to those recorded for OH 22 (see Table 17). Upper and lower borders of the body are approximately parallel. Several cracks which have spread and filled with matrix cause the lateral prominence to appear strongly developed. In its original (undistorted) state, the lateral corpus may have exhibited a prominence only slightly

Table 16. *Measurements (mm) of the teeth of SK 15*[a]

	M_1	M_2	M_3
Mesiodistal diameter	(11.9)	(13.0)	(14.3)
Buccolingual diameter	11.9	(12.9)	12.3

[a]Mesiodistal and buccolingual diameters are taken parallel to the crown base as maximum readings. No corrections for interproximal attrition are included. Where damage to the crown is appreciable, ( ) indicates that only an estimate is possible.

Table 17. *Measurements (mm) of the corpus of SK 15*

	P_4	M_1	M_2	M_3
Minimum breadth[a]	17	18.5	(23.5)	(23.5)
Minimum height[b]	(28)	(27.5)	(24)	(24.5)

[a]Taken with the shaft of the caliper held perpendicular to the long axis of the body but not necessarily parallel to the occlusal plane. Where damage to the specimen is appreciable, (   ) indicates that only an estimate is possible.
[b]Taken from the base to the lateral alveolar margin at the center of each tooth crown.

more pronounced than that of the Olduvai specimen. The base seems to be rounded rather than everted, and there are no marginal tubercles.

In profile, the symphysis is flattened and receding. There is damage inferiorly in this region, but no *mentum osseum* can be discerned. Whether other elements of a trigone are present can no longer be determined. Internally, the alveolar planum is at least as extensive as that of OH 22. This shelf is hollowed behind the empty sockets for the anterior dentition. A rounded superior transverse torus is evident, but a large crack passes obliquely through the genial fossa below. No spines are preserved, and the crack has also damaged the area at the midline where an inferior torus would be expressed. This second torus cannot have been prominent.

5

Northwest Africa

The first hominid from northwest Africa showing a resemblance to *Homo erectus* was discovered in 1933. The find was made by workmen quarrying in the consolidated dune of Kébibat, near Rabat on the Atlantic coast of Morocco (see Fig. 28). Only parts of a fragmented vault, the left maxilla, and the lower jaw of a subadult individual were recovered. Uncertainties concerning the dating of these fossils have still not been resolved, although it is agreed that they are of later Middle Pleistocene age. Controversy over the significance of the Rabat hominid has also persisted. The bones have been linked to *Homo erectus* by some workers, or viewed at least as intermediate in their morphology between archaic and more modern humans. Saban (1977) suggests that the occipital bone exhibits a pattern of endocranial vascular and cerebral markings which is primitive, while the external surface lacking a transverse torus is more advanced in form. The mandible also retains numerous archaic characters, although the symphysis 'foreshadows' the condition seen in *Homo sapiens*. Evidence of this sort is interpreted to show that a northwestern African *Homo* lineage became progressively more modern in the later Pleistocene. Other workers including Howell (1978) prefer simply to assign the fossils to *Homo sapiens*. The mandible does appear to be more lightly constructed than any of the jaws discovered 20 years later at Ternifine in Algeria. The corpus displays little lateral relief, and elements of a bony chin are clearly present. Given these and other features, it is difficult to see how an identification as *Homo erectus* can be justified.

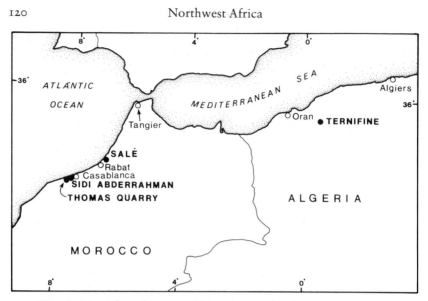

Fig. 28. Map of northwestern Africa showing localities where discoveries of *Homo erectus* have been made. Ternifine has produced three well preserved lower jaws, while the braincase from Salé is damaged. Remains from Sidi Abderrahman and the Thomas Quarries consist of teeth, broken jaws and bits of a frontal bone.

Remains found later are clearly more archaic. The site at Ternifine has yielded three mandibles, a parietal bone, and teeth, all apparently of early Middle Pleistocene date. Two fragments of another jaw were recovered at Sidi Abderrahman, near Casablanca, in 1955, and several interesting specimens have since come to light in the Thomas Quarries, located nearby. The only more complete cranium known from any of these Moroccan coastal localities was discovered near Salé in 1971. The Salé braincase is small and resembles *Homo erectus* in a number of respects. Unfortunately, it is likely that the rear of the cranium has been deformed pathologically. Identification of this fossil is therefore not straightforward, especially since much of the facial skeleton is missing.

Stratigraphy and dating

The hominids from Ternifine (now Tighenif) in Algeria are almost certainly the oldest to be recovered in northwest Africa. This site was investigated late in the last century, and a number of mammalian fossils were collected and described. The presence of stone industries was also noted. A more systematic survey was undertaken in 1931, but the site was not worked intensively until 1954 (Arambourg & Hoffstetter, 1963). Recent field research is detailed by Geraads *et al.* (1986). Deposits at Ternifine consist of clays and sands stratified in a small lake fed by artesian springs. The sequence apparently does not cover a long period of time. Although the sands are not suitable for paleomagnetic study, measurements made on clays from near the bottom of the section show these sediments to be of normal polarity. Geraads *et al.* (1986) argue that this evidence, coupled with studies of the Ternifine bovid and giraffid fossils (Geraads, 1981), is in keeping with an earliest Middle Pleistocene age for the deposits.

Other localities, all close to the Atlantic coast of Morocco, are not so ancient. Local stratigraphies are not well correlated, so the relative ages of several of these sites are disputed. A lack of reliable radiometric dates also makes it difficult to place the Moroccan hominids in a secure chronological framework. Information reviewed by Debenath, Raynal & Texier (1982) suggests that the sandy deposits from which the human fossils have been recovered belong to the Tensiftian continental cycle. The mandible from Sidi Abderrahman may be the oldest of the group, followed by material from the Thomas Quarries and Salé. A slightly different view is taken by Geraads, Beriro & Roche (1980) and by Geraads (1980), who argue on faunal grounds that the Thomas I and Thomas II assemblages are roughly contemporary and that both are about as old as the bones from Sidi Abderrahman. Jaeger (1981) places the Salé cranium with this group as well. So, the scattered remains of Moroccan *Homo erectus* may all be of approximately the same Tensiftian geological provenience. Hublin (1985) has recently advanced the claim that these coastal Tensiftian deposits may be close to 400 000 years old, rather than later Middle Pleistocene in age.

The Ternifine remains

The first and second Ternifine mandibles were found in the course of excavations conducted in 1954. The third jaw and the parietal bone were picked up during the following field season. All of this material has been described by Arambourg (1963), who also provides some comparisons with other hominids.

TERNIFINE 1 (Figs 29 & 30)

Although this mandible was badly cracked and broken when it was recovered, much of the original damage has been skillfully repaired.

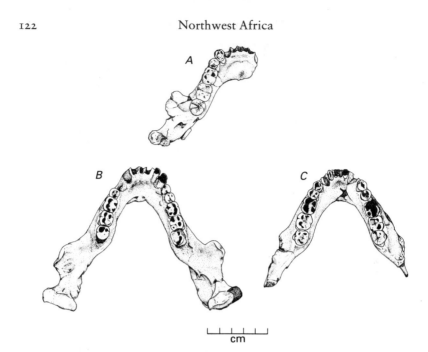

Fig. 29. The three lower jaws from Ternifine, drawn in occlusal view. (A) Ternifine 2 is likely to be female, while (B) Ternifine 3 and (C) Ternifine 1 are more massive mandibles probably attributable to male individuals.

Portions of both rami are still missing. In the right corpus, numerous cracks remain. These have been filled, but in some areas small plates of surface bone have been displaced. There is more damage anteriorly, where the jaw has been broken just to the right of the midline. Here a good deal of bone is missing from the internal aspect of the symphysis. Reconstruction is generally good, but the right and left sides of the mandible have not been perfectly aligned. While the crowns of the anterior teeth are missing or badly damaged, the crowns of P_3 to M_3 are intact on each side (Table 18). The teeth are set in an arcade which is evenly rounded at the front. In occlusal view, the tooth row passes posteriorly across the long axis of the jaw, so that M_2 and M_3 are very close to the inner margin of the mandibular contour.

In lateral view, upper and lower borders of the body are parallel, as in OH 22. Measurements confirm that the Algerian jaw is higher than OH 22 by several millimeters, but Ternifine 1 is similar in this dimension to OH 51 (see Tables 19 and 20). A striking feature is the lateral

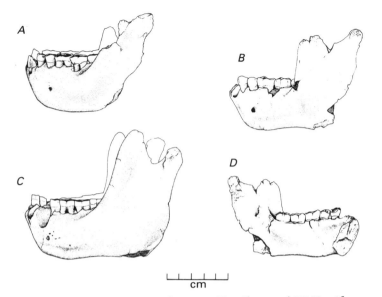

Fig. 30. Drawings of (A) Ternifine 1, (B) Ternifine 2 and (C) Ternifine 3, in lateral view. Shown also is the medial aspect of (D) Ternifine 2.

Table 18. *Measurements (mm) of the teeth of the Ternifine hominids*[a]

	P_3	P_4	M_1	M_2	M_3
Ternifine 1					
Mesiodistal diameter	8.5	8.3	(13.0)	13.0	12.0
Buccolingual diameter	10.2	10.1	12.5	13.0	12.2
Ternifine 2					
Mesiodistal diameter	(8.6)	(8.8)	(13.9)	14.1	13.4
Buccolingual diameter	11.1	11.0	12.8	13.3	12.5
Ternifine 3					
Mesiodistal diameter	8.0	(8.2)	(12.4)	(12.0)	(12.0)
Buccolingual diameter	10.2	10.0	12.0	12.2	11.5

[a]Mesiodistal and buccolingual diameters are taken parallel to the crown base as maximum readings. No corrections for interproximal attrition are included. Where crown damage is appreciable, ( ) indicates that only an estimate is possible.

Table 19. *Measurements (mm) of minimum corpus breadth for the Ternifine jaws*[a]

	Ternifine 1	Ternifine 2	Ternifine 3
Midline	18.5	17	19
I_1	18.5	16.8	19
I_2	18.0	16.5	19.1
$\bar{C}$	19.5	16	20
P_3	20	15	(19.5)
P_4	19	15	19
M_1	19	15.5	19.5
M_2	22	17.5	21
M_3	22.5	21.5	22

[a]Taken with the shaft of the caliper held perpendicular to the long axis of the body but not necessarily parallel to the occlusal plane. Where damage to the specimen is appreciable, (   ) indicates that only an estimate is possible.

prominence, which is a well defined bulge extending down and forward from the junction of the anterior border of the ramus with the body. This prominence is somewhat stronger than in OH 22, and as a consequence, the entire jaw is also thicker at this level, below the position of M_2. Anteriorly, the prominence is continued toward the mental foramen as a weak superior torus, which fades out below the

Table 20. *Measurements (mm) of minimum corpus height for the Ternifine jaws*[a]

	Ternifine 1	Ternifine 2	Ternifine 3
Midline	37.5	(31)	(35)
I_1/I_2	37.5	31	(34)
$\bar{C}$	–	–	(30)
P_3	33	(30)	–
P_4	33	32	35
M_1	35.5	33.5	–
M_2	–	31.5	38
M_3	(35)	–	(39)

[a]Taken from the base to the lateral aspect of the alveolar margin or interproximal contact zone. Where damage to the specimen is appreciable, (   ) indicates that only an estimate is possible.

premolars. Inferiorly, the marginal torus, which is said by Arambourg (1963) to be 'remarkably developed' in this individual, is in fact
not much more pronounced than that of OH 22. There is definite
localized swelling of the torus below P_3 and also below M_2, to produce anterior and posterior marginal tubercles. These tubercles contribute to a general thickening of the base, so that the inferior aspect
of the jaw is broad and rounded, more resembling the base of OH 51
than that of OH 22. Anterior marginal tubercle development is still
more exaggerated in OH 51, however.

The symphyseal profiles of Ternifine 1 and OH 22 are quite similar. In the Ternifine fossil, the symphyseal face is smooth and
rounded, and there is no suggestion of an incurvation or depression
between the alveolar margin and the base. A *mentum osseum* as
defined by Weidenreich is absent. On either side of the midline, there
are regions of very faint depression situated anterior to the canine
alveoli, as noted by Arambourg (1963). But true lateral (mental)
tubercles are not formed, and Ternifine 1 appears to possess none of
the components of a bony chin.

In internal aspect, differences between the Algerian and East
African mandibles are present, but not marked. The alveolar planum
of Ternifine 1 is slightly hollowed in the region below the incisors but
then curves evenly downward, without any noticeable interruption
by a superior transverse torus. Arambourg (1963) does describe a
lightly developed transverse crest or *margo terminalis* delimiting the
alveolar plane inferiorly, and his account is followed by Tobias
(1971a). But careful examination of the lingual symphyseal face does
not bear this out, and there is little division of the planum from the
region surrounding the 'foramen supraspinosum' below. Unfortunately the anatomy of the genial fossa and tubercles is largely destroyed. It is clear that a planum and superior transverse torus are less
strongly developed than in OH 22. In its expression of these features,
the Ternifine jaw seems more closely to resemble OH 23 or OH 51.

On the internal surface of the body, the alveolar prominence is
comparable in size and form to that of OH 22. This prominence
curves back and upward, forming the medial limit to a relatively
short retromolar space, before giving rise to a thick triangular torus.
This torus and its division into endocoronoid and endocondyloid
cristae is preserved for some distance on the internal aspect of the left
ascending ramus. On this side and also on the right, much of the buccinator gutter is present, passing as a smooth channel outward

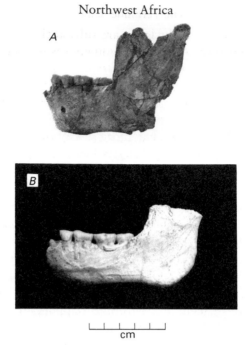

Fig. 31. Photographs of (*A*) Ternifine 2 and (*B*) Thomas Quarry I, both shown in lateral view.

between the anterior border of the ramus and the last two molar teeth. Width of the extramolar sulcus is 8 mm on the left, 6 mm on the right, at the level of M_3.

TERNIFINE 2 (Figs 29, 30 & 31)

This specimen consists of the left half of a mandible, complete to a point slightly beyond the symphyseal midline. Sockets for all of the incisor teeth and the left canine are preserved but empty, while P_3 to M_3 are still in place. The body is generally in good condition, and a transverse fracture between M_1 and M_2 has caused little loss of bone. Relatively more of the ramus is present than in the case of Ternifine 1. As Arambourg points out, this mandible is lighter in construction than the first. It is fully adult, but the unworn state of M_3 suggests that this individual was somewhat younger. Dental dimensions are given in Table 18.

Upper and lower borders of the body are parallel, as in the other jaws, while corpus height is close to that of OH 22 and OH 23. Ternifine 2 thus seems more comparable to the East African fossils in overall proportions, although the latter are substantially thicker and consequently more robust. A lateral prominence is less well defined than in the mandible of Ternifine 1 but stands out in as much or more relief than that of OH 22. Expression of the superior lateral torus and of the marginal torus is not remarkable. Small anterior and posterior tubercles locally accentuate the thickness of the base, but the inferior margin of the jaw is more lightly built than that of Ternifine 1. In basal view, the Ternifine 2 and OH 22 mandibles are similar, while OH 23 is still more gracile in appearance.

At the symphysis, the profile is flat and receding rather than rounded, and depressions on either side of the midline are a little deeper than in Ternifine 1. Inferiorly, the bone between these depressions broadens to form a triangular eminence which corresponds to the mental trigone described for several of the Zhoukoudian mandibles by Weidenreich. This external profile is closely similar to that of OH 22. Unfortunately the Olduvai fossil is broken just at the midline, but enough of the bone remains to show that the symphysis is again flattened rather than convex. Components of a trigone are less clearly developed than in Ternifine 2, but differences are slight and should not be emphasized.

An alveolar planum is more extensive on the posterior symphyseal face of Ternifine 2 than in jaw 1. This surface is again slightly hollowed below the roots of the anterior teeth and is divided into two parts by a faint median crest. The planum slopes gently rearward to about the level of the septum between P_3 and P_4, and then drops more sharply downward. The rounded buttress marking the inferior margin of the alveolar surface may be termed a superior transverse torus (not quite so clearly defined as in OH 22, although the two jaws are again similar in symphyseal construction). Below the torus, there is an oval depression, roughened throughout. Just at the apex of this hollow, in the midline, there is a small foramen, while at the inferior border there is a sharp crest, oriented vertically and partly broken. From this spine, the symphyseal profile curves abruptly forward toward the base. Arambourg comments on the presence of an inferior transverse torus, but a definite lower buttress is not distinct. Digastric impressions are strongly marked, however, and these areas of muscular insertion face posteriorly as well as downward.

Although the ramus is damaged, and some of the remaining sections are badly cracked and reconstructed, much of the coronoid process and even a part of the mandibular condyle are preserved. All of the angle is missing, and there is some bone lost from the alveolar prominence, where this curves back and upward to merge with the triangular torus. The prominence itself is sharply outlined, and its crest confines the retromolar fossa to a small area immediately behind M_3. Width of the extramolar sulcus is only about 5 mm. On the internal aspect of the ramus, the triangular torus is as heavily constructed as that of OH 22, and its posterior branch can be followed toward the broken condyle. Behind the torus, and just below its division into endocondyloid and endocoronoid cristae, part of the opening of the mandibular foramen is still filled with sandy matrix. Because the outer rim of this canal is broken, its exact form and that of the lingula cannot be determined.

TERNIFINE 3 (Figs 29 & 30)

Ternifine 3 is the largest of the three mandibles. It is slightly higher in the body than jaw 1 and equally thick at the level of the first molar. Ramus dimensions cannot be compared directly, because of damage to Ternifine 1. In any case, mandible 3 is said by Arambourg to be male, because of its 'robusticity' and absolute dimensions, and in these respects it is closer to OH 51 than to other Olduvai individuals. The fossil is quite complete, although there has been considerable crushing of the right corpus. Both internal and external aspects of the body exhibit cracking, and there is an area of heavy reconstruction near the symphysis. The very worn right I_2 and C appear to have been inserted into their sockets as part of this reconstructive effort. Both crowns now project well beyond the level of the posterior part of the tooth row, so occlusal relationships are not well preserved. Dental measurements are given in Table 18.

In side view, the surface of the body is relatively smooth, and the superior lateral torus is only moderately developed. A clear intertoral sulcus can be traced from the level of M_2 forward almost to the symphysis. A marginal torus is also present, although expression of the anterior and posterior marginal tubercles is less than in either of the other jaws. The base is thickened, but not to the degree seen in Ternifine 1. Anteriorly, the symphyseal face is flattened, much in the manner of jaw 2. While there is no incurvation of the bone below the alveolar margin, a slight median crest is formed, and this is expanded below to shape a mental trigone. As in the second mandible, the trigone is extended downward just in the midline to produce a basal eminence, flanked on each side by a marked depression following the line of digastric insertion. This mandibular incisure is not characteristic of Ternifine 1, nor does it appear to be prominent on OH 22. An upcurving of the base forward of the anterior marginal tubercle can be seen in OH 51, however, and this suggests that a similar incisure may be present. Unfortunately OH 51 is broken at the canine alveolus, and the symphyseal region is not preserved.

The posterior aspect of the symphysis is slightly concave above, near the incisor roots, although the alveolar planum is not extensive and slopes downward more steeply than in Ternifine 2. Below the rounded superior transverse torus, a genioglossal fossa is deeply excavated (as is clear to the left of the midline where the bone is intact and has not been reconstructed). Much of the space within the fossa is occupied by a vertical crest, broadened below in the region of the mental spine(s). As is the case with the other jaws, an inferior torus is not prominent, although there is some swelling of the symphyseal wall well below and to one side of the genial structures.

Arambourg remarks on the presence of a mandibular torus in Ternifine 3, and on the right alveolar border below M_1 there is a definite tubercle. Other signs of torus formation are not distinct. However, the alveolar prominence is exceptionally well developed as it passes behind M_3 onto the internal face of the ascending ramus. The triangular torus is also quite heavily constructed, and on both sides the lingula is prolonged superiorly to produce a pointed spine. Below and posterior to the mylohyoid groove, the inner aspect of the mandibular angle is roughened to mark insertion of *m. pterygoideus medialis*.

The retromolar spaces are again restricted, and in lateral view the leading edge of the ramus rises so as to obscure the rearmost portion of the crown of the third molar tooth. Between the anterior border of the ramus and the triangular torus, the bone is flattened rather then deeply concave or gutter-like, and the extramolar sulcus is wide (8 mm on the left, slightly less on the right). The coronoid processes are high and massive in construction, and the entire ramus is large by modern human standards.

TERNIFINE 4

The Ternifine right parietal bone is remarkably complete and well preserved. Several cracks have been repaired, and distortion is not apparent. The borders approaching the thickened mastoid angle do show signs of weathering, while the lambdoid angle seems also to be damaged. According to Arambourg, some bone was lost from this part of the parietal prior to fossilization. This interpretation is probably correct, although the border in this region does show sutural indentations, even if these are not deeply impressed into the compact tables. It may be questioned whether a sutural ossicle was present. Otherwise, the parietal margins are intact.

On the external surface, close to the sagittal suture, there is hollowing which suggests some heaping up of bone just in the midline. Such keeling could not have been pronounced. The temporal lines are clearly marked. Distance from the superior line to the sagittal border of the bone is minimally 53 mm. Arambourg's description of the division posteriorly to produce two lines is accurate. However, there is no formation of an angular torus. The depression between the superior and inferior lines is very faint, and there is no extension of a supramastoid sulcus (as an angular sulcus) onto the parietal. Although there are signs of weathering along the temporal border, this parietotemporal junction appears to have followed a straight course, as is common in *Homo erectus*.

Variation in the Ternifine assemblage

The Ternifine jaws are exceptionally well preserved. Even the Ternifine 2 hemimandible is more complete than Olduvai Hominid 22 (OH 22). Within this assemblage, there is substantial (size) variation. Ternifine 2 is not very robust and has a cross-sectional area below M_1 of only about 420 mm². Mandibles 1 and 3 are much more massively constructed with strong lateral prominences and thickened marginal tori. In Ternifine 3 there is a well developed arrangement of buttresses on the medial aspect of the ramus. Cross-sectional areas of the corpus at M_1 are 565 and 595 mm², respectively. A reasonable explanation for this variation is provided by sex dimorphism, and it is likely that Ternifine 2 is female. As noted by Arambourg, Ternifine 3 and probably also jaw 1 may be regarded as males.

Despite this variation, the fossils share a complex of archaic features. All three jaws are robust by modern standards, and the teeth are very large. The alveolar margin is parallel to the base. There is always some separation of the lateral tori by an intertoral sulcus. Symphyseal profiles are flattened and receding, and there is no incurvation below the alveolar margin to produce a bony chin. Internally, there is heavy buttressing of the symphysis, whether or not a superior transverse torus is defined. In no case is a double torus system clearly present, although there is an approach to this in Ternifine 2 and especially in jaw 3. All of the mandibles are easily distinguished from those of *Homo sapiens*.

In other respects, there are few significant departures from the modern condition. A lateral prominence is not much more pronounced than that seen frequently in *Homo sapiens*. Shape of the digastric impressions is highly variable, as is the anatomy of the genial region. Form and extent of the masseteric fossa is not extraordinary in the Ternifine jaws, and there is some eversion of the angle in mandible 3. The ascending ramus of this individual seems to be distinguished principally by overall size. Height and thickness of the Ternifine 3 coronoid process are striking, and the condyle is very large.

Remains from the Thomas Quarries and Sidi Abderrahman
(Figs 31 & 32)

Human fossils have been collected from Thomas Quarry I and from Thomas Quarry III. Circumstances surrounding the discovery of the Quarry I mandible are discussed by Ennouchi (1969), and the fossil has been described in detail by Sausse (1975). This specimen consists of most of the left half of a jaw. The body is broken cleanly at the septum separating C and P_3, and only part of the rear wall of the canine alveolus is intact. The P_3 socket is filled with matrix. The lateral surface of the corpus has been damaged so as to expose the buccal aspects of the P_4 and M_1 roots. About a one millimeter thickness of surface bone is also missing from an area extending below M_2 and up onto the anterior edge of the ascending ramus, which itself is broken. All of the coronoid process and the condyle are lacking. Portions of the ramus and body which remain, including the mandibular angle, are in good condition, and P_4 to M_3 are still in place. Dimensions of the tooth crowns are provided in Table 21.

Because the Thomas mandible is rather incomplete, full comparisons with other specimens are rendered difficult. Corpus measurements are given in Table 22. The jaw appears to be lightly built, in that the corpus is less thickened than that of most of the Ternifine and Olduvai hominids, even when surface damage is accounted for. Upper and lower borders of the body are not quite parallel, and there is a slight tendency for height to increase anteriorly. Corpus height at

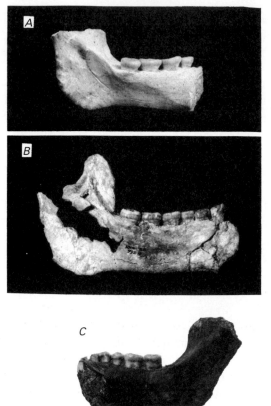

Fig. 32. Photographs of three lower jaws from northwestern and eastern Africa. (A) Thomas Quarry I, shown in medial view, is compared to (B) KNM-ER 992B from Koobi Fora and (C) Olduvai Hominid 22.

M_1 is about equal to that of OH 22 and only a little less than recorded for OH 23. The index of robusticity is consequently lower for Thomas I than for the Olduvai jaws. The Ternifine fossils are all higher at M_1, while Ternifine 1 and Ternifine 3 (not Ternifine 2) are a few millimeters thicker. Compared to Thomas I, all three have larger cross-sectional areas. Here Thomas I is closest to Ternifine 2, and an overall resemblance to this jaw suggests that Thomas I could well be female.

The original extent of lateral prominence development can no longer be ascertained. This does not appear to have been great, and only a shallow intertoral sulcus reaches forward toward the mental

Table 21. *Measurements (mm) of the Thomas Quarry I and Sidi Abderrahman teeth[a]*

	P_4	M_1	M_2	M_3
Thomas Quarry I				
Mesiodistal diameter	9.0	14.0	14.8	12.8
Buccolingual diameter	10.5	12.8	13.0	11.7
Sidi Abderrahman				
Mesiodistal diameter	—	12.8	13.5	12.3
Buccolingual diameter	—	11.8	11.7	11.2

[a]Mesiodistal and buccolingual diameters are taken parallel to the crown base as maximum readings. No corrections for interproximal attrition are included.

foramen situated below P_4. The foramen itself is sealed with the same reddish-brown matrix that adheres to other portions of the specimen. A marginal torus is present, but neither anterior nor posterior marginal tubercles are prominent. While there is slight localized swelling of the base below M_2, the inferior aspect of the body is generally less thickened than that of other African *Homo erectus*. Of the three Olduvai jaws, it is perhaps OH 23 which most resembles Thomas I in basal view.

Since the mandible has been broken well to the left side of the midline, none of the symphyseal region is preserved. It is not possible to comment directly on chin formation, nor can the alveolar planum or genial fossa be reconstructed accurately. It is clear from the orien-

Table 22. *Measurements (mm) of the corpus of the Thomas Quarry I mandible*

	P_4	M_1	M_2	M_3
Breadth[a]	16	(17)	—	18.5
Vertical height[b]	28.5	27.5	26.5	27

[a]Taken with the shaft of the caliper held perpendicular to the long axis of the body and parallel to the occlusal plane. Where damage to the specimen is appreciable, ( ) indicates that only an estimate is possible.
[b]Taken on the internal aspect of the body.

tation of the remaining cross-section that the symphyseal axis would be inclined rather steeply forward, however, and there is no sign of any protrusion of the lower part or base of the corpus at the level of P_3. Internally at this level, the surface of the body is evenly convex. No indications of transverse tori remain. Posteriorly, the alveolar prominence shows little relief, and the retromolar triangle is short. Even the broken border of the ascending ramus obscures the rear of the M_3 crown in lateral view, and it is likely that the ramus when reconstructed would rise from the body at a position adjacent to the center of this tooth. Width of the damaged extramolar sulcus is about 5 millimeters.

Little can be said concerning the upper portion of the ramus, which is broken just below the mandibular notch. Internally, the mandibular canal opens forward and downward into the thickened bone behind the triangular torus, and a plate-like lingula is present. The angle is blunt and evenly rounded in profile. On its medial surface, a series of peripherally placed impressions mark insertion of *m. pterygoideus medialis*. Laterally there is some eversion of the posteroinferior border of the masseteric fossa.

Additional human material, recovered from Thomas Quarry III, has been described briefly by Ennouchi (1972, 1976). One piece of frontal bone, with portions of the nasal and lacrimal bones still attached below glabella, is in poor condition. Only part of the eroded left squama is preserved, along with a section of the supraorbital torus and orbital roof. Attempts to clean this specimen have resulted in heavy damage to the torus. Apparently this brow is not greatly thickened. Posteriorly the frontal surface is flattened, and a supratoral sulcus is not developed.

There is also a fragment of maxilla containing the damaged alveoli for the left I^2 and C. These teeth are glued in place. Nine additional teeth include the left P^3 to M^2, the right C to P^4, right M^1 (or M^2) and right M^3. The dentition is generally well preserved. For all of the premolars, two roots are present. The P^3 roots are joined for most of their length, but bifurcation produces two apices. The P^4s show less tendency toward root bifurcation. The M^1 crowns are heavily worn, and dentin is exposed over most of the occlusal surface. Details of cusp structure can be made out only on the right M^3.

SIDI ABDERRAHMAN

This jaw consists of two fragments. The more important is a section of the right mandibular corpus, rather badly cracked and weathered.

Anteriorly, part of the alveolus for P_4 is preserved, although the tooth itself is lost. All three molar teeth are in good (but worn) condition (Table 21), although the arcade in which they have been reconstructed is distorted. The roots of M_1 and M_3 are exposed, and below M_3 the bone is shattered. None of the ramus remains.

Because this specimen is so poorly preserved, its proportions cannot be determined with much certainty. The Sidi Abderrahman jaw is higher at the position of the molars than Thomas I and is perhaps more comparable in both height and thickness to Ternifine 2. The alveolar margin and the base are parallel. There is some swelling of the surface below M_2 to mark the position of the lateral prominence, but all of the extramolar sulcus is missing. Other details of corpus morphology are obscured by weathering.

The Salé braincase

Human fossils from the Salé locality have been described by Jaeger (1975) and by Hublin (1985). Specimens of interest include a somewhat damaged cranial vault, a natural sandstone braincast, and part of the left maxillary alveolar process carrying I^2 to M^2. The frontal bone is broken anteriorly, and none of the supraorbital region has survived. Much of the left parietal and temporal are in place, but there is damage on the right. On this side, there is no contact between the upper part of the wall of the vault and the cranial base. The uppermost portion of the occipital squama is also broken, and none of the lambdoid suture is preserved. However, the cranial base including the lateral and basilar sections of the occiput, parts of both temporal bones and the body of the sphenoid is in satisfactory condition.

The cranium is small and thick-walled. Bone thickness near asterion is about 17 mm, while at bregma it is 7.5 mm. Endocranial volume as measured by Holloway (1981b) is 880 ml. A striking feature is the extent of postorbital constriction. The remaining frontal squama is narrow, flattened laterally, and exhibits some blunt keeling in the midline. This keeling is not continued onto the parietal region, where the vault is substantially wider. Maximum biparietal breadth is 128 mm, while an estimate of least frontal breadth is only 81 mm. Considerable bossing of the parietal bones is evident. Cranial measurements are given in Table 23.

On the left side, the temporal line describes a rounded arc and is only slightly raised (not crested) as it curves toward the parietotemporal suture. The mastoid crest is sharply defined. A supra-mastoid crest is prominent, and this takes the form of a localized protuberance which fades before producing any noticeable shelf over the external meatus. The auditory opening is oval in shape, with its long axis slanted slightly forward. For a cranium of relatively small size, the mastoid processes are quite large. These are strongly inclined medially as well as downward to terminate in conical tips. The greatest breadth of the Salé vault falls at the supramastoid crests.

The occipital bone is rounded in lateral view and does not display a transverse torus. Orientation of the nuchal lines is not clear, as noted by Hublin (1985). The superior lines appear to be quite low. The nuchal area (lower scale) of the occiput is thus restricted in extent, relative to the occipital plane (upper scale) above. There is also considerable bilateral asymmetry. On the left, there is some peculiar heaping up of bone along the nuchal line as this passes toward asterion. There is more abnormal bone development on the right, in the area of the inferior line. Hublin (1985) considers this pattern to be pathological, perhaps resulting from injury to some of the nuchal musculature. More symmetrically located on either side of the squama are rough, plateau-like structures which approach the occipitomastoid suture anteriorly. On the left, this crest is bounded by a wide channel, which may in part give passage to the occipital artery. Between this smooth channel and the deeper digastric notch, a juxtamastoid eminence is developed. The posterior face of the mas-toid itself is flattened and lies in the same plane as the adjacent nuchal region of the occiput.

Nearly all of the glenoid cavity is preserved on the right side. The fossa is relatively short in anteroposterior extent and is about 27 mm wide. The anterior articular surface is markedly concave from side to side, and there is no tubercle. A postglenoid process is not present. The entoglenoid process is located just at the junction of the temporal and sphenoid and is traversed by the sphenotemporal suture. On this side, the adjacent sphenoid anatomy is not clear, but on the left there is a prominent plate-like sphenoid spine. This gives the Salé cavity a modern appearance, which is reinforced by the structure of the tym-panic bone and petrous temporal. The more lateral part of the tym-panic plate is broken, but a large syloid sheath is developed.

These characters of the Salé braincase do not point unequivocally toward an identification as *Homo erectus*. The skull does display some of the features of more modern humans, as has been noted by other workers. Perhaps a few of these traits should be discounted, if the rear of the specimen has been deformed. The rounded occipital profile, lack of a strong transverse torus, and short nuchal plane may all be a consequence of pathology, as argued by Hublin (1985). However, the basioccipital is short, and the glenoid cavity and tympanic bone exhibit some aspects of modern form. There is also substantial bossing of the parietal walls. These traits contrast with others which are found routinely in *Homo erectus*. The latter include frontal form, shape of the temporal squama, and some features of cranial base anatomy as well as overall proportions of the braincase. The vault bones are thick, and the Salé endocranial capacity is well below the mean for *Homo erectus*. This individual may well be female. In my view, the fossil is best sorted with *Homo erectus*, even if uncertainties remain to be resolved.

6

Comparisons of African hominids with Asian *Homo erectus*

In the four preceding chapters, I have provided descriptive accounts of the morphology of fossils from Java, Olduvai Gorge, other East African localities and northwest Africa. These descriptions are in some cases quite detailed. Where appropriate, I have incorporated comparative information, including at least some discussion of general resemblances among specimens from a given site or geographic area. It should be apparent that a number of the individuals from Trinil, Sangiran and Sambungmachan are broadly similar. Particularly the larger crania from Sangiran and Sambungmachan also share features with the assemblage from Ngandong, although there are some differences. So far, I have taken the position that all of these Javanese hominids can be referred to *Homo erectus*.

The large braincase found by Louis Leakey in deposits of upper Bed II at Olduvai seems unequivocally to represent the same species. This has been emphasized in earlier reports (Rightmire, 1979), although OH 9 has not before been compared systematically to specimens from Indonesia. The most complete of the Olduvai mandibles also shows similarities to Asian *Homo erectus* (Rightmire, 1980), as do the jaws from Ternifine (Arambourg, 1963). Other remains from East Africa are perhaps less easily identified by species. Doubt concerning the affinities of the two rather complete crania from East Turkana has been expressed recently by Wood (1984). Whether these and other individuals from the Koobi Fora region should be assigned to *Homo erectus* or to another *Homo* species can be settled only after thorough comparisons with Asian fossils have been carried out.

Comparisons of the African and Asian hominids are here based on measurements and especially on my own observations of anatomical structure. I have tried to touch on all aspects of skull form, although of course some parts of the vault are much less frequently preserved than others. Fragile facial bones and cranial bases are poorly represented in the *Homo erectus* inventory. Mandibles are more numerous, and some are in quite good condition. Postcranial remains, unfortunately very scarce and incomplete at the Asian localities, are becoming better known from several sites in eastern Africa. All in all, there is on record a substantial body of fossil material. There is consequently a need to organize comparative treatment so as to avoid the confusion that will certainly arise if too many of the specimens are discussed simultaneously.

A reasonable basis for partitioning both the Asian and the African assemblages into subgroups is provided by gross size. Among the individuals recovered at Sangiran, for example, there are marked differences in braincase size and robusticity. Sangiran 2 has an endocranial volume of only a little over 800 ml and is considerably smaller than Sangiran 12 or Sangiran 17. This cranium is more appropriately lumped with Sangiran 10 or even with Sangiran 4, along with the Trinil skullcap, to constitute a sample that can be compared with fossils such as KNM-ER 3733 or KNM-ER 3883 from eastern Africa. Some or most of these individuals are likely to be females. Larger hominids such as Sangiran 12, Sangiran 17, Sambungmachan and several of the Zhoukoudian remains may be compared to one another and to the Olduvai Bed II braincase. Work of this sort, carried out systematically, will make clearer the extent to which the important East and northwest African fossils share in or depart from the morphology characteristic of Asian *Homo erectus*. If the African crania and jaws do substantially resemble those from the Far East, then it will be necessary to take note of this African material in compiling a more comprehensive definition of the species.

Crania from East and northwest Africa compared to Trinil 2 and the smaller Sangiran hominids

Of the two East Turkana crania referred tentatively to *Homo erectus*, KNM-ER 3733 is the more complete. This Koobi Fora individual exhibits many cracks, and there is damage both at bregma and to the frontal squama. The braincase is otherwise intact, although the occiput and cranial base show signs of deformation. It is apparent that the entire nuchal surface has been skewed to the left, and on this side of the midline the occiput is flattened. The foramen magnum is distorted, and both condyles are broken. The facial skeleton is only partially preserved. The nasal bridge and both zygomatic bones are present, but the maxillae are eroded. There is extensive damage to the zygomatic and maxillary alveolar processes, and all of the anterior teeth are missing. However, the contour of the bone below the nasal opening can be reconstructed reasonably accurately.

KNM-ER 3883 consists of part of a face and braincase from Ileret. Although the supraorbital region and right zygomatic bone are preserved, much of the rest of the facial skeleton is lost. The frontal process of the maxilla is complete enough only to outline the right orbit. Some of the bone of the vault has been plastically deformed, and pieces of the occiput have been displaced upward into the endocranial cavity. The left temporal bone is also damaged, but on the right side the glenoid cavity, auditory meatus and mastoid process are in relatively good condition.

The two Turkana crania, with internal capacities estimated by Holloway as 800–850 ml, may be compared directly to the small braincase from Salé. These three African specimens are all similar in size to Trinil 2 and to the more lightly constructed individuals from Sangiran. Trinil 2, the first cranium of *Homo erectus* discovered by Dubois in 1891, is rather badly broken. Much of the frontal squama is preserved, but only a little of the original contour of the supraorbital torus remains on the left side. Both parietals are present, and on the right, a fragment of the anterior temporal squama is still attached to the vault. The upper scale of the occipital is intact, but most of the nuchal area and all of the rest of the cranial base are missing. More of the Sangiran 2 braincase is preserved. Similarities of this specimen to Trinil 2 have already been noted in Chapter 2. Sangiran 4 consists of a maxilla, parts of both parietal bones and much of the rear portion of a robust cranium. It is appropriate to discuss this individual here and also in subsequent sections dealing with the larger Asian crania. Sangiran 10 has been reconstructed from many fragments. A little of the face, some of the frontal squama, most of both parietal bones, the broken temporals and the back of the occiput are present, although the base of the cranium has not survived.

THE SUPRAORBITAL REGION AND THE FRONTAL SQUAMA

The anatomy of the brow and supratoral region is clear in the case of the Turkana crania, but in Salé the supraorbital torus is not preserved. In the Indonesian specimens, this part of the frontal bone is frequently damaged or missing altogether. Overall proportions of the frontal cannot readily be compared in the two groups. It is apparent that the squama is flattened, as in other *Homo erectus* individuals. It is also evident that supraorbital tori are prominently developed, although there is substantial variation in brow thickness.

In KNM-ER 3733, the torus is especially gracile. Above glabella, there is some hollowing of the frontal surface, and this extends laterally behind the brows. However, the supratoral region is still shelf-like, and there is only moderate expression of a sulcus. The KNM-ER 3883 frontal is severely cracked anteriorly, but this damage does not greatly affect brow thickness at the center of the orbit. Here the torus is heavier, glabella is more massive, and there is less hollowing of the supratoral surface. In these respects, the KNM-ER 3883 frontal approaches the condition seen in the larger hominid from Olduvai Bed II.

The torus of Sangiran 2 is comparable to that of KNM-ER 3883, while Sangiran 10 displays a brow which is substantially thicker. In neither of these Sangiran individuals is there much supratoral hollowing. The Trinil brows are too eroded to be measured, but here some blunt keeling is present in the frontal midline. This extends posteriorly toward a prominent bregmatic eminence. Behind the vertex, the vault is flattened. Damage to Sangiran 2 makes it difficult to determine whether slight keeling also occurs in this cranium, but a low eminence is present at bregma.

In the two Turkana fossils, these features of the squama are variably expressed. The Ileret frontal is evenly rounded in the transverse plane, and there is no bregmatic swelling. KNM-ER 3733 does exhibit a sagittal keel, to either side of which the squama is quite flat. It is partly because of this elevation of the midline that the Koobi Fora frontal appears to rise relatively steeply from the supratoral shelf. Whether keeling extends all the way to bregma is uncertain, but there is no sign of it posteriorly on the parietals. The Salé frontal also shows some blunt keeling, but again this is missing from the parietal vault.

Pronounced anterior narrowing of the frontal bone characterizes all of the crania from Africa and Asia. Measurements are given in Table 23. When minimum frontal breadth is expressed as a percentage of maximum (coronal) width, the resulting breadth index is low for the Turkana individuals. Index values are somewhat higher for Salé and for the Indonesian hominids, and in most cases the degree of narrowing is not much different from that expected for modern *Homo sapiens*. Although frontal constriction assessed in this way seems to be pronounced in the East African skulls, this feature does not generally distinguish *Homo erectus* from later humans. When least frontal breadth is compared to upper facial breadth, contrasts are much clearer. Narrowing, as measured by an index of postorbital constriction, is again marked in KNM-ER 3733 and KNM-ER 3883. Here the temporal lines are strongly crested anteriorly and course medially for some distance behind the brows. In KNM-ER 3733, these lines reach almost as far inward as the center of the supraorbital margin before turning sharply posteriorly. In *Homo sapiens* crania, where biorbital breadths are lower and temporal crests are less prominently flared, postorbital constriction is much reduced.

Since upper facial parts are missing for the smaller Indonesian hominids, biorbital chord lengths cannot be taken. However, some of the lateral part of the torus and supraorbital margin are available for Sangiran 2. Although index values cannot be calculated, it is clear that postorbital constriction is marked both in this individual and in the Trinil cranium. In the case of Sangiran 10, the temporal crests are not preserved, and there is little indication of the shape of the temporal fossae. Only the contour of surviving portions of the frontal squama and the sphenoid suggests (substantial) postorbital narrowing. In several of the larger Indonesian specimens, the orbital region is complete enough to measure. Both Sangiran 17 and Sambungmachan have constriction indices which are higher than those for the African crania but still well below the average for recent humans.

MEASUREMENTS OF THE FRONTAL BONE AND PARIETAL VAULT

The parietal bones are at least partly preserved in each of the African and Indonesian crania. Measurements of the parietal vault and temporal bone as well as frontal dimensions are given in Table 23. Several of these vault breadths and measures of parietal size are displayed in Figure 33. In this ratio diagram, the horizontal scale records proportional difference(s) among a number of the fossils, relative to a

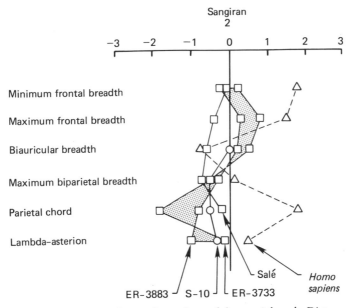

Fig. 33. Ratio diagram for six dimensions of the cranial vault. Distances on the horizontal scale are proportional to the ratios of the actual measurements. Sangiran 2 is taken as the standard against which Sangiran 10 (circles) and specimens from Africa (boxes) are contrasted. The envelope described by the two East African crania is shaded, to facilitate comparisons. These Koobi Fora individuals have broad frontal bones but short parietal chords, relative to the Indonesian standard. Note that modern humans (triangles) differ from all of the archaic hominids in having broader frontals, long parietal bones and narrow cranial bases.

single more complete Asian individual taken as a standard. In this case, Sangiran 2 is used as the standard against which Sangiran 10 and the African individuals are compared. All dimensions are converted first to logarithms. For each variate, distances between values plotted on the diagram are proportional to the ratios of the actual measurements. Therefore any individual having proportions similar to those of Sangiran 2 will be represented in the figure by a series of points all about equidistant from the vertical axis.

The figure suggests that Sangiran 10 differs least from Sangiran 2 in those regions that can be measured. KNM-ER 3733 and KNM-ER 3883 show some contrast to this pattern. These individuals are larger than Sangiran 2 in frontal breadths but smaller in parietal lengths. Here the relatively short parietal chord of KNM-ER 3733 is especially apparent. Although KNM-ER 3733 and KNM-ER 3883 describe

Table 23. Measurements (mm) for the smaller Homo erectus crania from Asia, East Africa and northwest Africa. Modern humans are provided for comparison

	Trinil 2	Sangiran 2	Sangiran 4	Sangiran 10	KNM-ER 3733	KNM-ER 3883	OH 12	Salé	Homo sapiens[a]
Whole vault									
Cranial length	—	—	—	—	182	182	—	—	185.9
Basion–nasion length	—	—	—	—	107	102	—	—	98.9
Basion–prosthion length	—	—	—	—	118	—	—	—	99.6
Maximum cranial breadth	—	141	147	140?	142	140	—	137	138.6
Biauricular breadth	—	126	132	126?	132	129	—	124	117.4
Frontal bone									
Supraorbital torus thickness									
central	—	12	—	19	8	11	10	—	—
lateral	—	8	—	—	9	7	—	—	—
Minimal frontal breadth	85	82	—	—	83	80	—	81?	97.6
Maximal frontal breadth	95	102	—	—	110	105	—	98	118.3
Biorbital chord	—	—	—	—	109	110	—	—	102
Frontal breadth index[b]	89.4	80.3	—	—	75.4	76.2	—	82.6	82.6
Postorbital constriction index[c]	—	—	—	—	76.1	72.7	—	—	96.2
Frontal sagittal chord	—	—	—	—	104	101	—	—	113
Frontal sagittal arc	—	—	—	—	119	118	—	—	129.3
Frontal subtense	—	—	—	—	18	18	—	—	26.6
Frontal angle	—	—	—	—	139	140	—	—	128.7
Parietal and temporal bones									
Maximum biparietal breadth	131	137	140	131	131	134	—	128	138.2
Parietal sagittal chord	100?	98?	—	93	82	90	—	96?	117.3
Parietal sagittal arc	—	103?	—	98	85	95	—	100?	129.8

Measurement									
Lambda–asterion chord	—	82?	80?	79	81	74	—	71?	86.1
Lambda–asterion arc	—	92?	87?	85	88	79	—	—	94.0
Mastoid length	—	12	27	—	—	30	25	28	28.8
Occipital bone									
Biasterionic breadth	—	122	126?	120?	119	115	—	—	107.8
Occipital sagittal chord	—	71	82	—	88	75?	—	77?	94.0
Occipital sagittal arc	—	—	108	—	118	101?	—	100?	112.3
Occipital subtense	—	—	30	—	35	31	—	26	27
Occipital angle	—	—	105	—	103	101	—	112?	119.5
Lambda–inion chord[d]	38?	45?	47	50	57	48	53?	58?	64.1
Inion–opisthion chord[d]	—	45?	56	—	53	51	—	32?	43.8
Occipital scale index[e]	—	100.0	119.1	—	92.9	106.2	—	55.1?	67.2
Inion–asterion chord[d]	—	75	79	—	73	67	60?	—	—
Foramen magnum length	—	—	40?	—	37	33	—	38?	37.1
Foramen magnum width	—	—	31	—	—	—	—	—	29.1
Facial skeleton									
Bimaxillary chord	—	—	—	—	101	—	—	—	95.4
Malar (cheek) height	—	—	—	—	34	—	—	—	22.2
Orbit breadth	—	—	—	—	44	45	—	—	40.3
Orbit height	—	—	—	—	35	36	—	—	35.5

[a] Figures for *Homo sapiens* are averages obtained from 15 crania of black males, measured in the Terry Collection at the Smithsonian Institution, Washington, DC.

[b] Frontal breadth index is calculated as the ratio of minimum frontal width to maximum frontal width.

[c] Postorbital constriction index is calculated as the ratio of minimum frontal width to biorbital chord length.

[d] Inion is here considered to lie at the center of the linear tubercle (the junction of the superior nuchal lines) rather than higher on the occipital torus.

[e] Occipital scale index is calculated as the ratio of inion–opisthion chord length to lambda–inion chord length.

roughly similar tracks, neither parallels the vertical axis. It is interesting that the Salé cranium, which has a frontal slightly smaller than that of Sangiran 2, seems to depart less strongly from the morphology of Asian *Homo erectus* than do the two more ancient specimens from East Africa. However, none of the archaic skulls has proportions resembling those of modern humans. Greater frontal breadths and larger parietal bones coupled with a relatively narrow cranial base cause *Homo sapiens* to describe a very different pattern on the diagram.

THE CRANIUM IN LATERAL VIEW

Details of parietal and temporal anatomy are relevant to comparisons of the African and Asian hominids. Of particular interest are the temporal lines and any expression of an angular torus, the shape of the mastoid process and its associated crest, the extent of the supramastoid sulcus, the supramastoid crest and the root of the zygomatic process, form and orientation of the auditory opening, and characteristics of the lateral tympanic plate. These structures are subject to considerable variation within assemblages, but it is difficult to establish the presence of consistent regional distinctions.

In lateral view, KNM-ER 3733 and KNM-ER 3883 exhibit the low cranial profile characteristic of early *Homo*. In both individuals, the front of the floor of the temporal fossa is deeply guttered to accommodate the converging fibers of the anterior portion of *m. temporalis*. The form of the temporal squama is like that of other *Homo erectus*. The upper margin of the bone is long and follows a fairly straight course posteriorly and downward, rather than describing a high arch as in modern *Homo sapiens*. The temporal line of KNM-ER 3733 is slightly raised as it passes from the frontal onto the parietal vault and becomes more prominent posteriorly, before turning downward near the lambdoid border. No strong angular torus is present, but on the right side a ridge above asterion may mark passage of the line forward toward the mastoid process. Given the small size of this (broken) process, the mastoid crest is well developed. Above it, the supramastoid sulcus is shallow. The supramastoid crest is prominent but does not extend posteriorly onto the parietal bone.

The Ileret cranium is similar. Partly because of damage, the temporal lines are less distinct, and there is no sign of an angular torus at the parietal angle. On the right side, which is best preserved, there is little expression of a mastoid crest, although the mastoid process is quite large. The supramastoid crest is weaker than that of KNM-ER 3733, and there is less projection of the posterior root of the zygoma. However, the rim of the auditory opening is recessed, and the porus itself is elliptical in form and oriented vertically. The part of the tympanic plate making up its anterior and inferior margin is broken.

The vault of Trinil 2 is weathered, and the temporal lines can barely be discerned. On one side, the line follows a low arc which can be followed toward asterion. Damage to the parietal mastoid angle makes it difficult to determine whether a broken crest located in this region is actually the posterior aspect of an angular torus. More of the parietal and temporal bone are preserved for Sangiran 2. In this individual, the temporal line is a low ridge which makes a close approach posteriorly to the superior nuchal line. These lines converge as they pass forward toward the bulge of the mastoid process. No distinct angular torus is present. The mastoid is small and nipple-like, and its axis is inclined medially. On the right, damage to the superior aspect of the process obscures the supramastoid sulcus, but enough of the zygomatic root is left to show that a weak shelf overhangs the auditory porus. On the other side, anatomy of the supramastoid region is clearer. Here the supramastoid crest is separated from the mastoid process by a very shallow sulcus, and the crest itself veers upward before terminating at the squamous border of the temporal.

Sangiran 4 displays prominent sagittal keeling of the parietal vault, and a roughened ridge extends almost to lambda. The temporal lines are indistinct. On the right, however, a definite bulge filling the parietal angle may be described as an angular torus. Sangiran 10 also exhibits some keeling in the parietal midline. This is most noticeable at and posterior to the vertex and is accompanied by parasagittal flattening. The temporal line, faintly marked, does not produce a torus at the parietal angle. As in Sangiran 2, a mastoid crest is only weakly developed, and the supramastoid sulcus is restricted in extent. Sangiran 10 differs from Sangiran 2 in that the supramastoid crest is a massive rounded structure which projects laterally above the (broken) mastoid. Cranial breadth measured at these crests is much greater than any width taken higher on the parietal vault. The crest merges anteriorly with the shelf-like zygomatic process. Since all of the tympanic bone is missing, shape of the auditory meatus cannot be determined, but the porus must have been at least slightly recessed below the zygomatic root.

MORPHOLOGY OF THE OCCIPITAL BONE

Measurements of the occipital bone are given in Table 23. As is true for cranial breadth, occipital width measured between the asteria is greater for *Homo erectus* than for *Homo sapiens*. Differences among the *Homo erectus* assemblages are small, but there is a suggestion that biasterionic width contributes less to overall skull breadth in the East African specimens. In the Turkana hominids, the occipital is narrow in comparison to breadth measured at the supramastoid crests. Sagittal chord lengths for both African and Asian fossils are lower than for modern humans, while sagittal arcs approach (or exceed) an average for Terry males. Such a disparity in chord/arc lengths indicates that the *Homo erectus* occiput is more strongly curved. An angle computed from sagittal chord and subtense values confirms this, and the more complete occipital bones from East Africa and Indonesia give angular readings of only 100–105°. Recent human occipitals are considerably flatter.

Curvature of the *Homo erectus* occiput is associated with formation of a transverse torus. While there is variation in size and form of this structure, some expression of a torus occurs even in the smaller individuals. KNM-ER 3733 exhibits a rounded torus which is most projecting near the midline of the occiput. Because of cracks and displacement of plates of bone just above the torus, the extent of sulcus development is not clear. Some definite supratoral hollowing is present, however. The lower margin of the torus is defined by the superior nuchal lines, which converge medially to produce a triangular eminence. This is best interpreted as a linear tubercle rather than an external occipital protuberance, and its downward facing apex is continuous with a crest which reaches toward opisthion. From the linear tubercle, each superior line describes a shallow arc which dips toward a strong retromastoid process before curving forward to approach the mastoid crest. The occiput of KNM-ER 3883 is less well preserved. On the right side, enough remains to show that the torus is not as prominent as in the Koobi Fora cranium. The shape of the linear tubercle cannot be ascertained, but probably no true external occipital protuberance is formed. From the vicinity of the tubercle, the superior line can be followed along an irregular course toward asterion, where there is no indication of a retromastoid process.

The upper portion of the occipital squama slopes gently forward in KNM-ER 3733 and exceeds the length of the nuchal plane by several millimeters. Here the ratio of lower to upper scale lengths as expressed by an occipital scale index is slightly less than 100. The nuchal plane displays considerable relief. In KNM-ER 3883, the upper scale is shorter, as is more usually the case for *Homo erectus*. The index of 106.2 calculated for the Ileret individual is much greater than that expected for modern *Homo sapiens*, where the occipital plane (almost) always dominates the nuchal plane by a substantial margin. Despite crushing of parts of the squama, it is apparent that the regions occupied by several of the deeper nuchal muscles are raised and rounded, as in the Koobi Fora specimen. Traces of an external occipital crest are preserved only near the border of the foramen magnum.

In the smaller Indonesian crania, much of the upper scale of the occipital is intact. Its length can be measured, and in Trinil 2 and Sangiran 2, this upper scale is shorter than in other hominids listed in Table 23. Unfortunately, the nuchal plane is incomplete. Since bone surrounding the foramen magnum is missing in these individuals, length of the lower scale cannot be determined very accurately. An estimate for Sangiran 2 is 45 mm, which yields a scale index of 100. More of the Sangiran 4 occipital is present, and here the distance from inion to opisthion is substantially greater than the length of the occipital plane.

In rear view, Sangiran 10 exhibits a straight torus which traverses most of the width of the occipital bone. This torus is blunt and most prominent near the midline. Its upper border is clearly outlined, but there is no external occipital protuberance. The superior part of the squama is inclined forward, suggesting a strong degree of occipital curvature. The torus is limited below by the superior nuchal lines. These are not deeply incised, and the underside of the torus does not overhang the nuchal plane to the extent seen in some of the larger Indonesian specimens. The areas covered by the nuchal muscles are gently convex, and an external crest is not developed.

COMPARISONS OF OCCIPITAL PROPORTIONS

A ratio diagram constructed for seven measurements of the occipital bone is provided in Figure 34. Sangiran 4, for which the occiput is better preserved than in Sangiran 2, is taken as the standard for comparison. Only two pairs of points can be plotted for Sangiran 2, and these suggest a pattern somewhat different from that of the larger

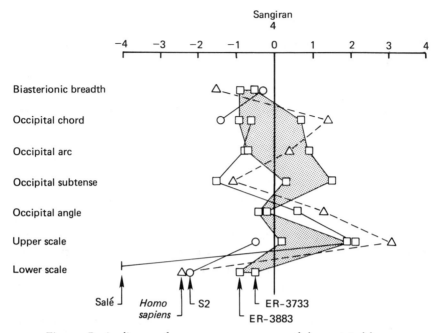

Fig. 34. Ratio diagram for seven measurements of the occipital bone. Sangiran 4 is taken as the standard, against which one other Indonesian cranium (circles) and individuals from Africa (boxes) are compared. Shading and symbols as in Figure 33.

Asian hominid. Sangiran 10 and the Trinil individual are not complete enough to be included in the diagram.

Neither of the two crania from the Koobi Fora region makes a very close fit to the proportions of Sangiran 4. Deviations from the zero line are most apparent for occipital subtense and lambda–inion chord lengths for KNM-ER 3733. However, neither the remaining dimensions of this cranium nor the ratios plotted for KNM-ER 3883 suggest important differences from Asian *Homo erectus*. The Salé occipital, which is relatively flatter and possesses a longer upper scale, produces a pattern which is much more similar to that for *Homo sapiens*. Here the lower scale is clearly even shorter than would be expected in modern humans. These peculiar proportions have been noted by Hublin (1985), who stresses that the Salé occiput is pathologically deformed. Resemblances in the ratio diagram to the modern condition should probably not be read as strong evidence against grouping this specimen with *Homo erectus*.

THE GLENOID CAVITY AND TYMPANIC PLATE

The mandibular fossa can be studied on both African and Indonesian crania, and here there are significant contrasts to the morphology of recent *Homo sapiens*. The glenoid cavity and surrounding structures are well preserved in KNM-ER 3733. Both ectoglenoid and entoglenoid processes are clearly defined. The sphenotemporal suture appears to pass directly across the apex of the latter process, but there is no appreciable development of a sphenoid spine. There is no raised articular tubercle, and the anterior wall of the cavity is deeply concave from side to side. Anteriorly, there is a smooth transition from the joint surface onto a flattened, upward sloping preglenoid planum. Laterally, a small postglenoid tubercle is present, while at its inner extent, the fossa is very constricted. Its form is similar to that of other *Homo erectus* in that a deep recess is produced between the entoglenoid pyramid and the vertical tympanic plate. The plate itself is thickened in comparison to that of modern humans, and in the region where the styloid should be located, there is a strong spine. This projection resembles the spine of the crista petrosa described by Weidenreich (1943). On its posterior aspect, there is a faint vertical groove, ending in a circular hollow. More medially and just anterior to the carotid and jugular openings, the tympanic bone produces another prominent spine, closely applied to the sphenoid portion of the entoglenoid process. Such a projection is not well developed in later *Homo sapiens*.

The glenoid cavity of KNM-ER 3883 is slightly damaged, but its morphology is similar. The Ileret entoglenoid process is entirely of temporal origin. The articular tubercle is a little less concave, so that the anterior joint surface is steeper and passes more abruptly onto the preglenoid planum. The postglenoid process is larger than that of KNM-ER 3733, and the medial part of the fossa is again deeply recessed. The tympanic plate is somewhat more horizontally aligned, and its inferior border is thickened. There is little doubt that a petrosal spine was developed. The medial aspect of the tympanic bone is even more thickened, as it terminates in a blunt process. Here the plate may be incomplete, but this tubercle is not as prominent as that exhibited by KNM-ER 3733.

Of the Indonesian specimens, Sangiran 2, Sangiran 4 and Sangiran 10 possess mandibular fossae which are at least partially complete. In Sangiran 10, neither the ectoglenoid nor the entoglenoid process is

preserved, but the intervening joint surface is strongly concave as in
KNM-ER 3733. No true tubercle is present. The postglenoid process
is expressed as a low ridge, but all of the rear of the fossa, constructed
from the temporal bone, is missing. In Sangiran 2, the glenoid cavity
is small but relatively deep. Apart from a distinct depression located
toward its medial aspect, the anterior joint surface is smooth and flattened. There is no bar-like articular tubercle. As in the East African
crania, the fossa extends medially as a crevice between the (broken)
entoglenoid process and the tympanic plate. Thickening of the lower
tympanic margin is even more pronounced than in KNM-ER 3733.
This crest is incomplete, but enough is left to suggest that a petrosal
spine was prominent. The tympanic plate of Sangiran 4 is elongated
vertically and thickened toward its lateral margin. The inferior aspect
of the plate is also heavily constructed, but a distinct petrosal spine is
no longer present. More medially, the tubercle representing Weidenreich's (1943) 'process supratubarius' is very large.

Olduvai Hominid 12

The small cranium from Olduvai Bed IV (OH 12) is very incomplete.
The facial skeleton is represented by part of the left maxillary
alveolar process, containing tooth roots, and by a frontal fragment
on which some of the superior rim of the right orbit is preserved.
Another piece of frontal bone includes bregma and a segment of the
coronal suture, to which parts of both parietals are attached. The
mastoid portion of the left temporal and some of the right temporal
squama are present, and the rear of the braincase has been reconstructed from many small fragments, some of which are badly
weathered. Holloway (1975) has provided an estimate of 700–800 ml
for the endocranial capacity of this individual. Given its size and gracile appearance, OH 12 may be a female.

   This hominid is best compared to the Turkana crania and to the
smaller skulls from Indonesia. The section of supraorbital torus from
the right side is only 10 mm thick, and on the bit of supratoral surface
that is preserved, there is a distinct sulcus. These features are most
closely matched by KNM-ER 3733, while in KNM-ER 3883 the brow
is a little heavier. The OH 12 torus is more lightly constructed than
that of any of the Indonesian individuals. The frontal squama is
weathered, but there may be traces of slight keeling in the midline.
Near bregma, the bone is relatively thick, and there is no sign of an

eminence. Some of the sagittal suture is preserved, but because of damage, length of the parietal chord cannot be determined. The parietal vault is rounded, and there is neither keeling along the suture nor any pronounced amount of parasagittal flattening. The temporal lines are very faintly marked. On the right, the line can be followed posteriorly for some distance before it is lost near asterion. Here the mastoid angle of the parietal is flared outward, and it is probable that an angular torus was developed.

In rear view, the OH 12 braincase appears comparatively narrow. The upper scale of the occipital is almost intact, and it is high (about 53 mm) relative to occipital width, taken from the midline. An estimate for the inion–asterion chord is 60 mm. This ratio of scale height to breadth is also high for OH 9 and for the Turkana crania, but upper scales are lower in Sangiran 2 and Sangiran 4. Here OH 12 falls in with the other African individuals, although it is not clear that these differences in occipital squama proportions are significant. Since the nuchal plane of the occiput is mostly missing, an occipital scale index cannot be calculated for the Bed IV specimen.

The transverse torus is marked near the midline by an area of swelling which stands out in low relief. This torus is blunt, almost flattened, and extends for a greater distance superiorly onto the occipital plane than is the case for other *Homo erectus*. It is bounded above by depressions corresponding (?) to the highest nuchal lines. An external protuberance is not expressed. The torus is limited below by the superior lines, which join centrally to produce a triangular linear tubercle. In the appearance of this tubercle, and also in the size of the mastoid process and definition of the mastoid crest and supramastoid sulcus, OH 12 is similar to KNM-ER 3733 from Koobi Fora.

Olduvai Hominid 9 and the larger Indonesian crania

The braincase from upper Bed II at Olduvai (OH 9) is considerably larger than either OH 12 or the crania recovered in the Koobi Fora region. It is likely to be male. In any case, OH 9 is most reasonably compared to some of the larger Indonesian specimens, including Sangiran 4, Sangiran 12 and Sangiran 17. Here the more important part of Sangiran 4 is the rear of the vault, which consists of two sections. One is reconstructed from portions of both parietals, united at the midline, together with the uppermost aspect of the occipital squama. The lower section is made up of most of the rest of the occiput, the parietal angles and the temporal bones. Fairly extensive areas of damage and weathering are present, and warping precludes a perfect joining of these two portions of the braincase. Sangiran 12 is also incomplete. The posterior region of the frontal squama is preserved, and the parietal and upper part of the temporal bone are in place on the left side. The occipital is represented by most of the squama. Sangiran 17 is rather less badly damaged. A good deal of the facial skeleton has been reconstructed, and the frontal bone has been pieced together from numerous fragments. Parts of the base are broken, but otherwise the braincase is reasonably intact. There is little indication that the bones have been plastically deformed.

The Bed II cranium may also be compared to the Sambungmachan individual and to the fossils from Ngandong in eastern Java. Sambungmachan 1 and several of the Ngandong hominids are quite well preserved, although faces are missing and damage to the cranial base is common. These specimens are similar to *Homo erectus* from Trinil and Sangiran. Metric evidence bearing on the appropriateness of referring them to this taxon is presented below. Once again, however, it is the relationship of the African material to that from Asia that is emphasized in the discussion.

SUPRAORBITAL ANATOMY

A striking feature of OH 9 is the heavy brow, which is thicker than the tori of other crania examined. Centrally, there is a massive glabellar prominence. The superior aspect of this prominence is slightly depressed, and this hollowing extends posteriorly onto the broad supratoral shelf. To either side, the supratoral sulci are shallow, while the temporal crests are prominent. Because bregma is missing, frontal chord length cannot be measured. But the frontal bone appears to be narrow, and postorbital constriction (least frontal breadth relative to biorbital diameter) is stronger than in other specimens listed in Table 24.

Little of the frontal is preserved for either Sangiran 4 or Sangiran 12. In Sangiran 17, the brow ridges are not quite as thick as those of OH 9, but there is again some depression of the supratoral surface just above glabella. Behind the brows, the frontal squama is quite flat, and there is no keeling in the midline. Breadth measured anteriorly at the temporal crests is a little greater than that of OH 9, while biorbital breadth is less. As a consequence, the postorbital constriction index is higher. Frontal narrowing is still less pronounced in

Sambungmachan 1. This is partly a result of greater anterior width but also reflects decreased lateral flare of the temporal crests. The same tendency toward broadening of the flattened, slightly keeled frontal bone is apparent in the Ngandong series, and in Ngandong 12 (the only specimen in which biorbital chord length can be measured), the index of postorbital constriction reaches 91.1. This value remains well below the figure usual for modern humans.

PROPORTIONS OF THE FRONTAL BONE AND MIDVAULT

Measurements registering torus thickness, vault breadth and parietal size are displayed in Figure 35. Sangiran 17, which is among the most

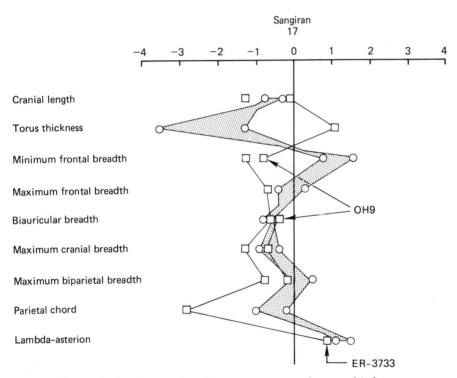

Fig. 35. Ratio diagram for nine measurements of supraorbital torus thickness, vault breadth and parietal size. Sangiran 17 is used as the standard against which other Asian and African crania are compared. The shaded envelope delimited by connected circles shows variation within the Ngandong assemblage (four crania) and includes values for Sambungmachan. It is clear that these individuals differ from Sangiran 17 principally in torus thickness and in relative frontal breadth. Other symbols as in Figure 33.

Table 24. Measurements (mm) of the larger Homo erectus crania from Indonesia, China and East Africa

	Sangiran 12	Sangiran 17	Sam-bung 1	Ngan-dong 1	Ngan-dong 7	Ngan-dong 11	Ngan-dong 12	Zhou-kou X	Zhou-kou XI	Zhou-kou XII	OH 9
Whole vault											
Cranial length	–	207	200?	196	192	202	201	199	192	195	206
Basion–nasion length	–	115	–	–	111	–	113	–	–	–	119?
Basion–prosthion length	–	129?	–	–	–	–	–	–	–	–	–
Maximum cranial breadth	146?	161	151	–	147	158	151	150?	145	147?	150
Biauricular breadth	–	140	137	130?	132	134	135	147	143	151	135
Frontal bone											
Supraorbital torus thickness											
central	–	17	15	13	15?	12	14	16.5	13.2	14.6	19
lateral	–	13	12.5	13	–	13	10	12	–	14.0	14
Minimum frontal breadth	–	95	102	106?	103	112	103	89	84	91	88
Maximum frontal breadth	–	119[e]	116	120?	116	122?	114?	110?	106	108	–
Biorbital chord	–	115?	114?	–	–	113?	113?	–	–	–	123?
Frontal breadth index[a]	–	79.8	87.9	88.3	88.8	91.8	90.3	80.9	79.2	84.2	–
Postorbital constriction index[b]	–	82.6	89.4	–	–	–	91.1	–	–	–	71.5
Frontal sagittal chord	–	118?	115?	114	116	120	113	115	106	113	–
Frontal sagittal arc	–	–	–	128	125	130	121	129	122	124	–
Frontal subtense	–	–	–	20	21	23	17	–	–	–	–
Frontal angle	–	–	–	141	140	138	146	–	–	–	–
Parietal and temporal bones											
Maximum biparietal breadth	139	142	146	149?	141	147?	139?	137	136	140	139
Parietal sagittal chord	97?	108?	96	106	98	105	102	106	86	91	–

Parietal sagittal arc	101?	—	102	114	103	110	105	113	92	102	—
Lambda–asterion chord	—	74[e]	79?	83	85	86	85	85	84?	87	—
Lambda–asterion arc	110	—	84?	89	92	94	91	93	99?	92	—
Mastoid length	—	22	20	—	28	29?	—	—	—	—	—
Occipital bone											
Biasterionic breadth	123?	—	127	128?	127	130?	126	111?	113?	115	123
Occipital sagittal chord	84	81?	—	79	84	78?	88	—	86	86	80?
Occipital sagittal arc	110	—	—	109	110	111?	119	—	118	118	110?
Occipital subtense	33	34	—	34	33	36?	36	—	—	—	—
Occipital angle	102	100	—	98.5	103	95?	100	—	—	—	—
Lambda–inion chord[c]	49	52	59	55	61	57	69	(see Table 25)	"	"	54?
Inion–opisthion chord[c]	56	57	—	47	46	49	47	"	"	"	52?
Occipital scale index[d]	114.3	109.6	—	85.4	75.4	85.9	68.1	"	"	"	96.3?
Inion–asterion chord[c]	—	—	—	—	—	—	—	—	—	—	—
Facial skeleton											
Foramen magnum length	—	39	—	—	43	—	49	—	—	—	—
Foramen magnum width	—	29?	—	—	30	—	29	—	—	—	—
Bimaxillary chord	—	116?	—	—	—	—	—	—	—	—	—
Malar (cheek) height	—	37	—	—	—	—	—	—	—	—	—
Orbit breadth	—	38	—	—	—	—	—	—	—	—	—
Orbit height	—	40	—	—	—	—	—	—	—	—	—

[a] Frontal breadth index is calculated as the ratio of minimum frontal width to maximum frontal width.

[b] Postorbital constriction index is calculated as the ratio of minimum frontal width to biorbital chord length.

[c] Inion is here considered to lie at the center of the linear tubercle (the junction of the superior nuchal lines) rather than higher on the occipital torus.

[d] Occipital scale index is calculated as the ratio of inion–opisthion chord length to lambda–inion chord length.

[e] Measurement from Thorne & Wolpoff (1981).

complete of the larger Indonesian hominids, is taken as the standard against which the other skulls are compared. Four of the Ngandong individuals are plotted in the diagram. These braincases are consistently quite similar in their proportions to one another and also to Sambungmachan 1, even if there is considerable variation in supraorbital development. It is clear that they differ from Sangiran 17 principally in this last feature and in relative frontal breadth, as noted previously. The lambdoid border of the parietal bone is also a little longer in the Ngandong group. Otherwise, deviations of the Ngandong and Sambungmachan crania from the zero line are not substantial.

OH 9 can be included in the figure, although entries for maximum frontal breadth and parietal border lengths are missing. Here supraorbital torus thickness has a moderately high positive value, while other differences from Sangiran 17 are relatively small. Cranial breadth dimensions closely parallel the pattern seen in Sambungmachan and the Ngandong series. KNM-ER 3733 is also plotted, in an attempt to provide some further information to supplement that obtained from Figure 33. The Koobi Fora individual shows negative values for nearly all dimensions, as expected for a cranium smaller than Sangiran 17. Torus thickness, much less than in the robust Asian hominid, is not plotted. Another clear departure from the standard occurs in the case of the parietal chord, which is shorter in KNM-ER 3733 than in any of the Asian crania. Length of the posterior border of the parietal is greater, so this bone is shaped rather differently in the African specimen. However, a general impression gained from the figure is that KNM-ER 3733 is nearly as similar to Sangiran 17 in its vault proportions as it is to Sangiran 2. With the exception of brow size, ratios of the Koobi Fora cranium are also close to those of OH 9, so far as the two can be compared.

THE CRANIUM IN LATERAL VIEW

When OH 9 is viewed from the side, the temporal line describes a flat arc, which is raised in relation to the more superior aspect of the vault surface. This line is prominent as it curves inferiorly toward the mastoid crest, but an angular torus is not present. The mastoid process is pyramidal in form, and its flattened posterior face is incorporated into the plane covered by the nuchal musculature. At the rear of the parietal the inferior temporal line can be followed for a short distance as it parallels the superior line and the mastoid crest blow. No angular sulcus is formed, and the supramastoid sulcus is very narrow posteriorly. This supramastoid sulcus broadens as it opens anteriorly toward the auditory meatus. The porus is oriented vertically and is overhung by the zygomatic root. The part of the tympanic bone which surrounds the porus is quite thick inferiorly.

Sections of both of the Sangiran 4 parietals are preserved, and a roughened midline keel is present. This is more prominent than the keels displayed by Sangiran 10 and Sangiran 17. Parasagittal flattening is apparent. The temporal lines are indistinct, but an angular torus does seem to be developed. The supramastoid crest is expanded posteriorly, to form a massive swelling which trends upward at an angle to the zygomatic root. The supramastoid sulcus is broad and continues for a short distance (as a shallow angular sulcus) onto the parietal bone. The large mastoid process is directed medially, so that the distance between the mastoid tips is much less than cranial width measured higher at the supramastoid crests. As in OH 9, the posterior face of this process lies in about the same plane as the nuchal area of the occipital.

Sangiran 12 displays an eminence at bregma, and there is an angular torus, faintly marked at the parietal mastoid angle. Here, and also in Sangiran 17, there is a heavy, rounded supramastoid crest. In the first individual, this crest turns sharply upward to produce a nearly vertical ridge in front of the deep parietal incisure. The crest of Sangiran 17 is more horizontally oriented. These crania show variation in form of the supramastoid sulcus, which may be open and shallow, or deep and relatively restricted in extent. However, in the frequency of angular torus formation and in the pattern of prominence and orientation of the supramastoid crest, the Sangiran crania are similar to those from Sambungmachan and Ngandong. There is here some contrast to the morphology of OH 9.

THE OCCIPUT AND CRANIAL BASE

Much of the upper part of the occipital bone of OH 9 is missing. Upper and lower scales can be measured only approximately, and the upper scale is slightly longer. These estimates yield an occipital scale index of just over 96, which is not greatly different from the value obtained for KNM-ER 3733. It is apparent that the bone is strongly flexed, although I have not tried to measure subtenses or calculate an occipital angle. The transverse torus is rounded and thickened centrally. On its lower border, inion can be located on a rough prominence corresponding to the junction of the superior nuchal lines. A true external occipital protuberance is not developed.

The occipital bone of Sangiran 4 is very thick. Its upper scale slopes forward and is quite short in comparison to the expanded nuchal plane below. Here the occipital scale index is high (119), while values for Sangiran 12 and 17 are a little lower. Occipital angles for these three Indonesian crania are comparable to those of the East African specimens and are all much lower than expected for modern *Homo sapiens*. A transverse torus is most strongly defined in Sangiran 4. Its superior aspect is shelf-like, and the bone is projecting rather than more rounded as in Sangiran 12 and 17. There is no distinct supra-toral sulcus. In Sangiran 12, a shallow sulcus is present near the midline. Here the torus is weathered, but on its surface there is a rounded tubercle, somewhat elongated from side to side. This is not the linear tubercle, which lies below. It may mark the junction of the highest nuchal lines, although these cannot be clearly discerned. If this is the case, the swelling corresponds to an external occipital protuberance, which is not usually present in *Homo erectus*.

Some or all of the occiput is preserved for a number of the Ngandong fossils. Where upper scale length is measured to inion located at the linear tubercle, values are a little higher than in the Sangiran specimens, especially in Ngandong 12. At the same time, lower scales are somewhat shorter than in the other large Asian hominids. These occipital proportions give index values which range from about 86 in Ngandong 11 to 68 in Ngandong 12. The scale index is lower than in the other Asian specimens and also falls short of the figures obtained for OH 9 and KNM-ER 3733. Here there is an apparent approach to the condition found in the occipitals of more modern humans. Such an interpretation of the measurements can be challenged, however, as results are strongly influenced by the morphology of the linear tubercle. In many of the Ngandong individuals, this tubercle is large and prolonged downward to merge with a prominent external occipital crest. Not only the tubercle but also the lateral parts of the transverse torus are extensively developed. Impressions left by the nuchal muscles are deep, so that the entire lower margin of the torus is sharp and overhangs the nuchal surface to an extent not seen in African *Homo erectus*. In Ngandong 12, these features are exaggerated, and enlargement of the linear tubercle displaces inion inferiorly. This affects the relative lengths of the upper and lower occipital planes. Although I have corrected for some of this displacement by locating inion a little above the actual junction of the nuchal lines, occipital scale index values are still very low. Higher indices result when inion is placed at opisthocranion, roughly at the center of the transverse torus (see Table 25).

Additional measurements of the occiput are treated in the ratio diagram of Figure 36. Sangiran 12 is taken as the standard. The Sangiran 17 occipital is not quite complete, but all of the measurements utilized in the plot can be obtained for four of the Ngandong specimens. Most of the Ngandong ratios lie within an envelope that includes and approximately parallels the zero line. That deviations from the standard are most striking in the case of scale lengths is not surprising, as the lambda–inion chord is substantially longer in the Ngandong hominids than in Sangiran 12. Sangiran 17, not plotted separately, is less extreme in these dimensions, while in its other measurements this individual falls within the range of variation displayed by the Ngandong series.

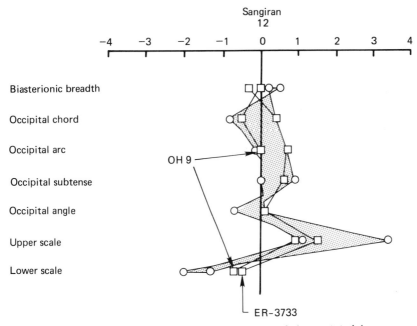

Fig. 36. Ratio diagram for seven dimensions of the occipital bone. Sangiran 12 is taken as the standard for comparisons. Four of the Ngandong crania (shaded envelope) differ little from the standard except in occipital scale proportions. Patterns described by Olduvai Hominid 9 and KNM-ER 3733 are similar. See Figure 33.

Table 25. *Measurements (mm) of occipital scale lengths for the Zhoukoudian crania, selected southeast Asian specimens and Olduvai Hominid 9. Location of inion follows Weidenreich (1943)*

	Sangiran 12	Sangiran 17	Ngan-dong 1	Ngan-dong 7	Ngan-dong 11	Ngan-dong 12	Zhou-kou XI	Zhou-kou XII	OH 9
Upper scale length	45	46	52	55	50	64	48	52.5	54?
Lower scale length	64	60	53	53	57	52	63	57	52?
Occipital scale index[a]	142.2	130.4	101.9	96.4	114.0	81.3	131.3	108.6	96.3

[a]Calculated as the ratio of lower to upper scale lengths. Compare to results given in Tables 23 and 24.

Five of the measurements can be taken on OH 9. Here again, the ratios (log differences) are small, and contrasts to Sangiran 12 are clearest for occipital scale lengths. The Olduvai braincase provides a pattern similar to but less exaggerated than that of the Ngandong individuals. Deviations of KNM-ER 3733 from the zero line are only slightly more pronounced. The occiput of this individual is narrower than that of Asian *Homo erectus*, but its sagittal chord, arc and subtense measurements are greater. The angle registering occipital curvature is nearly the same in KNM-ER 3733 as in Sangiran 12. Apart from differences in scale lengths, proportions of the two crania are much alike.

Other aspects of cranial base anatomy may be considered briefly. The glenoid cavity and tympanic plate are preserved in OH 9 and in several of the larger Sangiran hominids. There is some variation, but the cavity is constructed in much the same fashion as in Sangiran 2, Sangiran 10 and the Turkana skulls, already extensively discussed. Details of occipitomastoid morphology can also be observed. In OH 9, the digastric incisure is complete on one side, and the inner border of this notch is drawn (downward) to form a roughened ridge. On this juxtamastoid eminence, there is no sign of a groove for the occipital artery. Medially, the ridge is bounded by a shallow depression, which appears to merge with the insertion of *m. obliquus capitis superior*. The eminence itself must have been well developed, and since it is continuous posteriorly with the superior oblique line, I feel justified in using the term 'occipitomastoid crest', as employed by Weidenreich.

Unfortunately the course followed by the digastric groove is partly obscured in Sangiran 4. Here there is a massive juxtamastoid eminence. Nothing resembling an arterial channel is visible, and there is no clear evidence to suggest division of the eminence into paramastoid and occipitomastoid crests, as occurs in some of the Ngandong specimens. In Sangiran 12 and Sangiran 17, the eminence is lower and less distinct. No separate paramastoid ridge is formed.

Olduvai Hominid 9 and the Zhoukoudian specimens

Comparisons conducted so far have emphasized the African hominids and material from Java. The fossils from Trinil, Sangiran and other Indonesian localities constitute an important part of the *Homo erectus* hypodigm. Additional specimens universally agreed to belong to this species are known from China. I have already briefly discussed the discoveries at Zhoukoudian, Gongwangling, Chenjiawo and Lontandong Cave in Chapter 2. It is of course the cave complex at Zhoukoudian that has yielded the largest assemblage of fossils, augmented by several recent finds. Although nearly all of the original material is lost, Weidenreich's monographs provide much information. That I have made extensive use of Weidenreich's anatomical descriptions should be clear from the citations in earlier chapters. It now seems appropriate to refer more directly to Chinese *Homo erectus* in comparisons with East Africa, and in this section resemblances of OH 9 to the Zhoukoudian crania are documented.

In its principal linear dimensions, OH 9 equals or exceeds the size of the skulls treated by Weidenreich (1943). Cranial length lies beyond the range of 188–199 mm observed for five of the better preserved Chinese hominids, and maximum breadth matches the largest 'intercristal breadth' recorded by Weidenreich. Basibregmatic height cannot be measured accurately on OH 9 or on any of the Beijing specimens without the aid of plaster reconstruction. In its overall appearance, the African braincase is relatively robust, and its endocranial capacity is very near the mean of 1043 ml obtained for five Zhoukoudian individuals by Weidenreich.

Slight differences in the morphology of the supraorbital torus are present. The Olduvai brows are thicker and straight over the orbits, rather than arched as in the Chinese material. Comparisons with photographs and casts of the Zhoukoudian fossils show that OH 9 has a flatter frontal squama which rises less steeply from the supratoral shelf. A groove-like sulcus is more common in the Asian crania. Also, OH 9 exhibits no keeling in the frontal midline, while in the Zhoukoudian individuals a blunt ridge begins on the frontal and continues onto the parietal vault (as the 'sagittal crest' of Weidenreich). This keel is accompanied by parasagittal flattening on both sides of the midline.

Figure 37 provides information concerning the proportions of three of the Chinese crania and OH 9, as compared to one of the larger Indonesian hominids. Measurements of brow thickness, vault breadth and parietal size are the same as in Figure 35, and the standard is again Sangiran 17. Differences in supraorbital development register on the diagram, and the Zhoukoudian tori are more gracile than those of Sangiran 17. One of the Zhoukoudian crania also has a short parietal chord, while the posterior border of the parietal bone is

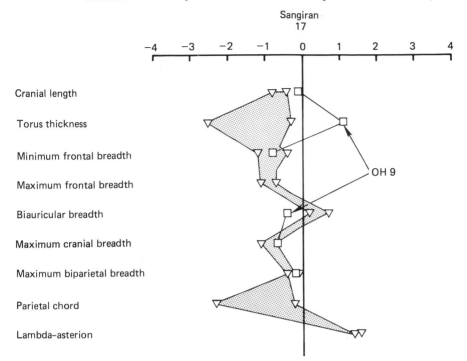

Fig. 37. Ratio diagram for nine cranial dimensions. Measurements of brow thickness, vault breadth and parietal size are the same as those of Figure 35, and the standard is again Sangiran 17. The shaded envelope delimited by connected triangles shows variation within the Zhoukoudian assemblage (three crania). Olduvai Hominid 9 (boxes) departs from the Zhoukoudian pattern in torus thickness but not in other measurements.

relatively long. Variation in other dimensions is slight, and the Chinese vaults are hardly more different from the Sangiran standard than those from Ngandong, displayed in Figure 35. OH 9 can be plotted for six of the measurements used in the diagram. Differences from Sangiran 17 are slight, as noted earlier. The Olduvai cranium departs from the Zhoukoudian pattern in supraorbital torus thickness but is otherwise proportionately similar to all of the Asian individuals.

Both the Olduvai and the Zhoukoudian occipital bones are strongly flexed. This is apparent from the occipital sagittal chord to arc ratios, which are low relative to other *Homo erectus*. Unfortunately, direct angular measurements cannot be compared. Occipital scale lengths are given in Table 25. The lambda–inion distance is

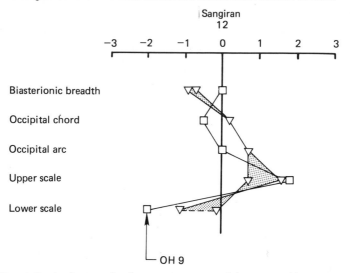

Fig. 38. Ratio diagram for five measurements of the occipital bone. Sangiran 12 is taken as the standard, against which two of the Zhoukoudian crania (triangles) and Olduvai Hominid 9 (boxes) can be
compared.

slightly greater for OH 9 than for the Zhoukoudian specimens, while
the inion–opisthion chord is shorter. Scale indices are therefore
higher for Chinese *Homo erectus*, but there is a lot of variation.
Measurements plotted in Figure 38 suggest that the Olduvai and
Zhoukoudian occipitals are much alike and that both differ primarily
in scale length proportions from one of the Sangiran crania taken as a
standard.

The Zhoukoudian transverse torus takes the form of a broad bulge
extending across the entire width of the occiput. There is a distinct
supratoral sulcus. Neither a linear tubercle nor an external median
crest is well developed. The morphology of OH 9 is somewhat different, in that a torus is only moderately expressed near the midline,
while signs of an external crest are clear. In rear view, the African
hominid shows more exaggerated development of the mastoid crests
and more flattening of the posterior mastoid faces, so that the nuchal
surface is very broad in relation to the parietal vault above.

Cranial base morphology is quite similar in the East African and
Asian specimens, as should be evident from the discussion of Chapter
3. The mandibular fossa is relatively large in OH 9, but details of its
construction can be matched in the Zhoukoudian fossils. No true

articular tubercle is present, and there is conspicuous narrowing of the posteromedial section of the fossa to form a cleft-like recess. The entoglenoid process is of squamous temporal origin, and there is no projecting sphenoid spine. The tympanic plate is thickened inferiorly, and a petrosal spine is prominent. The base of a broken styloid process is preserved for OH 9, although in the Chinese specimens this process does not seem to be developed.

The Olduvai and Zhoukoudian mandibles

The assemblage from Locality 1 at Zhoukoudian contains mandibles as well as crania. Eleven lower jaws, six of which are juvenile, have been described by Weidenreich (1936). The adult specimens are designated A II (a right mandibular corpus with M_1 to M_3 in place), B II (a broken left condyle only), G I (parts of body and ramus from both sides), H I (a right corpus with M_3) and H IV (badly damaged). Other fossils recovered later and not treated in Weidenreich's monograph include an adult jaw with teeth from Locus K and fragments from Locus M. More recently, the discovery of parts of a mandible has been reported by Woo & Chao (1959). In this section, only the more complete adult jaws originally available to Weidenreich are compared to the Olduvai remains.

In overall size, the half mandible from Olduvai Bed IV is more than a match for the Chinese specimens. Olduvai Hominid 22 (OH 22) is substantially thicker in the body than any of the three best preserved Zhoukoudian individuals and surpasses both A II and H I in height (Table 26). Differences in breadth are especially great, so that robusticity of the corpus measured as thickness/height is higher for OH 22 than for any Asian fossil. Robusticity figures for the other Olduvai jaw fragments are also relatively high but do not equal the extreme value obtained for OH 22. Olduvai Hominid 23 (OH 23) has an index of 62.8 measured at the position of M_1. Height of the body of OH 51 is difficult to ascertain accurately due to loss of alveolar bone, but an estimate for robusticity is 61.4. Both of these mandibles are comparable in absolute thickness to OH 22, while the corpus is higher, particularly in OH 51. This latter specimen appears to be larger in all of its measurable dimensions than even the G I jaw, designated as male by Weidenreich. Cross-sectional area of the OH 51 corpus exceeds that of G I and other Asian hominids, including Sangiran 5 and Sangiran 9.

Table 26. Measurements (mm) of Homo erectus mandibles from Asia, East Africa and northwest Africa

	Symphysis height[a]	Symphysis thickness	Corpus height[b] at M_1	Corpus thickness at M_1	Robusticity index	Cross-sectional area[c]
Sangiran 1 (B)	—	—	32.5	16.0	49.2	408.4
Sangiran 5 (1939)[d]	—	—	38.5?	19.3	50.1?	583.6?
Sangiran 9 (C)[e]	41.0?	—	34.0?	22.0	64.7?	587.4?
Zhoukoudian A II[f]	—	—	25.6	15.4	60.1	309.6
Zhoukoudian G I	40.0	13.7?	34.0	17.3	50.8	461.9
Zhoukoudian H I	32.3	14.0	26.0	14.9	57.3	304.2
Olduvai, OH 22	34.5?	19.0?	28.5	20.5	71.9	458.8
Olduvai, OH 23	—	—	32.0	20.1	62.8	505.1
Olduvai, OH 51	—	—	36.0?	22.1?	61.4?	624.8?
Baringo, KNM-BK 8518	29.5	17.5	29.5	20.0	67.8	463.3
Turkana, KNM-ER-730	33.0	18.0	32.0?	19.0?	59.3?	477.5?
Turkana, KNM-ER-992	38.0	—	32.0	20.0	62.5	502.6
Ternifine 1	38.0	19.0	36.0	20.0	55.5	565.5
Ternifine 2	34.0?	18.0	32.5	16.5	50.7	421.1
Ternifine 3	38.0?	19.0	37.0	20.5	55.4	595.7
Thomas Quarry	—	—	27.5	17.0?	61.8?	367.2?
Sidi Abderrahman	—	—	33.0?	16.0?	48.5?	414.7?

[a] Symphysis height is taken along the axis of symphyseal inclination, and thickness is measured approximately at a right angle to this axis.

[b] Corpus measurements are taken so as to be comparable to those of Weidenreich. Height at M_1 is treated as a vertical dimension, and thickness is measured with the caliper arm held parallel to the occlusal surface of the tooth row.

[c] Area (in mm^2) is computed as height × thickness × $\pi/4$.

[d] Measurements of Sangiran 5 are from Weidenreich (1945). Corpus height and thickness are taken at the level of the mental foramen.

[e] Sangiran 9 measurements are from a cast.

[f] All data for Zhoukoudian specimens are from Weidenreich (1936). Corpus heights are measured at the level of the mental foramen.

The anterior teeth of OH 22 are broken, and there has been some erosion of the alveolar border in the region of the incisors and canine. This damage makes precise reconstruction of the alveolar contour difficult. However, the shape of the arcade (the 'alveolar arch' of Weidenreich) is similar to that of the more complete Chinese specimens. The OH 22 arch seems relatively long and rounded anteriorly, rather than squared off and flattened at the front. In the other Olduvai jaws, only short segments of the alveolar contour are preserved.

A superior lateral torus and intertoral sulcus are prominent in OH 22 but are still more developed in at least one of the Zhoukoudian individuals. Relief in the form of a prominence and tori on the lateral surface of the corpus is especially strong in H I. An anterior marginal tubercle is present both in H I and G I, but in neither case is this tubercle as long and flange-like as in OH 51. Multiple mental foramina appear in all of the Chinese specimens. There are five separate apertures on G I, and Weidenreich considered this to be a primitive character. Multiple foramina seem also to be common in the Olduvai Pleistocene material.

Contrasts between the Zhoukoudian and Olduvai jaws in chin development are minor. The anterior corpus is preserved for two of the adult Chinese fossils, but in the case of H IV this region is severely damaged. Only H I is in good condition, although the chin can also be examined in one or two of the juvenile individuals. H I exhibits a flattened, receding symphyseal profile, and there is no noticeable hollowing of the bone between the alveolar and basal borders. Therefore a general projection of the basal part of the symphysis (the *mentum osseum* of Weidenreich) is lacking. But a low swelling of triangular form is located inferiorly in the chin region, and the presence of one mental component (the trigone) is thus confirmed even if the lateral tubercles are not well developed. The juvenile mandible B I is similar. Because of breakage at the midline in OH 22, symphyseal anatomy of this African individual is imperfectly preserved, and the crucial parts of OH 23 and OH 51 are missing altogether. Close examination of the Bed IV mandible shows no trace of a *mentum osseum*, however, and the sloping profile is devoid of any strong relief. Structures associated with chin formation are not evident in this Olduvai hominid.

Other differences are apparent in the morphology of the internal aspect of the symphysis. This region is preserved in two of the adult Zhoukoudian mandibles, and in H I the alveolar plane is slightly hollowed immediately below the sockets for the anterior teeth. This surface is extended downward and back to produce a smooth and diffuse swelling corresponding to a superior transverse torus. The same sort of shallow depression is present on the internal aspect of H IV, although in this specimen the bone surface is more steeply inclined. Consequently a flattened alveolar plane and superior torus are not clearly developed. But in the more robust mandible from Olduvai Bed IV, these structures are very prominent. The alveolar plane is again slightly concave below the incisor sockets but is expanded posteriorly to form a heavy shelf bounded by a well defined superior torus. The symphysis is thicker in cross-section than either of the Chinese jaws. Small but very distinct mental spines are found in the latter, while the number and arrangement of spines cannot be determined for OH 22. Digastric impressions on the basal margin of the corpus are elongated and narrow in H I, and these fossae lie entirely in the horizontal plane rather than partly on the posterior aspect of the jaw. Other Zhoukoudian adults are much the same, but digastric markings seem to be restricted in extent on OH 22. A faint impression reaches only to the level of the lateral incisor in this mandible, while the fossa extends to the region of M_1 in the most complete Chinese fossil.

Weidenreich's descriptions of the medial aspect of the corpus appear to hold for the Olduvai as well as for the Zhoukoudian remains. In OH 22 as in *Sinanthropus* H I, the posterior part of the alveolar prominence is quite projecting. This feature is subject to considerable variation, and the prominence is less exaggerated in the other Chinese jaws and in OH 23. Most of the relevant portion of OH 51 is missing. There is one important difference among the two assemblages. None of the three Olduvai specimens exhibit any sign of mandibular torus formation. This trait is strikingly developed in the Zhoukoudian material, where swellings and striations occur in the region of the premolars and anterior teeth of G I and H I. Similar but less marked tori are restricted to the vicinity of the molars in H IV and A II.

The alveolar prominence is continued onto the medial face of the ramus as a triangular torus, sharply defined in Zhoukoudian mandible G I. Division of this ridge into endocoronoid and endocondyloid cristae is apparent in both G I and H I, with the coronoid extension being more pronounced in each case. The same division of tori occurs on the ramus of OH 22, but the endocondyloid crista is here more heavily built, at least in so far as this structure is preserved.

The superior and posterior parts of the Olduvai ramus are broken, making further comparisons with Chinese *Homo erectus* difficult.

The mandibles from Ternifine

The three jaws from Ternifine have been discussed in Chapter 5. Mandible 1 is missing most of the ramus from both sides but is otherwise well preserved. All of the cheek teeth are still in place. Ternifine 2 consists of the left half of a jaw from which the anterior dentition has been lost. Ternifine 3 is quite complete, although parts of the right corpus have been reconstructed. There is some deformation of the ramus on one side.

All three mandibles are heavily built and show areas of strong muscle insertion. Robusticity is greatest for Ternifine 1 and Ternifine 3, which give ratios of about 55 at the level of M_1. Corpus cross-sectional areas are also large for these specimens, designated as male by Arambourg (1963). Robusticities of the Zhoukoudian jaws are similar, while corpus areas are substantially less, even for G I. The mandible of OH 22 is thick and relatively low. The Olduvai robusticity index of 71.9 at M_1 consequently exceeds the figures for each of the Algerian jaws as well as those for the Zhoukoudian fossils. The OH 23 and OH 51 fragments are also relatively more robust than the specimens from Ternifine.

Relief on the lateral surface of the body is particularly marked in mandible 1. In Ternifine 2 and Ternifine 3, the prominence and superior torus are not quite so well developed, although an intertoral sulcus is expressed. These structures are at least as pronounced as in OH 22. A roughened marginal torus and anterior tubercle are present in all three individuals. Ternifine 1 and Ternifine 3 each display a wide extramolar sulcus, maximally excavated at the level of M_3. This sulcus is broader than in the Olduvai or Zhoukoudian materials.

Symphyseal thickness reaches 19 mm in Ternifine 1 and Ternifine 3 and is only slightly less for mandible 2. These values are equaled by OH 22, while the symphyses of G I and H I from Zhoukoudian are thinner. The symphyseal contour of Ternifine 1 is rounded and receding, and neither a *mentum osseum* nor tubercles associated with a trigone are developed. In this respect the jaw is perhaps more similar to OH 22 than to its companions, which exhibit signs of more definite protrusion in the chin region. Ternifine 2 and Ternifine 3 are said by Arambourg (1963) to possess the components of a basal trigone, and here the profile is like that of the Zhoukoudian mandibles. Internally, a sloping alveolar plane is variably developed. This alveolar surface is concave but not bounded by a superior transverse torus in jaw 1, extensive in Ternifine 2, and more steeply inclined in Ternifine 3. Distinctions relative to the morphology of OH 22 are minor and difficult to describe in any systematic fashion.

On the medial aspect of the body, the alveolar prominence is strongly constructed in each of the Ternifine individuals and is especially heavy in mandible 3. This is to be expected in a large jaw, but Ternifine 3 also presents a tubercle in the vicinity of M_1, on the right side. Such traces of mandibular torus formation are common on Chinese *Homo erectus* jaws but cannot be discerned in the other northwestern African or Olduvai hominids. The ramus is preserved in mandibles 2 and 3, and crest formation on the internal face is comparable to that noted by Weidenreich (1936) for *Sinanthropus*. The division of the triangular torus into endocoronoid and endocondyloid cristae is also visible but less well marked on the broken ramus of Ternifine 1. Degree of expression of these bony crests is subject to considerable variation, and small differences between the Algerian and Olduvai individuals are not likely to have much significance.

Discussion

In summarizing these anatomical comparisons, it is important to keep in mind that only small numbers of fossils are available for study. Paleontological work of this sort is limited, in that samples drawn from extinct populations are nearly always inadequate. We are left in the position of hoping that the Turkana and Olduvai specimens are really representative of groups living in East Africa during the Early Pleistocene, since in fact little is known of the extent of sexual dimorphism or other individual variation in ancient *Homo erectus*. The situation in Asia is somewhat better. Much more material has been recovered from localities such as Sangiran and Zhoukoudian. However, the Indonesian hominids are scattered through a substantial thickness of sediments, accumulated over a lengthy period of time. These fossils exhibit wide variation, and there is still no firm consensus as to how many lineages may be present.

SORTING THE FOSSILS

In my own view, only one species of *Homo* need be recognized in the Pucangan- and Kabuh-age deposits of central Java. Apart from several damaged mandibles of uncertain provenience, the only material not immediately referable to *Homo erectus* is from Ngandong in eastern Java. Some authors see in this assemblage an approach to the morphology of more modern humans. I agree that the Ngandong crania do depart in a few respects from the appearance characteristic of other archaic Asian individuals. Supraorbital tori are not always thickened centrally, and the frontal bone may be relatively broad, without extreme postorbital constriction. The upper scale of the occipital is long in some Ngandong crania, resulting in a low scale index. This is at least partly a consequence of inferior projection of the large linear tubercle, as noted earlier. Also, in the construction of the glenoid cavity, there are small differences from the Sangiran specimens. The articular tubercle is never prominent and bar-like as in modern humans, but in one or two of the Ngandong crania this tubercle is more clearly defined than in most *Homo erectus* populations. In other features, including overall size and proportions of the braincase as well as many important anatomical details, the Ngandong people are not different from other Asian groups. In the descriptions presented in Chapter 2 and in the metric work carried out here, there is substantial evidence suggesting that this assemblage should be sorted with the Sangiran and Sambungmachan material as *Homo erectus*.

Another difficulty affecting regional comparisons is dating. Even when questions concerning sorting of the Asian hominids are settled, it must be remembered that all of the East African fossils (with the exception of OH 12, one or two of the Olduvai mandibles, and OH 28) are older than the Asian specimens. In the case of Turkana and the Sangiran Kabuh horizons or Zhoukoudian, this difference in geological age may amount to many hundreds of thousands of years. Comparisons of such assemblages are informative, but if morphological contrasts are noted, it will be hard to rule out the importance of evolutionary change through time. Anatomical differences resulting from advances in 'grade' may be confounded with variation due to geographic separation.

Despite these uncertainties, it is possible to draw some tentative conclusions. First, it is apparent that all of the crania are broadly similar. There are obvious differences of size, and endocranial volumes vary from about 800 ml (less in the case of OH 12) to more than 1200 ml. However, I have tried to avoid emphasizing this, by comparing African and Asian specimens which are roughly equal in cranial capacity. To some extent, I have probably compared females to other females, and males with males, but of course there is no certainty concerning sex identification. In any case, there are resemblances in many features, including frontal form, development of crests associated with the temporal lines, occipital curvature and presence of a transverse torus, occipitomastoid anatomy, construction of the glenoid cavity and form of the tympanic plate. Even the two Turkana crania (especially KNM-ER 3883) are not very different in their vault proportions from Sangiran 2, Sangiran 4 and Sangiran 12. The African individuals do have short parietal chords, and in KNM-ER 3733 the lambda–inion distance is relatively great. There is little expression of an angular torus on the parietal, and the occipital torus is not very prominent. However, given the extent of variation within the Asian assemblages, these differences should not be overemphasized. The Turkana crania seem to fit comfortably within the limits of anatomical and metric variability established for the Trinil and Sangiran hominids, and apparently only one taxon is represented. This conclusion holds for OH 9 as well. Extensive comparisons with the Sangiran, Sambungmachan and Ngandong fossils support the contention that the large Olduvai braincase should be lumped with *Homo erectus*.

Lower jaws are also similar. Several mandibles from Zhoukoudian and Sangiran are widely accepted as *Homo erectus*, and it is clear that the African fossils share features with these Asian specimens. Resemblances of the Ternifine jaws to those from Zhoukoudian have been stressed by Arambourg (1963) and noted by other workers. Parallels in symphyseal form, numbers of mental foramina, breadth and inclination of the ramus, and dental traits prompted Howell (1960) to suggest that North African and East Asian populations were closely linked in earlier Middle Pleistocene times, the differences between them indicating no more than minor geographic variation within a polytypic species. My own comparisons can be interpreted in the same way.

A resemblance of OH 22 to these northwest African and Asian fossils can be seen in the general size of the mandible and shape of the dental arcade, the extent of relief on the lateral corpus, the receding symphyseal profile, development of a shelving alveolar plane, and the presence of downward facing digastric impressions. In so far as the OH 22 ramus is preserved, its morphology is similar to that of other *Homo erectus*. In all of these features, OH 22 lies within the range of variation of the Ternifine specimens and the *Sinanthropus* mandibles described by Weidenreich (1936).

The same claim may be made for the jaws from Koobi Fora, Baringo and Swartkrans. KNM-ER 730 is similar to the Olduvai mandibles in nearly all respects. The more complete specimen numbered KNM-ER 992 does differ from KNM-ER 730 and OH 22 in lateral prominence development but resembles this group in the form of the chin and alveolar plane. The second mandible from the Kapthurin Formation, west of Lake Baringo, shares some features with OH 13 from Bed II at Olduvai, as noted in Chapter 4. This Bed II hominid has been referred to *Homo habilis*, mostly because the cranial vault associated with the jaw is small and lightly constructed. However, neither KNM-ER 992 nor KNM-BK 8518 can readily be distinguished from *Homo erectus*, and without more evidence it seems best to assign both individuals to this taxon. The SK 15 jaw from South Africa is poorly preserved. In overall size and proportions, it is also close to OH 22. Originally described as *Telanthropus*, SK 15 has since been referred to *Homo erectus*, and this conclusion has been supported by later workers.

THE ANATOMY OF *HOMO ERECTUS*

Characters common to the African and Asian assemblages may now be summarized, in an attempt to describe *Homo erectus* on the basis of all of the more important fossils:

- crania are long and relatively low in outline, and the average endocranial volume is close to 1000 ml. The basicranial axis is flattened in comparison to the more flexed base of *Homo sapiens*.
- the facial skeleton, preserved for only a few individuals, is robust, and alveolar prognathism is pronounced. The canine jugum is well enough developed to thicken the lower lateral aspect of the nasal aperture, which is relatively broad. Superiorly, the wall of the aperture is thin and everted. The nasal bones form a low keel in the midline. In sagittal profile, face form approaches that seen in *Homo sapiens*, although the nasoalveolar clivus is flattened. It can be argued that increase in the volume of the upper part of the nose may have allowed more efficient retrieval of moisture from exhaled air, thus enabling *Homo erectus* to inhabit relatively arid environments for the first time (Franciscus & Trinkaus, 1988).

- brow ridges tend to be quite heavy, even in smaller crania such as Sangiran 10 or KNM-ER 3883. There is hollowing above glabella, but supratoral sulci are shallow or not present.
- frontal profiles are flattened, and midline keeling is common. A bregmatic eminence is variably developed, and keeling may continue onto the parietal vault.
- the temporal lines may be crested anteriorly, and in some cases the lines reach medially almost to the center of the superior orbital margin before turning posteriorly. Least frontal breadth is low relative to the biorbital chord, so postorbital narrowing is marked.
- the (superior) temporal line follows a flat arc and may produce an angular torus at the parietal mastoid angle. The temporal and superior nuchal lines may converge near asterion, as in Sangiran 2. The mastoid crest is variably developed.
- height of the temporal squama is less than in modern humans, and the squamosal suture follows a rather straight course downward and posteriorly toward the parietal incisure.
- the zygomatic root rises from the horizontal as it approaches the supramastoid crest. This crest is prominent, especially in the larger Indonesian individuals. All crania give maximum breadth readings at this level, rather than higher on the parietal vault. Extension of the supramastoid sulcus onto the parietal bone (as an angular sulcus) occurs rarely.
- mastoid processes differ in size but may be quite large, as in Sangiran 4 and KNM-ER 3883. These processes are inclined medially, so that distance measured between the tips is substantially less than any breadth taken at the supramastoid crests.
- parietal sagittal chords and arcs are short compared to those of recent *Homo*. The posterior border of the parietal bone is relatively longer, particularly in the larger Asian hominids.
- the occipital squama is wider than in modern humans. Occipital angles are low, showing that the bone is strongly flexed. The upper scale tends to slope forward. Length of this scale relative to the nuchal plane below is variable, both in Asian and in African specimens.
- the transverse torus of the occiput is most projecting near the midline, where it is frequently blunt rather than shelf-like. Its lower border is defined by the superior nuchal lines, which meet at a central linear tubercle. There is no true external occipital protuberance.
- a juxtamastoid eminence, separated from the mastoid process by

the digastric incisure, parallels or traverses the occipitomastoid suture. In some crania, this eminence is continuous with the line of insertion of the superior oblique muscle and thus corresponds to the occipitomastoid crest of Weidenreich (1943).

— the anterior wall of the mandibular fossa may be hollowed, and there is a smooth transition from this joint surface onto the preglenoid planum. No raised articular tubercle is developed.

— the glenoid cavity is narrowed medially to form a deep recess between the entoglenoid process and the tympanic plate. The entoglenoid itself may be partly of sphenoid origin, but a sphenoid spine such as occurs in later *Homo sapiens* is not present.

— the tympanic plate is thick inferiorly. A petrosal spine is prominent, and the plate terminates medially in a blunt tubercle (the 'process supratubarius' of Weidenreich).

— the lower jaw is large and robust, with a long arcade which is rounded rather than flattened in the region of the anterior dentition. Where it is preserved, the ramus is very broad.

— the external symphyseal profile is receding. There is no incurvation of the bone between the alveolar border and the base (no *mentum osseum*), although in some individuals the components of a trigone are expressed.

— as described by Weidenreich (1941), the femora from Zhoukoudian have shafts which are straight, flattened anteroposteriorly, and narrowed distally so that the position of minimum circumference is relatively low. The medullary canal exhibits stenosis, and the cortical wall is correspondingly thickened. Several of these features also characterize the femur of OH 28 (Day, 1971) and some of the limb bones from the Koobi Fora region (Day, 1976; Kennedy, 1983). It is of interest that the femur of KNM-WT 15000 from Nariokotome has an exceptionally long neck, suggesting enhancement of the abductor mechanism compared to *Homo sapiens* (Brown *et al.*, 1985).

— the hip bone displays lateral flare of the iliac blade, a very prominent vertical iliac pillar, and a strong acetabulosacral buttress. The auricular surface is relatively small, and the ischial tuberosity faces laterally as well as posteriorly. At least some of these characters of East African *Homo erectus* occur also in pelvic bones thought to represent an archaic form of *Homo sapiens*.

— estimates of body size can be obtained by regression from measurements of femora and other postcranial bones, as noted in Chapters

3 and 4. An average for Asian and African individuals is about 48 kg (Rightmire, 1986a). When body weight is coupled with average cranial capacity, a quotient of encephalization (*EQ*) can be computed as the ratio of actual brain size to the size expected for an appropriately selected reference population. If modern *Homo sapiens* is taken as the group on which to base the exponent by which body weight is scaled to obtain expected brain size (equation 10 of Holloway & Post, 1982), the resulting *EQ* is about 0.87. That is, the brain of *Homo erectus* is relatively small, reaching a volume which on average is 87% of that in modern humans.

These as well as other features noted by Weidenreich (1936, 1943), Le Gros Clark (1964) and Howell (1978) serve to describe *Homo erectus* as known from sites in East and northwest Africa, China and Indonesia. Many of the traits do in fact differentiate *Homo erectus* from later humans. In this sense, the description stands as a diagnosis. However, some of the same characters also appear in earlier *Homo* from Africa or even in species of *Australopithecus*. Such traits, which may be interpreted as primitive retentions from a common ancestor, do not help to diagnose *Homo erectus* relative to other hominids. Characters likely to be derived (apomorphic) for *Homo erectus* are fewer in number but are more useful in assessing the relationships of this species to other groups. This question will be explored further in later chapters.

It should be emphasized that there is a lot of variation. Keeling in the midline, especially where present on the parietal bone, is characteristic of the Asian specimens but does not seem to occur regularly in the Olduvai or Turkana remains. Parasagittal flattening is especially marked on some of the Sangiran vaults. In several of the Asian skulls, the supramastoid crest is not only large but also turns sharply upward as it passes posteriorly from the zygomatic root. The tympanic plate of some Sangiran individuals may be described as more robust (thickened anteroposteriorly relative to height) than that of African specimens, as noted by Stringer (1984). Also, the upper scale of the occiput is lower and broader in Sangiran 2 and Sangiran 4 than in the Olduvai and Turkana individuals.

Differences which set the Zhoukoudian and Ternifine mandibles apart from Olduvai *Homo erectus* are apparent but not striking. The Asian and northwest African jaws are less robust at the level of M_I. Internally an alveolar plane is less extensively developed, especially in the Chinese material, and a superior transverse torus is usually not prominent. Other distinctions occur in the dentition. In Ternifine 1 and 2, the crown of P_3 is asymmetrical with a large compressed main cusp on the buccal margin. The smaller lingual cusp is located somewhat distally. The crown of P_4 is more symmetrical with a very large buccal cusp and an especially prominent posterior fovea. Buccal enamel ridges are apparent. The molars are variable in size and cusp pattern but, like the premolars, are said by Howell (1960) to resemble the teeth of eastern Asian *Homo erectus*. In contrast, the P_3 of OH 22 is more markedly asymmetrical and compressed in its buccolingual dimension. Features such as enlargement of the buccal cusp, attenuation of the mesiolingual margin, and the resulting oblique orientation of a line joining the cusps relative to the mesiodistal axis of the crown are greatly exaggerated, so that the Olduvai tooth is quite different. The second premolar (P_4) is also slightly asymmetrical in outline and not quite like its more rectangular counterpart in the Ternifine jaws.

How much importance should be attached to these anatomical differences is still not settled. The site at Ternifine is of course quite distant from Olduvai Gorge, and it is probable that the populations sampled in these areas were not contemporary. Uncertainties of this sort, and appreciation of the variation evident in mandibular form of (all) hominids, should counsel caution. It would be unwise to give great weight to the few distinctions exhibited by the Olduvai remains. Differences in cranial morphology are of the same order and should be expected within a species that is geographically widespread. Perhaps it is surprising that more variation is not apparent. One has to check quite carefully for signs of consistent regional change, and the evidence for overall similarity of African and Asian populations is much more striking.

7

Homo erectus as a paleospecies

As described so far, *Homo erectus* is an extinct species known from several areas of the Old World. Fossils from Java and China display a suite of archaic characters, by which these individuals can easily be distinguished from more modern humans. Many of the same traits can be recognized in the material from Africa. Jaws from Ternifine are very similar to those excavated in the cave at Zhoukoudian. More ancient crania, mandibles (and other body parts) from Olduvai and the Koobi Fora region also resemble the remains from Asia, and it is probable that just one species is sampled in all of these geographic areas.

If it is agreed that *Homo erectus* ranged widely over a long span of Pleistocene time, an important question may be raised. This concerns the way in which species should be defined by paleontologists, who must focus on the fossil record. Some workers regard paleospecies simply as divisions or segments of larger evolutionary lineages. Species treated in this sense have no clear origin and are assumed to be transformed gradually into descendent groups. Boundaries between such taxa are largely arbitrary. Alternatively, paleospecies may be seen as discrete entities, as sets of populations which are readily separated from other extinct or living groups using morphological criteria. Evidence bearing on this issue of the distinctiveness of *Homo erectus* is presented below. It is my contention that the fossils document more than just a grade or stage in human evolution.

Species in the fossil record

Species of living organisms are composed of interbreeding populations exhibiting reasonably constant morphology over a geographic
range. Such groups, separated from other species by discontinuities,
can be delimited without much difficulty. Species in the past, which
are often poorly sampled and known only from hard body parts subject to fossilization, are less easily recognized. A traditional view
summarized by Gingerich (1985) is that samples drawn from populations of successive species, when compared over time, provide little
basis for distinguishing one taxon from another. Gingerich cites
several examples showing that early mammals have evolved slowly
and that transitions between these taxa are as gradual as change
within groups. Early and late representatives of species are connected
by intermediate forms, and successive taxa are linked in the same
way. Recognition of such groups is largely arbitrary. In other instances, transitions are more marked, and some ancestor–descendant
species are not clearly connected by intermediates. However, it is
Gingerich's opinion that gradual change is to be expected, when the
record is complete and can be studied in adequate detail.

Similar reasoning has been extended to the hominids. Many
workers frame the later history of this group as one of gradual diver-
gence of two major lineages, after splitting from a common ancestor
in the Pliocene. One lineage, containing species of *Australopithecus*,
is presumed to have become extinct, while the second is thought to
have produced successive species of the genus *Homo*, including
modern humans. Within this second lineage, three species are recognized, but the boundaries between *Homo habilis* and *Homo erectus*
or between *Homo erectus* and *Homo sapiens* are not clearly demarcated. Gingerich (1979) describes such species as 'arbitrarily divided
segments of an evolving lineage that differ morphologically from
other species in the same or different lineages'.

The difficulties associated with carving taxa out of what is
assumed, given an intact fossil record, would be a continuous sequence of slowly changing forms have been further enumerated by
Tobias (1978, 1980). Tobias notes that both dating and morphology
should be employed in an effort to name and describe successive species, although he cautions against accepting Campbell's (1974) pro-
posal that *Homo* taxa be delimited on strictly chronological grounds.
In a later paper, Tobias (1982) discusses trends which characterize

the *Homo* lineage. Enlargement of the brain, differential development of areas within the cerebrum, and reorganization of the cranial vault and face are said to have begun at different times and proceeded at different rates within the lineage. However, these trends are sustained over long periods and 'transcend systematic categories'. Changes initiated at one stage of human evolution are continued in later species, to culminate in the appearance of *Homo sapiens*. Here Tobias clearly perceives continuous phyletic transformation rather than episodic change to be important, even if mosaic evolution has occurred.

Other workers generally agree with the partitioning of *Homo* into three species but place more emphasis on the gradual nature of evolutionary advance. Cronin *et al.* (1981) have reviewed much of the Plio-Pleistocene hominid evidence and have concluded that fossils displaying intermediate morphology are fairly numerous. Such transitional individuals are said to be common in the European Middle Pleistocene, and the material from Petralona and other localities is used to support a claim for steady change in populations linking (late) *Homo erectus* with (early) *Homo sapiens*. Wolpoff (1980b, 1982) argues that the division between these species is arbitrary, and for Europe at least, he proposes a chronological criterion (the 'end of the Mindel glaciation') to mark the species boundary. A few of the European fossils may be *Homo erectus* by this reasoning, but the entire mid-Pleistocene assemblage is considered to be part of a lineage ancestral to later Neanderthals and more modern humans.

Some anthropologists have carried this thinking a step further by stating that there is no need to recognize separate species in the Middle Pleistocene. In Jelínek's (1980a) opinion, all of the Middle and Late Pleistocene hominids from Europe may be viewed as *Homo sapiens*, although this European lineage displays marked sex dimorphism. In another paper addressing the remains from Ternifine and other sites in northwest Africa, Jelínek (1980b) suggests that in Africa as well as Europe, there are general 'evolutionary trends leading to *Homo sapiens sapiens*'. Only one species is represented, but at the same time local changes (trends) documented in the Maghreb are not the same as those occurring in Europe or the Middle East. While he does not discuss subspecies, Jelínek does point to the importance of the environment in shaping population differences. He sees evolution within *Homo sapiens* as a complex process, proceeding at different rates in different geographic regions.

More explicit hypotheses of gradual evolution with regional continuity have been advanced by Thorne & Wolpoff (1981) for southeast Asia and by Jelínek (1982) and Wolpoff, Wu & Thorne (1984) for China as well as Java and Australia. For Jelínek, all of the Chinese material can be accommodated in a single evolutionary stream, in which modern features are increasingly expressed. The Middle Pleistocene hominids of Java are primitive, but discoveries from Australia suggest continuity in southeast Asia also. Jelínek argues that there is no reason to separate earlier representatives of this lineage from later ones, and he places all Asian *Homo erectus* in a subspecies of *Homo sapiens*. Thorne & Wolpoff (1981) agree in part and describe Indonesian *Homo erectus* as contributing to a 'morphological clade' which also includes *Homo sapiens* populations such as that from Kow Swamp, Australia. Two taxa are recognized, but these chronospecies are no more than segments of a morphological continuum. Evidence for continuity is found in trends toward facial prognathism, eversion of the malar bone, rounding of the lower orbital margin and overall reduction of facial and dental dimensions.

This idea of an ancestral relationship between southeast Asian *Homo erectus* and Australian *Homo sapiens* is not new, of course, but Thorne & Wolpoff attempt to place some distance between themselves and Weidenreich or Carleton Coon by rejecting the use of subspecific designations. Instead, they state that genetic isolation is not a necessary assumption of their 'multiregional evolutionary hypothesis'. This model as proposed by Wolpoff *et al.* (1984) holds that differences distinguishing 'clades' in Australasia, East Asia and other regions will be maintained by a balance between gene flow and selection, acting in peripheral areas of the geographic range occupied by Pleistocene hominids.

PALEOSPECIES AS DISCRETE ENTITIES

The concept of paleontological species as segments of a single lineage, arbitrarily defined by changing morphology or stratigraphic breaks (gaps in the record), has not been accepted in all quarters. Some students of human evolution have questioned the prevailing view that (all) *Homo* species are sequentially related within a framework of gradual, progressive change. In particular, the assumption that *Homo erectus* populations all across the Old World merged imperceptibly with early *Homo sapiens* has been sharply criticized by Eldredge & Tattersall (1975, 1982) and Delson, Eldredge & Tattersall

(1977). These authors point to several characters found in *Homo erectus* crania (an undivided supraorbital torus, sagittal keeling, a small mastoid process) which do not seem to be present in the skulls of early *Homo sapiens*. This choice of traits may be questioned, but if such non-shared morphological specializations can be identified, then at least some groups of *Homo erectus* are not likely to be the direct ancestors of *Homo sapiens*. Delson *et al.* (1977) seem to doubt that there can be any continuity between the two species, although Delson (1981) has since suggested that early evidence for speciation may be found in Europe. He hypothesizes that populations of *Homo sapiens* may have evolved there first, as a result of isolation due to glacial conditions. What should be emphasized here is not the timing or geographic location of speciation but rather the view that *Homo erectus* is a taxon distinct in important ways from other species. The transition from archaic to more modern forms may have taken place just once, in a restricted geographic province, rather than gradually in many areas.

Bonde (1981) has reviewed much of the current thinking about species in paleontology, and his conclusions as applied to the genus *Homo* also merit close consideration. Bonde supports the idea that species exist as coherent entities, not only in the present but also the past. Paleontological species, in accord with Wiley's (1978) revision of Simpson's (1961) definition, are single lineages, which cannot be subdivided arbitrarily. That such a species may survive one or more branching events is considered unlikely. Here Bonde sticks to the cladist principle that splitting of a lineage must always give rise to forms which, for purposes of formal classification, are distinct from the common stem or ancestor.

Application of this approach to the hominids results in the recognition of at least four species of *Homo* in the record of the last 1.5 million years. *Homo erectus* as known from the earlier African localities and from the Far East is viewed as one product of a split also yielding *Homo heidelbergensis*. This latter species is represented by the mid-Pleistocene remains from Europe. Branching of this European lineage is hypothesized to have given rise to two new stems, classified as *Homo neanderthalensis* and *Homo sapiens*. One question which comes to mind immediately is whether these branching points can indeed be identified from the sparse evidence available. Certainly the European fossils differ morphologically from *Homo erectus* as known from Asia and East Africa. It is not unreasonable to view the Middle Pleistocene people of Europe as part of a distinct lineage (as is done by some of the most committed gradualists)! It is also widely acknowledged that the Neanderthals display a suite of derived anatomical characters which are not shared with fully modern humans. As does Bonde, a few authorities would set the Neanderthals apart as a separate species on these grounds. Tattersall (1986) has recently defended this position. Other anthropologists object to assigning these Late Pleistocene Europeans to any taxon other than *Homo sapiens*. Linking the Neanderthals with our own species has been accepted practice for some time. A further concern is that Bonde's phylogeny does not completely accommodate mid-Pleistocene populations from regions outside of Europe. Fossils from sub-Saharan Africa, for example, do not seem to belong in any of the taxa named.

One solution to these problems, discussed by Bonde, is to reclassify all of these assemblages as allopatric or successive subspecies of *Homo sapiens*. This logic assures that an entire lineage is represented, especially if *Homo habilis* as well as *Homo erectus* populations are included. In such a scheme, *Homo sapiens* has great antiquity and can be recognized as a lineage spanning the entire Pleistocene. This concept of the evolutionary species is subject to the same objections that apply to Jelínek's view, in which very diverse remains are lumped together in one world-encompassing evolutionary stream. There is no serious attempt to sort the fossils, and any branching which has actually occurred since the origin of *Homo* is ignored. The inevitable result is that individuals assigned to one 'species' differ substantially more in size and form than do representatives of living groups. As rightly pointed out by other workers (eg. Gingerich, 1985; Tattersall, 1986) this reduces the utility of the species concept.

Even where branching points cannot be identified with certainty, it will be best to rely on morphology as a guide to the judicious separation of taxa. Samples should be sorted together, or assigned to different species, on the basis of similarity in one or more characters. Sorting of course is a process that depends heavily on familiarity with individual fossils, although several different procedures may be used. One approach to comparing *Homo erectus* specimens by means of measurements and anatomical features is given in Chapter 6. Species erected from assemblages extending over long time periods may, as more evidence is collected, appear to be anagenetically related. The boundaries between such taxa may become less distinct as resolution of the record is improved. However, where change is episodic, interspersed with periods of stasis, species can be distinguished nonarbitrarily from earlier (or later) members of the same evolutionary line.

Definitions of *Homo erectus*

Debate over the definition of paleontological species will surely continue, and the phylogeny of *Homo* will be a focus of discussion. At present, there is a substantial body of evidence favoring retention of the taxon *Homo erectus*. That this species can be distinguished from most Late Pleistocene populations of *Homo sapiens* and from modern humans is not in doubt. Descriptions based on the principal (Asian) fossil assemblages and provided decades ago by Weidenreich and others are quite adequate for this purpose, although of course these earlier studies take no account of new discoveries. Comparisons undertaken by Arambourg (1963) and Le Gros Clark (1964) have helped to demonstrate similarities of the Asian and African representatives of *Homo erectus*, while comprehensive reviews documenting the distinctions of this entire body of material have been published by Howell (1978, 1986) and Howells (1980).

Work of my own is intended to build on these earlier findings. While there are obvious differences of size within both Asian and African assemblages, it is apparent that the better preserved skulls from these regions are remarkably similar. Resemblances extend not only to general form of the cranium but also to many small anatomical details, including nasal projection, postorbital constriction, parietal proportions, expression of crests and tori on the vault, occipital flexion, and shape of the glenoid cavity and tympanic plate. These and other traits do differentiate *Homo erectus* from *Homo sapiens*. In this restricted sense, the description serves as a diagnosis, as already noted. However, some of these characters are also found in earlier *Homo* from Africa, or even in other hominid taxa. Such traits, considered to be plesiomorphic, do not help generally to define *Homo erectus* relative to other hominids or hominoids.

In most cases, a formal species diagnosis should be based on traits which are novel or apomorphic, rather than plesiomorphic. Apomorphic or derived characters which are expressed only in the group under consideration are unique. Many workers hold that such autapomorphies provide the evidence necessary for defining a taxon, whereas attributes interpreted as derived and shared by two or more species may be taken to demonstrate a close phylogenetic relationship between these groups. The latter claim is widely accepted, although the importance of unique traits may be questioned. If it is insisted that species be defined (only) from autapomorphies, then it may be difficult to identify links to other taxa. We are likely to be confronted by a paradox (Rightmire, 1986b). As a species is diagnosed more completely, by recognizing additional autapomorphies, it will be increasingly difficult to place it in any ancestor–descendant sequence.

The merits of the cladistic research program and problems associated with it have been discussed extensively in the recent literature and need not be reviewed here. Although I do not follow a strict interpretation of Hennig's views as given in the much cited work of Schaeffer, Hecht & Eldredge (1972), I do see advantages to applying cladistic principles to the study of hominid phylogeny. Characters which are plesiomorphic should where possible be separated from those that are derived, and the latter should be emphasized in diagnosing *Homo erectus* in a differential sense. The extent to which *Homo erectus* exhibits evolutionary novelties has been debated before, but no consensus has been reached. Several earlier reports are summarized below.

Delson *et al.* (1977) cite a paper by Macintosh & Larnach (1972) in support of their identification of at least six 'possibly autapomorphic' cranial features. These include an undivided supraorbital torus, marked postorbital constriction, midline keeling, a mound-shaped occipital torus, a small mastoid process and overall thickness of the vault bones. If these traits are in fact unique, then *Homo erectus* is not likely to have given rise to *Homo sapiens*. The authors note that possession of even a single non-shared specialization can disqualify one taxon as ancestral to another.

In a more recent paper, Wood (1984) lists some 30 traits, culled from Weidenreich (1943) and other sources, which he considers may be autapomorphic for *Homo erectus*. These range from general form of the cranium (long and low) and shape of individual vault and facial bones (flattened and rectangular parietal, low temporal squama, broad nasal bones) to details of anatomical structure. Some of the latter are still rather broadly defined (marked supramastoid and mastoid crests), while others are clearly subject to much variation within the species. Wood himself points out that a number of these features are expressed in similar fashion in *Homo habilis* or in crania usually referred to (early) *Homo sapiens*. After such shared traits are deleted, Wood's list still includes morphology of the occipital torus, its association with an angular torus and continuity with the mastoid crest, and at least four additional aspects of cranial anatomy.

Stringer (1984) also reviews a long list of characters said to be present in *Homo erectus*, in an attempt to isolate autapomorphies. He finds that a dozen or so traits, confined mainly to a sample of Asian hominids, can be considered distinctive. Other traits shared with the earlier African fossils or with later European specimens are likely to be plesiomorphic. Stringer's count is reduced further by Andrews (1984), who asserts that most of the characters commonly cited in definitions of *Homo erectus* are primitive, being present in other hominids or in recent hominoid primates. Unique specializations include only sagittal keeling on the frontal and parietal bones, the presence of an angular torus, separation of inion from endinion on the occipital, development of a fissure between the mastoid process and the tympanic plate, narrowing of the medial aspect of the glenoid cavity to produce a deep recess, and thick vault bones. For Andrews, as for Delson *et al.* (1977), possession of such autapomorphies removes at least some *Homo erectus* from any lineage leading towards modern humans. Andrews suspects that Asian *Homo erectus* became extinct in the Middle Pleistocene, while another lineage perhaps restricted to Africa evolved into early *Homo sapiens*.

A rather different interpretation has been advanced by Hublin (1986), who declares that *Homo erectus* displays very few if any unique characters. Hublin notes that an angular torus, for example, is variably expressed even in the Asian hominids, and he again emphasizes that many of the other traits distinguishing this group are lacking in specimens from eastern Africa. He feels that *Homo erectus* is best viewed as a grade, defined by features which are primitive relative to *Homo sapiens*. Neither the Asian fossils nor the African remains should be excluded from the role of ancestor to later humans, and it is unnecessary to retain separate species status for any of the Middle Pleistocene assemblages.

DIAGNOSING THE TAXON

Given these differences of opinion, the identification of characters diagnostic of *Homo erectus* is not straightforward. Perhaps the search can be facilitated by first listing those aspects of cranial anatomy that seem to be derived *Homo erectus*, relative to earlier *Homo*, on the strength of evidence discussed so far. Such a list follows:

- the brow is thickened and continuous, and there is a flat supratoral shelf behind.
- the frontal exhibits midline keeling.
- there is an angular torus at the posteroinferior corner of the parietal bone.
- the occipital squama is wide and sharply angled.
- morphology of the transverse torus of the occiput is distinctive, as noted by Wood (1984) and others, although there is a good deal of variation.
- the glenoid cavity is narrowed medially to produce a deep fissure between the (large) entoglenoid pyramid and the tympanic plate.
- the tympanic bone, which presents a strong petrosal crest, terminates in a blunt process supratubarius.
- vault bones are relatively thickened.
- endocranial volume is increased to approximately 1000 ml.

It should be understood that there is variation, and not all characters are expressed in each of the individuals assigned to *Homo erectus*. Supraorbital tori are not equally heavy in all of the Sangiran hominids, and there are differences within the East African assemblages as well. Keeling of the frontal bone and prominence of an angular torus are also subject to variation, as noted in the descriptions of individual specimens. In my view, this is to be expected for populations extending over a large geographic range. Nevertheless, a suite of most of these traits will serve to distinguish any fossil which is reasonably well preserved.

Crania of earlier *Homo* are quite different, being small and thin-walled in comparison to *Homo erectus*. Faces, present in a few cases, exhibit variation, but at least one individual from Koobi Fora (KNM-ER 1470) has a lower face which is markedly flattened rather than projecting. Brows are thinner at the center of the orbit than near glabella and are never massive. Neither frontal keeling nor an angular torus are observed, and the occiput is rounded rather than sharply flexed. There is no strong occipital torus. Other differences are less easily documented, because of damage to the specimens. The glenoid cavity is in fact similar in form to that of African *Homo erectus*, as noted by Hublin (1986), although the postglenoid process tends to be relatively large in earlier *Homo*. The tympanic plate, usually not well preserved, seems to be less thickened inferiorly.

If it is accepted that these features do distinguish *Homo erectus* from *Homo habilis*, then it is appropriate to touch briefly on the question of synapomorphy relative to *Homo sapiens*. Some of the traits interpreted as derived for *Homo erectus* are certainly shared with later humans. Increased brain size is one example, although cranial capacity is still substantially lower in *Homo erectus* than in modern man. While I have not listed it, flexion or kyphosis of the cranial base may constitute another trend. Laitman (1985) has found that changes in the basicranial line are first apparent in *Homo erectus*, even if specimens such as OH 9 are still primitive in this feature.

Many workers have stressed that other characters of *Homo erectus* also occur in early representatives of *Homo sapiens*. It is true that crania from Broken Hill and Lake Ndutu in Africa, and Petralona and Arago Cave in Europe, possess heavy brows, flattened frontals, an angled occiput and (in some cases) thick vault bones. At the same time, these later Middle Pleistocene hominids differ from *Homo erectus*. They exhibit a number of novel traits, shared only with recent humans. It is this evidence which has prompted many authorities to group these 'archaic' individuals with *Homo sapiens*.

Strictly speaking, characters which are shared by the two species cannot be considered autapomorphic for *Homo erectus*. Such specializations may be labeled synapomorphies, but it must be recognized that they have only a (very) limited distribution in *Homo sapiens*. Other derived aspects of frontal form and parietal and occipital morphology, together with the anatomy of the glenoid cavity and tympanic plate, are useful for distinguishing *Homo erectus*. Individually or as complexes, these traits should be listed in any species diagnosis. Many additional features which are clearly primitive, in the sense of being shared by *Homo erectus* with earlier *Homo* or australopithecines, need not be emphasized as diagnostic but do of course provide descriptive information. All of this anatomical information defines a species spread from Africa to Asia by the onset of the Middle Pleistocene. *Homo erectus* crania are built to a common plan, which is substantially different from that seen in other hominids.

Trends in *Homo erectus*

If it is agreed that *Homo erectus* is a real taxon, distinct from other representatives of *Homo*, then it must be determined whether important morphological changes have occurred within the species or whether instead relative stability has prevailed over long periods. This can be done quantitatively, by measuring aspects of skeletal or dental form for individuals drawn from assemblages of different age. Of course the success of such an approach to evolutionary trends will depend on how securely the fossils can be dated. While there are still problems, many of the more important specimens can be placed at least tentatively in chronological frameworks. Comments on the stratigraphic setting of *Homo erectus* discoveries are presented in earlier chapters, and it is appropriate to summarize the information relevant to dating which is now available.

CHRONOLOGICAL FRAMEWORKS

Remains of *Homo erectus* have been recovered from sites which are widely dispersed geographically, and there is evidence which suggests that these collections differ greatly in absolute age. Some comparisons for Africa and Asia are provided in Figure 39. It is clear that fossils from the Turkana basin are among the oldest on record. KNM-ER 3733 and KNM-ER 3883 are from the upper part of the Koobi Fora Formation. The first cranium, recovered in Area 104 at Koobi Fora, was located in sediments just below the Koobi Fora Tuff Complex and is likely to be more than 1.6 million years old. Feibel, Brown & McDougall (1989) now estimate the most probable age to be 1.78 million years. The second individual, from a slightly higher stratigraphic horizon at Ileret, is somewhat younger. Cranial and postcranial remains attributed to *Homo erectus* are known also from Beds II, III, IV and the Masek Beds at Olduvai Gorge. The Hominid 9 (OH 9) braincase from LLK in upper Bed II is about 1.2 million years old and therefore postdates the Turkana material by several hundred thousand years. The very incomplete cranium of OH 12 and the postcranial material of OH 28 are derived from Bed IV deposits. As is the case with the upper part of Bed II, these sediments cannot be dated directly by radiometric methods. However, estimates of 0.83 and 0.62 million years for the lower and upper boundaries of Bed IV have been obtained by measuring sediment thicknesses.

Nearly all of these East African fossils are more ancient than those

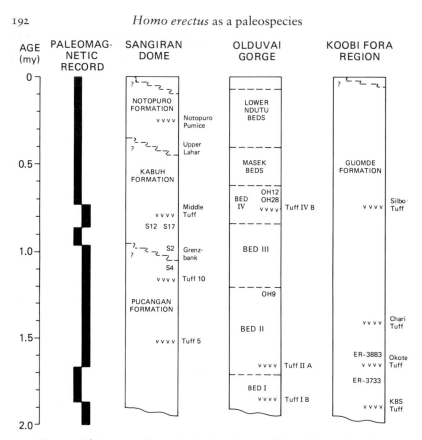

Fig. 39. Pleistocene chronologies for Java and East Africa, based on radiometric dates for marker tuffs and paleomagnetic determinations. Positions of only a few of the more important fossils attributed to *Homo erectus* are shown. This species is present in the Turkana basin more than 1.6 million years ago, but its first appearance at Sangiran is considerably more recent.

from Ternifine and the Atlantic coast of Morocco. The latter are probably close in age to the assemblages from Zhoukoudian in China. Dates for the Indonesian hominids are less certain. Recent studies of fauna collected from Dubois' excavations suggest that Trinil may be older than neighboring localities such as Kedung Brubus. If this 'new' biostratigraphy is correct, then *Homo erectus* at Trinil may be older than hominids associated elsewhere with a 'Jetis' fauna. Comparisons with Sangiran indicate that elements of a Trinil fauna as currently defined occur in Grenzbank deposits, where they are roughly contemporary with the first humans at this locality.

At Sangiran, *Homo* is present mainly in the Kabuh Formation, while a few individuals may be derived from Pucangan levels. The locations of some of the discoveries are not known precisely. Recent attempts to clarify relative ages of the Sangiran hominids by analysis of bone fluorine content seem promising. Matsu'ura (1982) shows that Sangiran 4 may be from the uppermost Pucangan Formation, and he notes that the fluorine content of Sangiran 2 best matches that of material from Grenzbank or lower Kabuh levels. The Sangiran 12 and Sangiran 17 crania give fluorine measurements compatible with derivation from lower or middle Kabuh horizons. Some questions raised by magnetic polarity determinations and radiometric dates remain to be resolved, but it now looks as though most of the Sangiran hominids may be less than 1.0 million years in age.

EVOLUTION OF THE BRAIN

One character which is of special interest in any discussion of evolutionary trends is brain size. It is widely recognized that the brain of early *Homo* is larger than that of *Australopithecus*, and there is a clear tendency for endocranial volume to increase in the *Homo* lineage (Tobias, 1971b). This increase seems to be relative as well as absolute (Pilbeam & Gould, 1974; Holloway and Post, 1982; Martin, 1983). However, the situation with respect to individual species is less well documented. Fossils attributed to *Homo habilis* exhibit much variation in cranial capacity. These differences are usually explained as a consequence of sex dimorphism, but there is now substantial doubt that crania as small as KNM-ER 1813 and as large as KNM-ER 1470 can be accommodated in a single taxon (Wood, 1985; Stringer, 1986a). If two groups of early *Homo* are recognized, then within-species trends of the sort identified by Cronin *et al.* (1981) and Tobias (1982) will be less easy to describe, and it will no longer be possible to view all of the specimens as part of a lineage also containing *Homo erectus*.

Brain volume for *Homo erectus* has been investigated by several workers, who have reached rather divergent conclusions. A tentative suggestion of my own is that later members of this species show an increase in cranial capacity in comparison to earlier ones, although this trend is not significant. Especially when individuals better assigned to early *Homo* or to archaic *Homo sapiens* are omitted from consideration, there is little evidence for gradual, progressive change (Rightmire, 1981). This finding has been criticized by Wolpoff (1984) and by Bilsborough & Wood (1986). The latter authors argue that a more definite trend will be apparent if 'small, late and taxonomically contentious' specimens are put aside. This may be correct, but of course it will be a mistake to ignore individuals which are smaller than expected, because they fall in a late time period. I agree that sorting is crucial, and hominids which are so incomplete as to preclude identification as *Homo erectus* should be dropped from the analysis.

Wolpoff (1984) offers his own assessment of change among Early Pleistocene, early Middle Pleistocene and later Middle Pleistocene subsets of this material. By his reading of measurements obtained from some 22 crania, brain size undergoes a dramatic and continuous increase throughout the history of the species. Wolpoff notes that the average cranial capacity for late *Homo erectus* is about 30% greater than the mean calculated for the Early Pleistocene assemblage, and contends that this is clear evidence for gradualism. However, if three of the fossils are excluded from this tabulation for reasons detailed elsewhere (Rightmire, 1986c), this picture is sharply altered. There is actually a decrease in brain volume in the group of early Middle Pleistocene age, as compared to the Early Pleistocene specimens from East Africa and Indonesia. Average capacity is somewhat greater in the later Middle Pleistocene subset, and the difference between the two Middle Pleistocene assemblages is significant, as Wolpoff demonstrates. But when the Early Pleistocene crania are compared to the most recent group, the difference is small and does not quite reach significance when a *t*-test is applied (Rightmire, 1986c). Interestingly, it is just this contrast that one would expect to be most pronounced, if brain increase were linked to time.

Confusion surrounding this issue can be dispelled only if there is agreement about specimens to be included in the taxon. The present study is based on the material listed in Table 27. Justification for sorting most of these individuals to *Homo erectus* is provided in previous chapters, while the two crania from Gongwangling and Hexian that I have not treated earlier are universally acknowledged to belong to the same species. The assemblages are arranged in an approximate chronological sequence. Since dating is uncertain, especially for the Asian hominids, even this ordering of the fossils is subject to change as better information is obtained.

A search for trends in the data may involve comparing early and late groups, as proposed by Wolpoff and other workers. In order to put aside entirely questions of absolute age, it is advantageous simply

Table 27. *Endocranial volume estimates for the more complete* Homo
erectus *crania from Asia and Africa*

Locality and specimen number[a]		Cranial capacity (ml)	Reference
Ngandong	I	1172	Holloway (1980)
Ngandong	6	1251	,,
Ngandong	7	1013	,,
Ngandong	11	1231	,,
Ngandong	12	1090	,,
Hexian		1025	Wu & Dong (1982)
Zhoukoudian	V	1140	Chiu *et al.* (1973)
Salé		880	Holloway (1981b)
Zhoukoudian	II	1030	Weidenreich (1943)
Zhoukoudian	III	915	,,
Zhoukoudian	VI	850[b]	,,
Zhoukoudian	X	1225	,,
Zhoukoudian	XI	1015	,,
Zhoukoudian	XII	1030	,,
Olduvai	12	727	Holloway (1973)
Sangiran	10	855	Holloway (1981a)
Sangiran	12	1059	,,
Sangiran	17	1004	,,
Gongwangling		780	Woo (1966)
Trinil	2	940	Holloway (1981a)
Sangiran	2	813	,,
Sangiran	4	908	,,
Olduvai	9	1067	Holloway (1973)
East Turkana	3883	804	Holloway (1983)
West Turkana	15000	900	Walker (pers. comm.)
East Turkana	3733	848	Holloway (1983)

[a]Specimens are listed in approximate chronological order.
[b]This value for Zhoukoudian VI is estimated by Weidenreich (1943, p. 114).

to lump specimens by region or locality and to proceed without reference to divisions of Pleistocene time. For example, the four crania from the Turkana basin and Olduvai Bed II can be treated as one group, with an average capacity of about 905 ml. When this group is compared to a later Asian assemblage composed of all (five) measurable Sangiran individuals, there is a very modest increase amounting to just over 20 ml. This difference is small and insignificant ($t = -0.318$, $p > 0.3$). If instead the East African subset is contrasted to the Zhoukoudian population, the difference is somewhat greater.

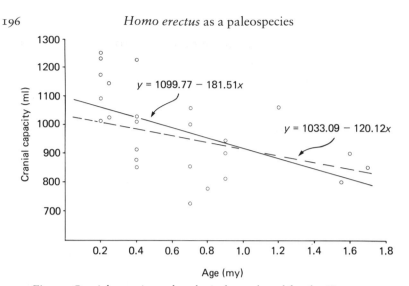

Fig. 40. Cranial capacity and geological age plotted for the *Homo erectus* specimens listed in Table 27. The regression relationship calculated for all 26 crania (solid line) shows that brain size increases in the more recent individuals. When the poorly dated Ngandong skulls are dropped from the analysis, the (dashed) regression line is flatter, and the slope is no longer significantly different from zero. Here there is less evidence for a trend toward brain expansion.

The (seven) Locality 1 specimens give an average volume of about 1029 ml, which exceeds the African mean by 124 ml. Here there are more definite signs of change, although the difference is still short of significance ($t = -1.618$, $p > 0.1$). The Ngandong crania are larger, and there is little doubt that brain expansion can be documented for some of the latest *Homo erectus* populations of the Far East.

Another approach to trend analysis is more rigorous but does require that absolute dates be assigned to each locality. Least-squares regression of endocranial volume on geological age is a method that I have applied before, to similar material (Rightmire, 1981, 1985). When dates are supplied for all 26 of the fossils listed in the table, a linear equation relating brain size (y) to time (x) can be constructed:

$$y = 1099.77 - 181.51x$$

This relationship is plotted in Figure 40. Here it is evident that a number of the more recent specimens have large cranial capacities, and the regression slope shows brain volume to be increasing at a rate of about 181 ml/my. The 95% confidence limits calculated for this coefficient (-181.51 ± 113.87) do not include zero, so it may be concluded that the trend is real.

A note of caution should be emphasized at this point. This result is heavily influenced by the date assigned to the Ngandong hominids, which places them at the near end of the Pleistocene time scale. In fact, the (true) age of the Ngandong assemblage is unknown but may well be greater than 200 000 years. Given this uncertainty, it is appropriate to recompute the regression relationship for the 21 individuals for which firmer dating is available. If the Ngandong crania are dropped from the analysis, the equation becomes:

$$y = 1033.09 - 120.12x$$

which is also plotted in Figure 40. This (dashed) line has a lower slope, and the 95% confidence limits (-120.12 ± 125.78) do include zero. There is now no evidence that the increase in brain size is statistically significant. Neither least-squares regression nor other approaches to the data of Table 27 support unequivocally a claim that there is continuous expansion of the vault within *Homo erectus*.

OTHER DIMENSIONS OF THE CRANIUM

Along with brain volume, other characters should be included in a survey of trends. Bilsborough (1976) has discussed change in the teeth, face, cranial base and other complexes for early and late *Homo erectus*, while Wolpoff (1984) has examined 12 linear dimensions of the cranium, lower jaw and dentition. The latter include four separate assessments of vault breadth, length and height of the braincase, measurements of the mandibular corpus, and M_1 breadth. Wolpoff finds that, with some exceptions, the average differences between Early Pleistocene and later Middle Pleistocene assemblages are 'marked and significant'.

My own study of the vault is limited to four measurements which can be taken for most of the individuals listed in Tables 23 and 24, as well as for additional specimens. What constitutes a 'key' character can always be questioned, but supraorbital torus thickness, cranial base breadth, width of the occipital squama and curvature of the occiput are all features incorporated in the description of *Homo erectus* provided in Chapter 6. Patterns of variation in these dimensions should supply important clues concerning morphological change or stasis in the braincase.

Averages of the four measurements for six groups of *Homo erectus*

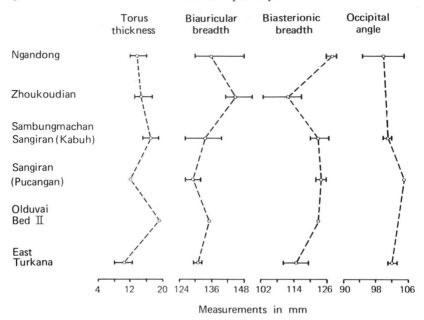

Fig. 41. Patterns of change in four characters of the cranial vault. *Homo erectus* assemblages are arranged in approximate chronological order, beginning with the most ancient specimens from East Africa and ending with later fossils from Zhoukoudian and Ngandong. Averages and observed ranges are plotted for each group.

are plotted in Figure 41. The supraorbital torus is lightly built in the three Turkana specimens but much heavier (19 mm) in the case of OH 9. The brow is thinner again in Sangiran 2, thicker in the Kabuh group, and then only slightly smaller in the later crania. Here the pattern is one of fluctuation, and there is no trend, as noted also by Wolpoff (1984). Biauricular breadth seems to increase in the larger crania, first in Africa and then in Asia. The broadest bases are found at Zhoukoudian, where the average for four individuals is 145 mm. It is this increase which leads Wolpoff to conclude that the difference between early and late *Homo erectus* is significant, but it should be pointed out that biauricular breadth decreases again in the Ngandong assemblage. The latter value (136 mm) is about the same as the means recorded for the Kabuh crania and for OH 9. Bilsborough & Wood (1986) suggest that basicranial breadth is in fact a character in which little change would be expected.

Biasterionic width shows a somewhat different pattern. There is lateral expansion of the occiput in OH 9 and in the earlier Asian groups, relative to the condition found at East Turkana and at Zhoukoudian. Wolpoff's data for this feature do not match my own, but the changes he detects do not reach significance. A substantial jump in biasterionic breadth does occur in the Ngandong crania. Here the nuchal plane is deeply excavated as well as broad, and development of a transverse torus is extreme for *Homo erectus*. Whether this increase in the area occupied by the nuchal muscles is correlated with enlargement of the anterior dentition, as argued by Wolpoff (1984), is not possible to say. No teeth for the Ngandong hominids are available for study.

The occipital angle records curvature of the occipital bone. Larger angles indicate rounding of the profile, while smaller values are associated with greater flexion. Two of the Turkana crania can be measured, and the average (102°) is not very different from results obtained for the Indonesian groups. Comparable figures are not given by Weidenreich (1943) for Zhoukoudian, but the Ngandong mean (100°) is almost identical to that for the much earlier Turkana specimens. Certainly no trend toward greater rounding of the occipital profile in later *Homo erectus* can be discerned.

THE MANDIBLE AND DENTITION

Measurements of the mandible and lower molar teeth are plotted in Figure 42. The fossils are again grouped by localities, arranged in a rough chronological progression. Jaws from the Koobi Fora region are the oldest, followed by material attributed to Grenzbank or Pucangan deposits at Sangiran. Specimens from Olduvai Beds III/IV (undivided) and Ternifine are somewhat younger. Placement of Zhoukoudian before the Moroccan sites is arbitrary, as these assemblages are likely to be of comparable antiquity. Data for the mandibles are taken mostly from Table 26. Measurements of a few other individuals, including KNM-ER 1506 and KNM-ER 1808 from Koobi Fora and K I, M and the 1959 jaw from Zhoukoudian, are also used in the analysis.

Corpus height can be taken for all (four) of the East Turkana fossils, and the average is 31.5 mm. This figure increases modestly to 35.0 mm for the three Sangiran jaws, drops again at Olduvai, and then fluctuates through the Middle Pleistocene. There is substantial overlap of the ranges observed for the several assemblages, and overall change is slight. Corpus breadth is also rather stable, at least to the

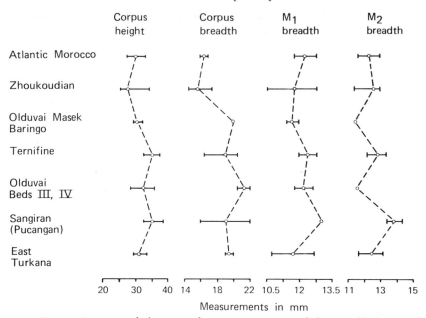

Fig. 42. Patterns of change in four measurements of the mandibular corpus and lower molar teeth. *Homo erectus* assemblages are arranged in approximate chronological order, beginning with the most ancient specimens from East Africa and ending with later fossils from Zhoukoudian and the Atlantic coast of Morocco. Averages and observed ranges are plotted for each group.

time of the lower Masek Beds at Olduvai. Averages at Zhoukoudian and at the Moroccan sites are somewhat lower, however, and here a trend toward decreasing breadth is more apparent. These results stand in contrast to the situation reported by Wolpoff (1984), who finds that both height and breadth of the corpus decrease 'dramatically' through the *Homo erectus* span. My own data, drawn from all of the principal sites, provide only marginal support for Wolpoff's conclusions.

Means and ranges plotted for lower molar breadths are calculated for teeth *in situ* in the jaws. Left or right (not both) sides are utilized, and isolated specimens are ignored. Measurements for Zhoukoudian are those reported by Weidenreich (1937, 1945). Figure 42 shows that buccolingual breadth of M_1 increases from 11.7 mm at East Turkana to 12.9 mm for the early Sangiran specimens. Averages for all of the later assemblages are intermediate between these values, and no trend can be documented. For M_2, the pattern is similar, and there is not much evidence for systematic reduction in width of the posterior teeth within *Homo erectus*.

The importance of this observation has been questioned by Bilsborough & Wood (1986), who suggest that M_1 breadth is relatively stable for all hominids and is therefore not a good character on which to base a discussion of stasis. This claim can in turn be challenged. Means for buccolingual breadth of the cheek teeth of *Australopithecus* species have been compiled by other workers (eg., White, Johanson & Kimbel, 1981), and there is substantial variation among these taxa. M_1 breadths for specimens assigned to *Homo habilis* generally fall within the range recorded for *Homo erectus*, but the molars of later humans are markedly reduced in size. The fact that there is little change in this character for *Homo erectus* does add to our understanding of Pleistocene evolutionary tempos.

Current status of *Homo erectus*

In this chapter, I have touched on several topics which are subject to continuing debate by paleontologists and paleoanthropologists. One is the question of whether extinct species are best defined as arbitrary grades or rather as discrete entities. Another issue concerns the necessity or even the utility of recognizing characters which are unique (autapomorphic) for *Homo erectus*, if this species is to be diagnosed adequately relative to other taxa. A third topic centers on evolutionary tempos and whether gradual change can be documented within *Homo erectus* over a long span of Pleistocene time. Answers to these questions must remain tentative, pending new discoveries and a more sophisticated understanding of the evolutionary process.

I have presented a case for viewing *Homo erectus* as a real taxon. The description of this species lists many characters which are primitive and which are not shared with modern humans. It is also possible to identify some traits which are clearly derived for *Homo erectus* in comparison to earlier *Homo* or *Australopithecus*. These include a heavy brow, midline keeling and parietal tori, strong flexion of the occiput and development of a prominent transverse torus, features of the cranial base and expansion of cranial capacity. Such characters serve to diagnose the species in a more precise way, and it can be argued that *Homo erectus* is not simply an arbitrarily defined segment of a lineage. This paleospecies had ancestors and probably left descendants, but these groups can be distinguished from one another on the basis of morphological comparisons.

Crania referred to *Homo habilis*, widely regarded as ancestral to *Homo erectus*, differ from the latter not only in overall size but also in frontal form, occipital curvature and other ways. There is much variation among individuals which are usually assigned to this species, as I have already pointed out. Both large and small-brained morphs are present in the East African record. This may suggest a high level of sex dimorphism, but differences seem to extend to shape as well as size, and several of the smaller skulls (eg., KNM-ER 1813) depart from the morphology of larger *Homo habilis* (eg., KNM-ER 1470) in characters that are not obviously related to sex. It is possible, even likely, that two taxa are represented. If this is the case, then only one group can be ancestral to later *Homo*.

How such species may be related to one another or to *Homo erectus* must be decided on anatomical grounds. Brain size may be used to link *Homo habilis* with *Homo erectus*, for example, or resemblances in the facial skeleton may be taken as evidence that the smaller-brained taxon is the better antecedent of later humans. At the moment, there is no consensus on this issue. A complicating factor is that some early *Homo* specimens overlap in time with *Homo erectus*. OH 13 from middle Bed II at Olduvai must be about the same age or even younger than specimens such as KNM-ER 3733 and KNM-ER 730 from the Koobi Fora region and the boy from Nariokotome. Other fossils including KNM-ER 1470 are older, but the transformation leading to *Homo erectus* must have taken place relatively soon after the first appearance of the genus *Homo*.

Following the emergence of *Homo erectus*, systematic change is not easily documented. There is a trend toward endocranial expansion, which is apparent particularly in the later assemblages at Zhoukoudian and Ngandong. When the Ngandong crania are included with all other *Homo erectus* individuals in a linear regression of brain size on time, the slope shows brain volume to be increasing at a rate of about 180 ml/my. However, there is much doubt about the age of the Ngandong hominids, and assigning them a latest Middle Pleistocene date does bias the analysis. If the regression line is constructed without reference to Ngandong, the slope drops to about 120 ml/my. This result cannot be distinguished from zero, and there is no evidence that the trend is statistically significant.

Other characters change slowly or not at all. Thickness of the supraorbital torus and the angle expressing flexion of the occiput undergo minor fluctuations throughout the history of *Homo erectus*. Vault widths show more variation, and biauricular breadth does tend to increase in the later Asian groups. Height of the mandibular corpus remains relatively stable, while corpus breadth decreases more regularly with time. For the lower molar teeth, no patterns can be discerned. Buccolingual breadths of M_1 and M_2 are about the same at Zhoukoudian as in the much earlier Turkana hominids, and certainly there is no indication of any dramatic reduction in posterior tooth size.

Toward the close of the Middle Pleistocene, there are signs that some of these traits begin to change more rapidly. It is during this period that populations of *Homo erectus* must have given way to the first representatives of a new species. How this transition occurred, and whether it took place gradually in several different geographic areas or perhaps in a more restricted region, are important problems. Fossils which provide information about archaic *Homo sapiens* are known from Europe and Africa as well as Asia. Some of the key specimens are discussed in Chapter 8.

8

The transition to more modern forms

Early in the Middle Pleistocene, *Homo erectus* can be documented from fossils found in the south, eastern and northwestern parts of Africa, in the Far Eastern tropics, and in the cooler reaches of northern China. Populations inhabiting these far-flung regions of the Old World are anatomically similar, and the morphology of the species seems to have changed little over more than a million years. Differences in behavior are apparent from careful study of the prehistoric record, however. In Africa, Middle Pleistocene humans utilized an Acheulian technology, while at sites such as Zhoukoudian in China, the chopping tools associated with *Homo erectus* do not include handaxes. The extent to which these changes reflect divergent practices of procuring food or processing other materials is still not clear. In Java, few stone tools of any sort are found in the deposits yielding ancient hominids. It has been argued that these people of the southeast Asian forests used bamboo or other woods, rather than stone, to manufacture implements. These lines of evidence suggest that groups of *Homo erectus* were adapting differently to local circumstances. Some bands presumably coped more efficiently than others, although the pace of technological and cultural advance seems to have been slow in most regions. Over the course of millenia, many local populations probably decreased in size or died out altogether.

A plausible scenario is that such extinctions became more common later in the Middle Pleistocene, as a new form of *Homo* evolved and spread across the landscape. Hominids which differ significantly from *Homo erectus* are known from Europe, where some of the more

spectacular discoveries have come from Petralona in Greece and
Arago Cave in France. Other localities, such as Mauer, Bilzingsleben
and Vertesszöllös, are likely to be equally ancient, although the
fossils recovered at these sites are less complete and consequently less
informative. Dates are very approximate for all of these European
specimens. Even the oldest (Mauer?) may be less than 450 000 years in
age (Cook *et al.*, 1982). Crania which display an advanced morphology have turned up also in Africa, at Bodo in Ethiopia, Lake Ndutu
near Olduvai Gorge, Broken Hill (now Kabwe) and Elandsfontein. In
China, important discoveries have been made at Dali and other sites.
As in Europe, dating is very imprecise, although it can be established
that the fossils cover a substantial span of Middle Pleistocene time.

The transition from *Homo erectus* to more modern humans must
have occurred across much of the Old World, but this event can be
reconstructed only in rough outline. The record has been interpreted
in very different ways. Many workers argue that there has been continuity in different geographic regions. It is assumed that change was
gradual and that populations of late *Homo erectus* were succeeded by
local populations of *Homo sapiens* in an unbroken progression. Few
if any groups became extinct. Here the distinction between the two
species is seen as arbitrary or is simply ignored. Emphasis is placed
instead on differences among the people of major geographic provinces, who are thought to have evolved in (partial) isolation for long
periods. This is the view of Weidenreich and Carleton Coon, and it
has been developed more recently by Milford Wolpoff and his colleagues (see references in Chapter 7).

An opposing view, adopted here, is that *Homo erectus* is a stable
taxon, distinct in important ways from all later Pleistocene humans.
In this scenario, archaic people were pushed toward extinction and
actually replaced by members of an anatomically advanced species.
In some, probably many, regions such extinctions were complete, and
there was no local continuity. If this version of events is more or less
correct, then one would expect to see more abrupt changes in the
record. Traits characteristic of *Homo erectus* would not always be
carried into later populations of the same geographical area, where
instead new trends in morphology should be established. Such novel
features would be shared by all members of the descendant
species, who would have dispersed widely following a later Middle
Pleistocene origin.

These are large questions, and a full review of the pertinent evidence would be out of place in this work on *Homo erectus*. Descriptions of only a few of the more important fossil crania and jaws from Africa and Europe are provided here. My emphasis is again comparative, and I have tried in each case to note similarities or differences to *Homo erectus*, as well as to comment on other archaic individuals from the later Middle Pleistocene. These descriptive sections are followed by discussion of the anatomical characters which distinguish post-*erectus* species of *Homo* and trends exhibited within these groups. My aim is to add to our understanding of speciation in *Homo*, even if it is not possible to consider all areas of the Old World in great detail.

The hominid from Lake Ndutu (Fig. 43)

Lake Ndutu is located at the western end of the Main Gorge at Olduvai. Excavations conducted near the lake yielded a human cranium in 1973, and the circumstances surrounding this discovery have been recounted by Mturi (1976). The greenish sandy clay in which the remains occur is overlaid by a hard, root-marked tuff, which may

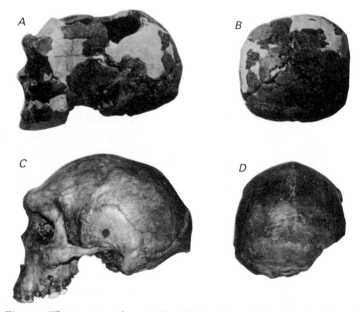

Fig. 43. The cranium from Lake Ndutu photographed in (A) lateral and (B) posterior views, compared to the hominid from Broken Hill (C & D).

represent the Norkilili Member as known from the upper part of the Masek Beds exposed at Olduvai. If this is the case, then the assemblage may approach 400 000 years or so in age (Hay, 1976; M. D. Leakey & Hay, 1982). However, Lake Ndutu lies outside of the immediate Olduvai tectonic zone, and it is not possible without more fieldwork to be entirely certain of this correlation with the well established Olduvai sequence. Hay (pers. comm.) notes that the mineral content of the Ndutu tuff is similar to that of the Norkilili Member and different from that of the tuffs of the Masek lower unit. This suggests that the hominid is no older than the top of the Masek Beds. At the same time, mineralogic analysis does not fully distinguish between the upper Masek tuffs, and tuffs of the overlying Ndutu Beds at Olduvai. It is therefore possible that the cranium is younger than Masek age, but the Ndutu lower unit covers a lengthy span of time, perhaps several hundred thousand years. Just where within this range the hominid may fall cannot be established, but a later Middle Pleistocene age is likely.

The cranium itself has been reconstructed by Clarke (1976), who views it as *Homo erectus*. The specimen is rather incomplete, and only parts of the facial skeleton are preserved. The frontal bone is also poorly represented, mostly by a section of supraorbital rim from the left side. Both temporal bones are damaged, but the squama and mastoid region are nearly intact on the left. The parietal is fairly complete on one side, while the occiput, lacking only its basilar portion, is quite well preserved. Measurements of the vault are provided in Table 28. Cranial capacity for the Ndutu hominid has not been determined directly, although at least a partial endocast can probably be obtained from the reconstruction. Using instead my estimate for internal biasterionic breadth, Ralph Holloway has calculated a range of values for brain volume, and I am indebted to him for this help. Holloway's figures, based on regression and using both hominids and pongids as a guide, range from about 1070 ml to 1120 ml. An average is close to 1100 ml (Rightmire, 1983).

Because the frontal bone is broken, the maximum extent of supraorbital development cannot be determined. On the one side where it can be measured, the rounded torus is about 10 mm thick near the frontozygomatic junction. It could not have been much heavier over the center of the orbit. There is a good deal of postorbital constriction. Posteriorly, the frontal profile is steep, but a liberal amount of plaster has been incorporated into the supratoral

Table 28. *Measurements (mm) of the crania from Lake Ndutu, Broken Hill and Petralona*

	Lake Ndutu	Broken Hill	Petralona
Whole vault			
Cranial length	183?	205	208
Basion–nasion length	105?	108?	110
Basion–prosthion length	–	116	116
Maximum cranial breadth	144	145	165
Biauricular breadth	128	140?	150
Frontal bone			
Supraorbital torus thickness			
central	–	23	21
lateral	10.5	16	14
Minimum frontal breadth	–	98	110
Maximum frontal breadth	112?	118	120
Biorbital chord	–	125	126
Frontal breadth index[a]	–	83.0	91.6
Postorbital constriction index[b]	–	78.4	87.3
Frontal sagittal chord	–	120	110
Frontal sagittal arc	–	139	129
Frontal subtense	–	21	20
Frontal angle	–	141	140
Parietal and temporal bones			
Maximum biparietal breadth	–	145?	151
Parietal sagittal chord	–	113	106
Parietal sagittal arc	–	120	114
Lambda–asterion chord	83	91	89
Lambda–asterion arc	91	100	99
Mastoid length	27	27	–

region, and probably frontal fullness has been exaggerated in the reconstruction. Whether there is keeling in the midline cannot be ascertained.

There is no trace of any keeling or heaping up of bone on the parietal vault, where the sagittal suture is preserved along a length of some 65 mm. On the left parietal, which is least complete and to which much plaster has been added, no superior temporal line can be discerned. Near asterion, there is no evidence for formation of any angular torus. Further forward, there is a slight depression in the border of the temporal bone, and this may mark the passage of an inferior line. This line is continuous with the supramastoid crest. Both the crest

Table 28. (cont.)

	Lake Ndutu	Broken Hill	Petralona
Occipital bone			
Biasterionic breadth	113	–	120
Occipital sagittal chord	87	87	92
Occipital sagittal arc	111	–	128
Occipital subtense	30	–	41
Occipital angle	111	–	97
Lambda–inion chord[c]	61	–	65
Inion–opisthion chord[c]	45	–	55
Occipital scale index[d]	73.7	–	84.6
Inion–asterion chord[c]	65	–	–
Foramen magnum length	38?	42?	44
Foramen magnum width	29	–	35
Facial skeleton			
Bimaxillary chord	–	107	120
Malar (cheek) height	–	29	39
Orbit breadth	–	48	44
Orbit height	–	38	34

[a]Frontal breadth index is calculated as the ratio of minimum frontal width to maximum frontal width.
[b]Postorbital constriction index is calculated as the ratio of minimum frontal width to biorbital chord length.
[c]Inion is here considered to lie at the center of the linear tubercle (the junction of the superior nuchal lines) rather than higher on the occipital torus.
[d]Occipital scale index is calculated as the ratio of inion–opisthion chord length to lambda–inion chord length.

and the posterior root of the zygoma are rounded but are not strongly projecting.

On the right, where more of the outer table of the parietal is present, the superior line is still hard to trace. There is some thickening at asterion, but a true torus is not developed. Instead, this region is distinctly flattened, almost hollowed in appearance. This feature is best described as a broad and only slightly depressed angular sulcus, limited anteriorly by the extension onto the parietal bone of the supramastoid crest. Below the crest, the sulcus passes across the face of the mastoid process toward the auditory porus. This (supramastoid) sulcus is shallow and contains no tubercles. The mastoid crest below is irregular and roughened, and it extends right to the tip of the relatively short, pyramidal mastoid process.

The upper scale of the occipital is approximately vertical, while the extensive, flattened nuchal area does not rise quite to the level of the horizontal plane. There is a well developed transverse torus. This is prominent centrally and is still slightly raised at a distance of about 10 mm from the occipital margin. The superior border of the torus is clearly marked near the midline, where there is a roughened external occipital protuberance. Above this protuberance, there is an oval depression or supratoral sulcus. Here there is no uplifting of the surrounding bone to produce a triangular plateau of the sort usually associated with a suprainiac fossa, as described for Neanderthal crania by Santa Luca (1978). The morphology of this supratoral sulcus and the presence of a 'true' external protuberance combine to give the Ndutu occiput an appearance which is also unlike that of *Homo erectus*.

The mound-like transverse torus is bounded inferiorly by the superior nuchal lines. These are slightly raised and converge toward a linear tubercle which is small and indistinct. Below the torus, the impressions left by the *semispinalis* complex are clearly defined. The inferior nuchal lines can be followed laterally, and there are no retromastoid processes. The nuchal surface is generally smooth. There are no bulges associated with *m. rectus capitis posticus major*, and the areas occupied by the superior oblique muscles are outlined only in low relief.

Near the junction of the occiput with the mastoid portion of the temporal bone, there is a short, deep digastric incisure. The medial wall of this groove contributes to what is best called a broad juxtamastoid eminence. This structure is preserved on both sides, but detail is sharper on the right. Here the eminence is divided into medial and lateral parts by a deep (arterial?) channel. Only the more medial ridge may join posteriorly with the superior oblique line, which is very faintly marked. An occipitomastoid crest as described by Weidenreich is thus not strongly expressed.

The glenoid cavity is deep and also comparatively short in anteroposterior extent. The lateral part of the articular tubercle and the ectoglenoid process are broken away, but enough of the articular surface remains to show that the forward wall of the cavity is gently convex. The tubercle itself is slightly raised and more prominent than is usually the case for *Homo erectus*, where the front of the cavity grades smoothly onto the preglenoid planum. The floor of the fossa is straight from side to side and channel-like, and its width (ecto-

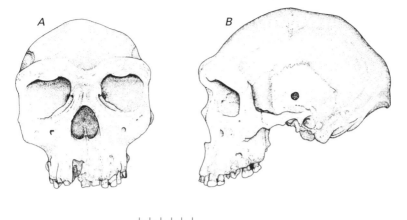

Fig. 44. Drawings of the Broken Hill cranium, as viewed from (A) the facial aspect and (B) the left side.

glenoid–entoglenoid) can be estimated as 25–30 mm. The medial wall of the cavity is damaged, and part of the entoglenoid process is missing. The sphenotemporal suture seems to bisect this process, but whether a sphenoid spine of the sort found in modern *Homo sapiens* was developed from this region can no longer be determined. A prominent postglenoid process is present.

The tympanic bone is more complete, and the lateral side of the plate surrounding the auditory porus is clearly thickened. Its inferior border is much thinner than is usually the case for *Homo erectus*. A styloid sheath is preserved, and on one side the root of the styloid process is still in place. Here there is no departure from the anatomy expected for modern humans.

The Broken Hill assemblage (Figs 43 & 44)

Another collection of bones and artifacts was recovered at Broken Hill in 1921. The famous cranium is very well preserved and is a most important find. In addition to this specimen, a broken maxilla, a parietal bone, and postcranial remains of several individuals were discovered in cave deposits at the site (now Kabwe), north of Lusaka in Zambia. The fossils are known to have come from different sections of the cave fill, and analysis of the chemical content of the bones has never satisfactorily settled the question of whether the postcranial parts are contemporary with the skull. The pelvic and limb material has been regarded as essentially modern anatomically, but Stringer (1986b) has pointed out that one of the innominate bones has a thickened iliac pillar, similar to that expressed in *Homo erectus*. Dating is also problematical. Radiometric methods cannot be used at Broken Hill, but fauna collected from the deposits suggests considerable antiquity. More than 20 species of large mammal are present, and several of these are extinct forms (Klein, 1973). A reasonable estimate is that the Broken Hill cranium, and possibly the right innominate, are of later Middle Pleistocene age.

The adult cranium is low in outline, with massive brows. The supraorbital torus is thicker than that of most other Pleistocene hominids and is even a little heavier than that of OH 9. The facial skeleton is large and is especially broad across the orbits. Relative to a chord linking the auditory openings, neither nasion nor subspinale is as far forward as in European or Near Eastern Neanderthals (Howells, 1975, 1982). The radius taken from this same chord to prosthion does approach or even exceed Neanderthal values, however, and it is evident that the alveolar process of the Broken Hill maxilla is long and projecting. Nearly all of the upper teeth are still in place, but many of the crowns are severely eroded.

Behind the brows, the frontal bone is flattened to either side of a blunt midline keel. This part of the braincase appears relatively narrow, and the postorbital constriction index comparing minimum frontal width to the biorbital chord is 78.4. Although this figure is higher than any recorded for African *Homo erectus*, the Broken Hill frontal is somewhat more constricted than that of archaic specimens from Asia. The parietal bone is expanded, however, and both sagittal and lambdoid margins are longer than in *Homo erectus*. There is no further keeling along the sagittal suture. The parietal surface shows little bossing, and maximum cranial breadth lies in the supramastoid region rather than higher on the vault. The course of the superior temporal line is clearly marked, and on the left side a rounded angular torus occupies the parietal mastoid angle. A faint angular sulcus is also developed. This sulcus becomes deeper and groove-like as it passes forward onto the temporal bone, and above it the supramastoid crest is prominent.

Much of the upper scale of the occipital is intact, but the lower right half of this bone as well as the rear of the parietal and all of the right temporal are missing. Surface damage extends also from the junction of the upper and lower scales over an area that would include the center of the transverse torus. The part of the torus remaining is sharply defined and overhangs the nuchal plane below. A faint supratoral sulcus extends laterally toward the lambdoid suture. Unfortunately, neither the extent of sulcus formation near the midline nor the design of the (missing) linear tubercle can be determined.

The nuchal plane of the occiput is flattened and shows only slight relief resulting from muscular insertions. The area below the torus occupied by the *semispinalis* complex is clearly delineated, and along the midline, extending for a distance of several millimeters back from the foramen magnum, there is a sharp crest rising between the depressions for *m. rectus capitis posticus minor*. The principal branch of the inferior nuchal line can be followed laterally to a position behind the insertion for *m. rectus capitis posticus major*, where it produces a low eminence. An anterior extension of this line, marking the lateral border of *rectus capitis* attachment, converges toward the occipitomastoid suture and the adjacent mastoid groove.

The anatomy of the mastoid region is perfectly preserved on the left, although the mastoid process itself is pathologically affected. The superior nuchal line can be traced from the occipital onto the lateral aspect of the process, where it merges with the mastoid crest. This crest is elevated superiorly, where it is accentuated by the deep supramastoid sulcus. However, the crest is continued down and forward toward the tip of the mastoid process and does not present a distinct protuberance or tubercle localized behind the auditory meatus, as in European Neanderthal crania. The posterolateral surface of the mastoid is flattened and heavily scarred by muscle attachment.

The digastric fossa, up to 5.3 mm wide, can be followed for a distance of 39 mm toward the stylomastoid foramen. Medially, a parallel segment of the occipitomastoid suture is deeply incised, and this narrow channel may mark the passage of the occipital artery. No occipital groove is otherwise apparent. There is some heaping up of bone on the medial side of the suture, but an occipitomastoid crest in the sense of Weidenreich (1943) is not developed. Protrusion of the entire medial margin of the digastric incisure is not nearly so extreme as in Neanderthals and rather resembles the condition seen in many modern crania.

In comparison to OH 9, the glenoid fossa of Broken Hill is shallow, while its width is nearly the same. Breadth of the articular tubercle is 31 mm. The tubercle is somewhat hollowed, especially as it approaches the zygomatic root, but is still prominent enough to stand out against the preglenoid surface. The inner wall of the fossa is made up of squamous temporal, and the entoglenoid process is primarily of temporal origin. The sphenotemporal suture passes within a millimeter or so of the medial extent of the glenoid surface, serving to separate this cavity from a downward projecting sphenoid spine. This spine does not contribute directly to the fossa wall and is not particularly large. Such a spine is not present in *Homo erectus*, but in the Broken Hill individual it is oriented in about the same way as in modern humans. Its medial border appears to be flattened to form with the adjacent temporal a narrow groove for the cartilaginous part of the auditory tube.

The postglenoid tubercle is irregular in form and extends downward about 8 mm from the upper border of the auditory meatus. Much of the rest of the posterior wall of the glenoid cavity is made up of the tympanic plate (broken laterally, just where it should define the anterior border of the meatus). This plate is prolonged medially and thickened to create a heavy vaginal process or sheath for the styloid. Although the styloid itself is broken, a circular opening marks its original position. Still further medially and just anterior to the carotid canal, the tympanic bone produces an irregular tubercle, closely applied on one side to the root of the sphenoid spine and on the other to the petrous portion of the temporal. Here there is some departure from the more typical modern human case, where the sphenoid spine is larger and underhangs the adjacent tympanic or petrous temporal.

Petralona (Fig. 45)

The large cave at Halkidiki, near Petralona in northern Greece, has been a focus of anthropological interest for nearly three decades. Following the discovery of a fossil cranium, several sets of excavations have been carried out, and quantities of animal bones have been collected. The stratigraphy of parts of the deposits has been investigated, and a number of workers have tried to provide dates for different levels in the site. Unfortunately, many of the published reports are in disagreement. There is little doubt that some of the fauna is quite ancient, as argued by Kurtén & Poulianos (1981). However, clear association of the hominid with other animal fossils has never been

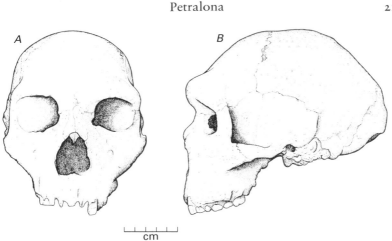

Fig. 45. Drawings of the Petralona cranium, viewed from (A) the facial
aspect and (B) the left side.

established. A date of about 200 000 years for calcite encrusting the
human cranium has been obtained by Hennig *et al.* (1981), but this
approach must yield only a minimum age for the remains. At present
it can be concluded that the Petralona specimen is of Middle Pleistocene antiquity, and perhaps the balance of evidence points toward a
date later in this interval.

The cranium is exceptionally complete. The facial skeleton is
intact, and nearly all of the stalagmitic matrix which originally coated
this region has been removed. A little of the matrix remains in cracks,
in between the teeth on the left side, and inside the nasal cavity. There
is some damage to the zygomatic process of the right maxilla, and on
this side the temporal process of the zygomatic bone is missing. All of
the incisors have been lost, as has P³ on the right side. The crown of
right C is broken, and the crown of right M¹ has also been badly
damaged, apparently during cleaning of the specimen.

Although the frontal bone is undistorted, the rear of the vault
shows slight deformation. This causes the right parietal to bulge a
little more than the left, and on the right side the temporal squama is
displaced laterally, as noted by Wolpoff (1980b). The occipital is well
preserved and clear of matrix over all but its basilar portion. Unfortunately the temporal bones are damaged, and the mastoid processes
are broken on both sides. The petrous and tympanic parts of both
temporals, and the glenoid cavities, are still coated with a layer of
stalagmite, as are the sphenoid body and the pterygoids. Inside the

cranium, patches of matrix adhere to the endocranial surface, but a reasonably complete endocast can be obtained. Brain volume is estimated as close to 1230 ml.

Since earlier studies of Petralona carried out by Stringer, Howell & Melentis (1979), Wolpoff (1980b) and de Bonis & Melentis (1982) have tended to emphasize comparisons with other European fossils, especially the Neanderthals, it is appropriate here to discuss similarities and differences with African remains. All of the *Homo erectus* specimens cannot be touched on, but limited comparisons to OH 9 can be carried out. Certainly there are some general resemblances to this large cranium from Olduvai. However, the affinities of Petralona are more likely to lie with *Homo sapiens* than with *Homo erectus*, as has been pointed out by other workers. My descriptive comments are prepared with this in mind, and I have made particular reference to later Middle Pleistocene hominids such as Broken Hill.

The Petralona frontal bone is flattened, and there is little expression of a supratoral sulcus. The brows are very heavy. Torus thickness on the left side must nearly match that recorded for Broken Hill. Division of the torus into separate arches is noted by Stringer, Howell & Melentis (1979), but in fact this separation is not pronounced, and glabella projects strongly above the nasal root. To this extent, there are similarities to archaic African crania, including Broken Hill and Bodo. But the nasion–bregma chord length is less than in Broken Hill, while frontal breadth is greater. The Petralona frontal is thus relatively broader, and there is less postorbital constriction. The anterior temporal lines are not so clearly marked, and there is no keeling in the midline. In these features, Petralona seems to differ from Broken Hill in the same way as does Arago 21.

The facial skeleton is large, and biorbital breadth is about the same as in the Kabwe cranium. The orbit is relatively small, however, and perhaps here as in the dimensions of the nasal cavity there is more resemblance to Arago 21. The mid-facial region is massively built, and cheek height measured either on the maxilla or as a minimum on the zygomatic bone exceeds that of Broken Hill. The maxilla is quite broad, and there is no canine fossa. Wolpoff (1980b) suggests that some features of the maxilla 'foreshadow' the morphology expected in Neanderthals, although he notes that measurements of facial projection are less extreme for Petralona. In fact, radii recording the positions of nasion and prosthion relative to an axis joining the auditory openings are comparable to those of Broken Hill, while subspinale is a little further forward. Other chords locating the lower margin of the cheek and the first upper molar tooth in this same (sagittal) plane of reference are again similar in Petralona and Broken Hill. These values do not demonstrate a strong resemblance to European or Near Eastern Neanderthal populations (Stringer, 1983). Below the nose, the surface of the maxilla is flat, and there is little corrugation associated with the incisor roots. Here there is some contrast to Broken Hill, where the subnasal clivus is deep and forward sloping.

Behind bregma, there is some heaping up of bone along the suture, to form a blunt keel. The superior temporal line can be followed along most of its course and produces a moderate angular torus at the mastoid angle of the parietal bone. This torus is distinct on the right, but on the left side it has been damaged. Both mastoid processes are missing, and some matrix still coats the broken stumps and fills the region just behind the auditory openings. Fortunately, the squamous temporal is better preserved. Its superior border is high and arched as in *Homo sapiens*. A striking feature of the Petralona cranium is the flange-like projection of the posterior zygomatic root. This can be described as a thickened supramastoid crest, which swings upward as it approaches the squamosal suture. This crest is continued only faintly and for a short distance onto the parietal, but between it and the angular torus below, there is a shallow sulcus.

The upper scale of the occipital bone is nearly vertical, as in other archaic *Homo sapiens*. The length of the lambda–inion chord is greater than the length of the nuchal plane. The transverse torus does not stand out in high relief and instead presents a mound-like appearance, rather different from that of Broken Hill. Above it, there is a shallow depression, extending for some distance from the midline. Neither this faint sulcus nor the torus itself reaches as far laterally as asterion. There is no true external occipital protuberance. The superior nuchal lines meet centrally, at a roughened linear tubercle, which is continued forward to join with an external occipital crest. This crest can be followed to the rim of the foramen magnum. Laterally, the superior lines terminate in small, poorly defined retromastoid processes. Beyond these low tubercles, the bone below asterion is damaged or obscured by matrix, so the path taken by the nuchal lines into the mastoid region cannot be ascertained.

The nuchal plane is strongly impressed by muscle markings. The areas occupied by the *semispinalis* complex are hollowed, and depressions located on either side of the external crest, behind the foramen magnum, apparently correspond to the attachments of *m. rectus capitis posticus minor*. More of the nuchal surface is taken up by twin rounded swellings, which contribute posteriorly to formation of the inferior nuchal lines. These areas of swelling subside laterally as they approach the scars left by superior oblique attachment. Because of damage, details concerning form of the digastric incisure and of the occipitomastoid junction are mostly lost. A little of the digastric fossa (filled with matrix) seems to be preserved on the right, and to its medial side there is a trace of raised bone that may represent a juxtamastoid eminence.

Both glenoid cavities are coated with a thin layer of stalagmite, but on the left, enough of the bone is exposed to show that there is an articular tubercle. Without more cleaning, it will be hard to say more about the anterior border of the cavity. Clearly the preglenoid surface (infratemporal fossa) is very restricted in its anteroposterior dimension, in comparison to the more extensive and flattened surface found in OH 9. On this side, both ectoglenoid and postglenoid processes are damaged, although both may be preserved under matrix on the right. The relative contributions of sphenoid and temporal bone to the entoglenoid pyramid remain unknown. The tympanic plate is probably 'thin and relatively vertical' as noted by Stringer *et al.* (1979), but there is definitely a thickened styloid sheath. Details of the anatomy in this region are subject to verification when the fossil has been prepared further.

The Arago remains

Arago Cave is situated in the eastern Pyrenees, near the village of Tautavel in France. This site has been excavated by the de Lumleys, who began work there in 1964. The rather complete but distorted facial portion of a human cranium was found in 1971. More fossils including cranial bones, two partial mandibles, teeth and postcranial parts have since been discovered, along with a large fauna and many artifacts. Studies of the animal remains have not led to a consensus regarding the age of the Arago deposits, and numerous attempts to obtain radiometric dates for bones or travertines have met with only limited success (Cook *et al.*, 1982). As at Petralona, a middle to later Middle Pleistocene age is likely.

THE CRANIUM

In comparison to the large braincase from Bed II at Olduvai, the Arago cranium is less massively constructed. Differences extend both to supraorbital structure and to other aspects of frontal form. The torus itself is thinner, especially laterally near the frontozygomatic margin. Glabella is less prominent, but a central supraglabellar depression is more pronounced, so as to separate the brows. The latter are more strongly arched than is the case for OH 9. The supratoral region is shorter and less shelf-like in appearance. Sulci are faint and restricted in extent, and the frontal squama is already slightly elevated just behind the brows. The inferior temporal line does not stand out in high relief, and this together with the shallower contour of the temporal fossa suggests that at least the anterior portion of *m. temporalis* was not so large in the Arago hominid. Least frontal breadth as measured on a cast of the reconstructed face is greater than that of OH 9 by nearly 20 mm, and the proportions of the two specimens are different. The *Homo erectus* frontal is relatively narrow and displays much more postorbital constriction.

Contrasts in size and form of the parietal bone are also apparent. Since neither bregma nor lambda is preserved on the Olduvai vault, length of the parietal chord can be estimated only roughly. Asterion is present, so the length of the lambdoid margin of the parietal can be determined somewhat more accurately, on the left side where the bone is most complete. In both of these dimensions, the Bed II parietal is almost certainly shorter than Arago 47, and in the case of the lambdoid border, this difference must be more than 15 mm. The smaller Olduvai bone also slopes inward as it rises from the squamosal border, while the side of the Arago vault is more vertical.

The curve of the temporal line is low, in relation to the vertex of the Arago cranium. Over most of its length, this superior line is rounded rather than crested, while a more pronounced, mound-like torus is present at the mastoid angle. Inside the arc produced by the line and angular torus, there is some suggestion of an angular sulcus. This extension of the supramastoid sulcus onto the parietal does not occur in OH 9, although such a depression is found in other *Homo erectus* individuals. It is also expressed in Broken Hill and some other archaic crania usually referred to *Homo sapiens*.

The facial skeletons of Arago 21 and Broken Hill can be compared, although most of the face of OH 9 is missing. The Arago frontal shows no midline keeling, and the arched brows are considerably less thickened than those of the Zambian individual. Biorbital breadth is also less. In other respects, the Arago face is again lighter in construction, with smaller orbits separated by a narrower interorbital region. The frontal process of the maxilla is relatively delicate, and the subnasal clivus is very short. Damage has skewed the Tautavel maxilla slightly to one side, but if this warping is corrected, it does appear that the nasal aperture and midparts of the face are set in a slightly more forward position relative to the cheek bones and lateral margins of the orbits. As noted earlier, the Broken Hill face is longer below the nasal opening, and prognathism is mostly confined to this part of the maxilla.

LOWER JAWS

The two mandibles from Arago may be compared to *Homo erectus* specimens from Olduvai. Measurements are given in Table 29. The corpus of Arago 2 is about the same height as OH 22 but is considerably less robust. Here as in the Olduvai individual, the upper and lower borders of the body are parallel. The lateral prominence is well developed posteriorly and is continued forward as a superior lateral ridge, which fades out below P_4. Neither an intertoral sulcus nor a marginal torus is pronounced, however. The anterior corpus of Arago 2 is cracked and has sustained some loss of bone near the midline, but there is definite incurving of the symphyseal face below the alveolar border. Elements of a mental trigone are present, in contrast to the condition seen in OH 22.

The jaws differ also in details of internal symphyseal form. The Olduvai individual exhibits an extensive alveolar plane, hollowed slightly below the anterior teeth but more rounded laterally. This shelf is bounded behind by a superior transverse torus, clearly visible in cross-section where the bone is broken. Below this shelf, the profile drops steeply toward a small but well defined posterior projection, which is all that remains of an inferior torus. Unfortunately the bone is incomplete just at the midline, and the morphology of the genial region is obscure. On the base, digastric fossa is only faintly marked. This fossa is narrow and faces almost directly downward rather than posteriorly.

The alveolar planum of Arago 2 is a more steeply sloping shelf, shorter than that of OH 22. Even at the midline, posterior projection

Table 29. *Measurements (mm) of the Arago mandibles*

	Symphysis height[a]	Symphysis thickness	Corpus height[b] at M_1	Corpus thickness at M_1	Robusticity index	Cross-sectional area[c]
Arago 2	30.5?	14.0	29.9	15.9	53.1	373.4
Arago 13	–	19.0?	31.1	22.0	70.7	537.4

[a]Symphysis height is taken along the axis of symphyseal inclination, and thickness is measured approximately at a right angle to this axis.

[b]Corpus measurements can be compared to those of Table 26. Height at M_1 is treated as a vertical dimension, and thickness is measured with the caliper arm held parallel to the occlusal surface of the tooth row.

[c]Area (in mm^2) is computed as height × thickness × $\pi/4$.

of the planum is restricted, although a superior torus is present. Below the torus, there is a large shallow depression, within which the genial foramen and tubercles are situated. There is also an inferior torus, which serves to thicken the mandibular base locally at the symphysis. Digastric impressions are perhaps a little deeper than in OH 22 and extend further posteriorly along the undersurface of the body, almost to the level of M_2.

In other respects, the African and European jaws are generally similar, at least in so far as can be determined from the parts preserved. The alveolar process of the Olduvai mandible bulges internally to form an alveolar prominence which is strongest at the position of M_3. This prominence is slightly crested as it swings up and rearward onto the ramus. Here it is continuous with a heavy ridge, termed the triangular torus by Weidenreich. Between this torus and the anterior border of the ramus, the bone is hollowed to produce a buccinator gutter, which narrows as it passes alongside the socket for M_3. The maximum width of this extramolar sulcus is 5 mm.

The body of Arago 2 also shows moderate development of an alveolar prominence. This internal buttress is continued forward from the position of M_3 to merge with the superior transverse torus, which spans the symphysis. Protrusion in the form of uneven swellings is pronounced below the premolar alveoli, and the anterior subalveolar fossa is deep as a result. Here there is some contrast to OH 22, in which the internal contour of the corpus is more rounded, and the anterior subalveolar fossa is not clearly outlined. The medial aspect of the ramus is badly cracked, but a strong triangular torus is present in the Arago specimen. Division of this torus into endocoronoid and endocondyloid cristae is apparent, although the latter is less heavily constructed than in OH 22. Form of the lingula is not exceptional. Anteriorly, a retromolar fossa fills the space behind the M_3 alveolus. This fossa is distinct from the more lateral buccinator gutter, which is approximately 9 mm wide as it opens onto the external surface of the body.

The Arago 13 mandible is larger than Arago 2 and has been described as male by the de Lumleys. The body of this jaw is lowest at the level of M_2/M_3 but gains height further forward, in the region of the premolars and canine alveolus. Upper and lower borders of the corpus thus diverge anteriorly and are not parallel. At the position of M_1, the corpus is both thicker and higher than that of OH 22, and the robusticity index is about the same. A lateral prominence, apparent as a diffuse swelling below the root of the ramus, is slightly less well developed than in the smaller Arago individual. This area of swelling subsides evenly into the lateral contour of the jaw without producing a superior branch, and the wall of the corpus is quite flat. Just under the mental foramen, there is a faint horizontal sulcus. This is shallower than the intertoral sulcus of OH 22 but does define the upper limit of a rounded marginal torus. Anteriorly, bone loss has exposed much of the empty canine alveolus, but the deep and relatively massive canine jugum must have bulged inferiorly. Another sulcus separates this alveolar swelling from the anterior marginal tubercle, poorly defined below. Unfortunately the jaw is broken at the symphysis, so details of chin formation are not quite clear. This region is flattened, although the elements of a (partial) mental trigone may be present in very low relief.

The Arago 13 alveolar plane is hollowed and slightly more extensive than that of Arago 2. A superior transverse torus is visible in cross-section, while the inferior torus is less sharply defined than in the smaller mandible. Digastric impressions are broad and roughened and encroach slightly onto the anterior margin of the base. On the medial aspect of the corpus, the bone of the alveolar border is damaged so as to expose the M_3 roots. An alveolar prominence must have been strongly developed in this region, and the anterior part of the subalveolar fossa is preserved below M_1/M_2. A striking feature of the jaw is the extent to which this alveolar prominence is enlarged as it passes forward, to form a mound-like swelling maximally inflated at the level of the premolars. On the superior aspect of this mound, there are several palpable tubercles, separated by vertical striae. These structures stand out in somewhat greater relief than in the case of Arago 2 and may be described as a mandibular torus. Similar tori occur with varying frequency in modern human populations, in mid-Pleistocene mandibles (eg., several of the Zhoukoudian individuals described by Weidenreich in 1936), and in Pliocene hominids such as Lucy from the Afar in Ethiopia (Johanson et al., 1982). Such tori are not found in any of the Olduvai Homo erectus mandibles, however.

Another point of contrast between Arago 13 and OH 22 concerns the retromolar fossa. In the Arago jaw, this triangular space behind M_3 is large and deeply excavated. The extramolar sulcus is not especially broad, and the anterior border of the ramus is inclined backward. As in Arago 2, the root of the ramus rises from a relatively posterior location, so that almost all of the crown of M_3 is visible when the mandible is viewed from the side. The M_3 crown of OH 22 is missing, but here the ramus is oriented more vertically and would obscure the distal part of the tooth.

Sorting the specimens: one species or several

In the descriptive accounts presented so far, I have provided evidence that the hominids from Lake Ndutu, Broken Hill, Petralona and Arago Cave differ in their morphology from *Homo erectus*. This position is further summarized below. I have also referred to the fossils as representative of *Homo sapiens*, although it is obvious that they display a number of archaic characters. In fact there is legitimate doubt about how Broken Hill or the Arago people should be sorted and how these populations should be named. A number of authorities argue that the European specimens are *Homo erectus*, for example, while others suggest that a name like *Homo heidelbergensis* may be more appropriate. In this section, the question of assigning the mid-Pleistocene fossils to one or several different species is explored in more detail.

THE AFRICAN RECORD

The Ndutu vault is similar in many respects to other discoveries from Africa. In superior view, the cranium is somewhat more rounded than that of Broken Hill and is comparable to the Elandsfontein braincase from South Africa. A resemblance of Ndutu to Elandsfontein is again apparent when the two are viewed from the rear. Both crania have walls which rise steeply from the supramastoid region and appear better filled than those of Broken Hill. Parietal bossing is emphasized especially in Clarke's (1976) reconstruction of Ndutu, which must be approximately correct. The parietal bones could probably be flattened, but these adjustments would have to be minor. Clarke's claim that the Ndutu vault shows more bossing than expected for *Homo erectus* is accurate. Occipital morphology is broadly similar in all three of these African individuals. The upper scale varies in orientation but is close to vertical, rather than forward-sloping as in *Homo erectus*.

In details of occipital and mastoid anatomy, Ndutu is particularly like Broken Hill. The nuchal area is extensive and flattened, and in Ndutu there is a true external occipital protuberance. The mastoid crest is developed along the full length of the mastoid process, and the posterolateral face of this process is flattened rather than convex.

Near the junction of the temporal bone and occiput, there is a deep digastric incisure. The medial wall of this groove contributes to a juxtamastoid eminence. In Broken Hill, the eminence is accentuated by hollowing of the adjacent muscle attachment, but in neither case is there a strong occipitomastoid crest. The juxtamastoid ridge is not as well expressed as in European Neanderthal crania and instead resembles that seen in many modern humans.

The glenoid cavity (deeper in Ndutu) is bounded anteriorly by an articular tubercle which is prominant enough to stand out against the forward surface of the temporal. There is a strong postglenoid process. The medial wall of the Ndutu cavity is broken, so it is not possible to tell whether a sphenoid spine is developed from the entoglenoid region. In Broken Hill, this spine is not very projecting but is oriented in about the same way as in recent *Homo sapiens*. The inferior border of the tympanic plate is thin (as in modern humans) and there is no development of what Weidenreich termed a 'spine of the crista petrosa'. But a styloid sheath is preserved, and in Ndutu the root of the styloid process is still in place.

All of this suggests that the Ndutu hominid should be grouped with other archaic humans from eastern and southern Africa. The small size and relatively low cranial capacity estimated for Ndutu may indicate that this individual is female, whereas the larger specimen from Broken Hill is likely to be male. Characters of the occipital, mastoid and tympanic parts of the cranium, which are quite well preserved, seem to set these hominids apart from *Homo erectus*. A next question is how the African fossils may compare to assemblages from other parts of the Old World, including Europe.

EUROPE

Petralona and Arago 21 are two of the best crania from the European Middle Pleistocene. Brows are large, especially in Petralona where the torus is almost as thickened as in Broken Hill. Division of the brow into separate arches is more noticeable in the case of Arago 21, but here as in Petralona and the African faces, glabella is strongly projecting. The frontal squama is relatively short and broad in both European individuals and postorbital constriction is a little less pronounced. Neither Petralona nor Arago 21 exhibits any midline keeling.

Faces are massively constructed, although the orbits are somewhat smaller than in Broken Hill. Petralona resembles the Zambian specimen in measurements of facial projection except at subspinale, which is slightly further forward relative to an axis through the auditory openings. Comparable measurements cannot be taken for Arago 21, since the temporal bones were not recovered. The Arago face is damaged, but there are signs that the maxillary wall to either side of the nasal opening is more inflated than in other specimens. In Broken Hill, projection of the face is prominent, but there is less involvement of the nose itself or its surrounding architecture.

Neither the Petralona nor the Arago parietal is quite as large as that of Broken Hill. Nevertheless, sagittal chord lengths fall toward the upper end of the range noted for *Homo erectus*, while the lambdoid margins are longer. Clearly the mid-portion of the vault is expanded relative to *Homo erectus*, as is shown also by the overall increase in endocranial capacity. An archaic feature of the parietal bone is the angular torus, which is developed in the European specimens and in Kabwe. An occiput is not preserved for Arago, but this part of the cranium can be measured for Petralona. Upper scale length exceeds that of the nuchal plane by about 10 mm, when inion is located on the linear tubercle. The Broken Hill occipital bone is damaged, and a ratio of scale lengths cannot be determined.

The Arago mandibles present a mix of archaic and more modern characters. Development of the lateral prominences, marginal tori and tubercles, internal symphyseal buttresses and digastric impressions is comparable to that seen in *Homo erectus* and cannot be used to distinguish consistently between the Tautavel and Olduvai assemblages. A few other features may be more useful. These include the symphyseal profile (more incurvation below the alveolar border to produce a chin eminence in Arago 2) and the appearance of a larger retromolar space. In the Arago jaws, the root of the ramus occupies a more posterior position relative to the last molar teeth. This trait is shared by the Arago people with the later Neanderthals. However, it is difficult to recognize other Neanderthal characters in the Tautavel material.

HOW MANY LINEAGES?

If the fossils are not *Homo erectus*, then it must next be agreed whether multiple lineages of more modern *Homo* are to be recognized in the later Middle Pleistocene. Here very different views have been expressed. One commentator is Wolpoff (1980b), who would include all of the hominids of Europe in a single, highly dimorphic group. To Wolpoff, it is unimportant whether the root of this lineage is termed *Homo erectus* or *Homo sapiens*. All of its members are said to be connected in an unbroken evolutionary stream, both with the Neanderthals and with modern humans. Stringer (1981) disagrees and notes that there are substantial differences between Petralona and smaller crania such as Steinheim. Size and other characters serve to distinguish two morphs that are unlikely to be simply males and females. One source of uncertainty is dating, as remarked by Stringer. It is quite possible that these two groups are time-successive rather than contemporary.

Elsewhere, Stringer (1983, 1985) has emphasized differences between later Middle Pleistocene hominids such as Swanscombe and Biache, which clearly share apomorphic characters with the Neanderthals, and a more archaic assemblage including Arago and Petralona. These latter individuals show few if any of the specialized traits associated with the Neanderthals of Europe and the Middle East. Instead, they may be lumped broadly with archaic humans from other geographic regions, including sub-Saharan Africa. Stringer *et al.* (1979) have suggested that fossils such as Petralona, Arago, Mauer, Broken Hill and Bodo may represent a primitive grade of our own species.

Another perspective is provided in a recent essay by Tattersall (1986), who argues that taxic diversity within *Homo* has been seriously underestimated. Tattersall attributes this to the fact that paleoanthropologists have focused their attention on variation within species, rather than differences between species, when dealing with the fossil record. This application of within-groups variability as a yardstick, coupled with disregard for the observation that morphological distinctions among closely related species may be slight, has resulted in much lumping of the fossils. Tattersall notes that this situation is unfortunate, as legitimate species must be identified and described before the phylogeny of hominids can be investigated. As an example, he points to archaic *Homo sapiens*, taken by most workers to encompass nearly all Pleistocene discoveries which are neither anatomically modern nor representative of *Homo erectus*. This loosely defined assemblage must contain several distinct morphs, and Tattersall would recognize one or perhaps two species in Europe in addition to the highly specialized Neanderthals. He is quite open to the possibility that additional taxa may have occupied Africa or the Far East after the time of *Homo erectus*.

On the basis of my own observations and measurements, I am inclined to agree with Stringer, at least in part. It is reasonable to assign Ndutu, Broken Hill, Petralona and the Arago remains to a single taxon distinct from *Homo erectus* and later Neanderthals, even if the Arago specimens display a few Neanderthal characters. There is no clear justification for separating the African and European assemblages. I also endorse Tattersall's point that groups exhibiting the archaic morphology of Broken Hill or Petralona should be set apart from anatomically modern people. To lump all recent humans, Neanderthals, and an assortment of Middle Pleistocene fossils together in one taxon is to ignore important differences.

Stringer *et al.* (1979) have attempted to deal with this obvious diversity by allocating the hominids to a series of grades within *Homo sapiens*. By placing Broken Hill, Petralona and other 'primitive' specimens in *Homo sapiens* grade 1, these authors do recognize similarities linking the fossils, although such shared characters are not treated in detail. There is no explicit effort to define a unit appropriate to evolutionary study. The relationships of populations making up grade 1 are not clarified, and the members of this grade cannot be regarded as ancestral to those of a succeeding level. Such a scheme does not tell us very much, as I have argued before.

In earlier papers (Rightmire, 1976, 1983), I have advocated the use of a subspecies label for archaic populations of Africa, so as to distinguish this group from the Neanderthals of Europe. If this procedure were to be followed consistently, it would now be necessary to swell such a subspecies to encompass not only Middle Pleistocene Africans but also Arago and Petralona. If the Mauer jaw were added, this group could be termed *Homo sapiens heidelbergensis*. However, this expansion of a paleontological subspecies to include fossils from very distant provinces is inappropriate. The criteria by which such taxa should be recognized have never been fully agreed upon, but subspecies are generally taken to be restricted geographically. Whether this category should be used to denote time-successive subdivisions of a species is also debatable. In cases where many successive subspecies are named, there is danger of ignoring real branching events and obscuring divisions among lineages, as noted in Chapter 7.

What is important is that the fossils are sorted into groups that can be described and studied as evolutionary units (not grades). Samples of later Middle Pleistocene humans from Africa and Europe are admittedly small, and most of these individuals are incomplete.

Under the circumstances, it is difficult to make very extensive comparisons or to reach definite conclusions concerning classification. However, it can be argued that this material is best placed in a taxon of species-level rank. If some of the confusion surrounding designation of certain hominids as 'archaic' relative to other members of the same species can be done away with, then relationships of *Homo heidelbergensis* to *Homo erectus*, the Neanderthals and modern people can be assessed in a more straightforward fashion.

Characters defining later Middle Pleistocene *Homo*

The fossils from Africa and Europe share a number of features with *Homo erectus*. Resemblances are evident in the relatively low vault carrying thickened supraorbital tori, the flattened frontal, parietal angular torus, and other crests and buttresses. The cranium tends to be broadest at the level of the supramastoid crests. In other respects, the later Middle Pleistocene hominids depart from the morphology detailed for *Homo erectus*. Characters which can be interpreted as derived for *Homo heidelbergensis* include increased width of the parietal bone, coupled with parietal bossing. Rounding of the rear of the vault as measured by the occipital angle is greater for Ndutu than for any *Homo erectus*, with the exception of the (deformed?) Salé cranium. The upper scale of the occipital is vertical and expanded relative to the nuchal plane. A bar-like articular tubercle marks the anterior margin of the glenoid cavity, and the inferior border of the tympanic plate is thin. Evidence concerning mandibular form is limited, but a mental trigone and/or a chin eminence are present in the Arago specimens. Other cranial features are obscured, or lacking from some individuals, but do occur sporadically. Both Petralona and Arago have rather broad frontals with reduced postorbital constriction. Ndutu exhibits an external occipital protuberance, and Broken Hill has a sphenoid spine which is oriented in the modern fashion. Finally, cranial bases appear to be shortened, and the basioccipital proportions of Broken Hill, for example, are comparable to those of recent people (Laitman *et al.*, 1979). Brain volume is expanded beyond that expected for *Homo erectus*.

Some of these characters are synapomorphies linking the Middle Pleistocene group to modern humans, while others are indicative of trends common to both taxa. The African and European specimens display few if any derived traits which are not shared with *Homo sapiens*. As a consequence, it will be difficult to distinguish between these populations except by reference to the (many) primitive features retained by *Homo heidelbergensis*. This is a problem which may become tractable only as the Middle Pleistocene record is pieced together in greater detail. Fossils from the Far East will surely be informative, when more complete descriptions are available. The cranium from Dali in China, for example, shows some primitive characters but has been called (early) *Homo sapiens*. Such discoveries will help to document the extent of variation present in later Middle Pleistocene populations, and systematic study of all the fossils will make it clearer whether the view of *Homo heidelbergensis* advanced here is accurate. Without more work and until dating of key specimens is much improved, it will be hard to trace evolutionary branching events which may have occurred late in the history of the *Homo* clade.

Trends in brain size

Even if it is not possible to be precise about the geographic origin of the first more modern people, it is evident that populations of sub-Saharan Africa and Europe were changing, probably at a time when *Homo erectus* was disappearing in most areas of the Old World. In some ways, the crania from Broken Hill and Petralona are similar to *Homo erectus*, as already noted. Brows are still thickened, for example, and adding the later Middle Pleistocene specimens to Figure 41 would show little deviation from the norm established in earlier groups. Much the same holds for cranial base breadth, which is large for Petralona but reduced in the African individuals. An average is close to the Ngandong value and lower than Weidenreich's (1943) figure for Zhoukoudian. Of the dimensions plotted in Figure 41, only the occipital angle, which can be measured for Ndutu and Petralona, would show substantial change relative to the *Homo erectus* condition.

Another important character is brain size. Reliable measurements can be obtained for the more complete Petralona and Broken Hill individuals, and volumes for Ndutu and Arago 21 have been estimated by Holloway. All four crania have capacities which lie near or beyond the upper limit of the range observed for *Homo erectus*. While there is some overlap with values reported for several of the largest specimens from Zhoukoudian and Ngandong, it appears

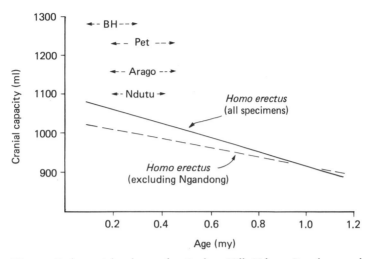

Fig. 46. Endocranial volumes for Broken Hill, Ndutu, Petralona and Arago, compared to values predicted for *Homo erectus*. Regression lines are constructed as in Figure 40. It is clear that the four archaic human specimens have brains which are larger than expected for *Homo erectus* of about the same geological age.

that the brain has expanded in populations of the later Middle Pleistocene.

This hypothesis is strengthened when cranial capacities are plotted against time in Figure 46. Dates are very approximate and should really be treated as intervals, which in most cases could span several hundred thousand years. Nevertheless, it is clear that the fossils lie well above the linear regression lines calculated for *Homo erectus*. Not only the larger Broken Hill and Petralona crania but also Ndutu and Arago have capacities which are greater than expected for *Homo erectus* of about the same antiquity. This holds for the regression relationship obtained for all *Homo erectus*, and the difference is even more striking when the later Middle Pleistocene hominids are compared to a line drawn for African and Asian assemblages excluding Ngandong.

How these data are to be interpreted is open to some controversy. It may be argued that a trend toward increasing brain size can be documented for *Homo erectus* and that this pattern is simply continued in groups of later people. Several workers have constructed exponential regressions for cranial capacity and geological age and have noted that these curves can be fitted to archaic *Homo sapiens* and even to representatives of pre-*erectus Homo* as well as to *Homo erectus*. Such results prompt speculation that the mode of brain evolution in humans has been neither gradual (linear) nor punctuated. Instead an autocatalytic model may be most appropriate, if size has increased at a rate which accelerates with time.

A case in point is Lestrel's (1976) paper. Lestrel's regressions are based on log-transformed values for both endocranial volume and age, and his data seem to show that the brain has expanded in a regular fashion first in *Australopithecus* and later in the *Homo* lineage. Only after about 200 000 years ago is there an indication that capacity has reached a maximum and begun to fluctuate independently of time. This paper has been criticized by Godfrey & Jacobs (1981), who point out that log–log transformations are inappropriate and will cause problems especially when the scale of time is very different from that of brain size. These authors note that the pattern observed by Lestrel is largely an artifact stemming from the transformations used, which makes it difficult to distinguish gradualism from other modes of evolutionary change.

Given these cautions, it is probably best to avoid the log–log approach to scaling. It is also a good idea, when searching for patterns that characterize species, to restrict treatment to species-level assemblages. There is no doubt that cranial capacity has increased during the history of the hominids, but showing this for some *Australopithecus*, some early *Homo* and selected modern humans mixed together in one plot may not provide much information about change or stasis in any (one) of the species represented.

When untransformed data for all measurable *Homo erectus* crania are taken as the basis for linear regression, there is some evidence for change through time. The brain increases in size at a rate of about 180 ml/my (see Chapter 7). There is no indication of any departure from this trend at Sangiran or even at Zhoukoudian. Several of the Ngandong individuals do fall above the regression line in Figure 40, and one might argue that these specimens are atypical of *Homo erectus*. In nearly all other respects, however, the Ngandong crania are very like those from Trinil and Sangiran.

In the case of Ndutu, Broken Hill and the European fossils (Figure 46), cranial capacities are substantially larger than expected for (late) *Homo erectus*. This increase in brain size cannot readily be attributed to continuation of a linear trend established in earlier populations. Whatever selective mechanisms are postulated, and whether or not the overall mode of change for the hominids is autocatalytic (Falk, 1987), there is evidence that rates of brain evolution increased in the later Middle Pleistocene. This shift produced populations that differ from *Homo erectus* in parietal proportions, occipital rounding and morphology of the cranial base as well as brain size. The hominids at Broken Hill and Petralona are among the earliest to display a suite of derived characters shared with later humans. *Homo heidelbergensis* may well have evolved in Africa or Europe and then replaced groups of *Homo erectus* in these areas. This species is clearly a close relative to *Homo sapiens* and should probably be regarded as the source from which modern people are descended. Whether *Homo heidelbergensis* spread also to Asia is presently uncertain. Individuals such as Dali may document the expansion into China of populations different from *Homo erectus* but still bearing some archaic features. In any case, there is not much basis for postulating direct evolutionary continuity from *Homo erectus* to *Homo sapiens* in the Far East, either in the north or in Australasia. To the extent that the role advocated here for *Homo heidelbergensis* is correct, any multiregional hypothesis is weakened.

9

Summary and prospects for further research

Nearly a century has passed since this species was first described by Eugene Dubois, but the story of *Homo erectus* is still incomplete. This is so partly because the record itself is sparse. The fossils assembled by Dubois, von Koenigswald and later collectors in Indonesia, and the specimens recovered at Olduvai Gorge and in the Turkana basin, are sampled from only a tiny fraction of the populations which lived during the Early and Middle Pleistocene. Despite a fairly steady flow of lesser finds, highlighted by occasional spectacular discoveries, the *Homo erectus* hypodigm is far smaller than the body of material available to any paleontologist investigating other mammalian groups. There are also continuing problems with chronology, particularly at the Asian sites. In Indonesia, the fossils from Ngandong and Sambungmachan are undated, and there is still doubt concerning the stratigraphic provenience of specimens picked up at Sangiran. In East Africa, fortunately, the situation is clearer, as many of the sites contain tuffs that can be dated unambiguously.

Other uncertainties stem not so much from gaps in the record as from questions about species and the evolutionary process. The nature of species, how speciation occurs, rates of evolutionary change and how these should be measured are topics much discussed by molecular biologists, geneticists, ecologists and other students of living organisms. It is not surprising that paleontologists may (also) disagree on how species are to be defined or about the course of evolution within a lineage, even when plenty of fossils are available. These are problems of broad concern, and contributions

234

toward resolving them will come from all areas of evolutionary biology.

On some fronts, definite progress has been made. In this final chapter, I will summarize important points concerning the history of *Homo erectus*. I will also comment on specific questions, presently difficult to answer, which can profitably be addressed in future research programs. New fossils and improved dating frameworks will help in many instances, and it is likely that the picture of *Homo erectus* will soon come into clearer focus.

One issue concerns the origin of *Homo erectus*. This species must be descended from an earlier form of *Homo*, present late in the Pliocene of sub-Saharan Africa. One possible ancestor is *Homo habilis*, as represented by large-brained crania including OH 7 from Olduvai and KNM-ER 1470 and KNM-ER 1590 from the Koobi Fora region. However, *Homo habilis* is still poorly known, and the situation is complicated by the presence of fossils which may best be referred to another taxon. This second group, made up of specimens such as OH 13 and KNM-ER 1813, is characterized by smaller brains and teeth (much) reduced in size compared to those of *Australopithecus*. The role played by this species *vis à vis Homo habilis* and/or *Homo erectus* is obscure.

Whether or not new light is shed on the question of origins, it is almost certain that further discoveries in eastern and perhaps also in southern Africa will add to the inventory of early *Homo erectus*. Increasing the size of samples from the Turkana basin should quiet recent controversy centering on the claim that specimens from Koobi Fora lack autapomorphies expressed in assemblages from the Far East. This suggestion challenges the long-held view that *Homo erectus* inhabited Africa as well as Asia. Fossils from Ternifine and Olduvai were judged to be similar to Chinese *Homo erectus* by Arambourg (1963) and by Le Gros Clark (1964). All of the African material was again referred to this species by Howell (1978). Current application of numerical cladistic analysis to the hominids links crania such as KNM-ER 3733, KNM-ER 3883 and KNM-WT 15000 to specimens from Sangiran and Zhoukoudian (Stringer, 1987). Further evidence confirming this conclusion is provided in Chapter 6. I expect that additional discoveries from the Turkana region will include crania comparable in size and robusticity to OH 9, so that it will be increasingly difficult to argue for any formal distinctions among the African assemblages or between East Africa and Asia.

As described in Chapter 6, the *Homo erectus* cranium is long and relatively low in outline, and the average endocranial capacity is close to 1000 ml. The facial skeleton, preserved in only a few cases, is robust and projecting in its lower parts. The wall of the nasal cavity is thickened below but is everted and plate-like superiorly. The nasal profile approaches that seen in later humans. Brows are quite heavy, even in smaller individuals that may be females. The frontal squama is flattened and may exhibit a keel in the midline. Least frontal breadth is low relative to the biorbital chord, so postorbital narrowing of the cranium is marked.

The parietal chord is short compared to that of later *Homo*, and the superior temporal line often produces a rounded torus at the parietal mastoid angle. The rear of the vault is sharply flexed. The occipital squama is relatively wide, and its upper scale slopes forward. A transverse torus is most projecting near the midline, where it may be blunt or shelf-like. There is no true external occipital protuberance. Crests associated with the mastoid process tend to be prominent, and the process itself is inclined medially.

In some individuals at least, the base of the skull is flattened in comparison to the more flexed condition of *Homo sapiens*. Other features of the base are also distinctive. The glenoid cavity is narrowed to form a medial crevice, and a sphenoid spine is not developed. There is no prominent articular tubercle. The tympanic plate is thick inferiorly, and a petrosal spine is strong. The mandible is large and robust and carries a broad ascending ramus. There is usually little indication of a bony chin.

Although there is variation in all of the assemblages, these as well as other traits can be used to distinguish *Homo erectus* from more modern humans. However, some of the same features of vault form or mandibular anatomy can be found in earlier *Homo* or even in species of *Australopithecus*. Such plesiomorphic characters are not helpful if one wishes to define a taxon in a more formal way or assess its relationships to other groups. A species diagnosis should be based on features which are apomorphic. Aspects of anatomy that seem to be derived for *Homo erectus* include the thickened brow backed by a flattened supratoral shelf, frontal keeling and expression of a parietal angular torus. The occiput is angled, and morphology of the transverse torus is distinctive. Shape of the glenoid cavity and of the tympanic plate also appear to be specialized in *Homo erectus*. In comparison to earlier *Homo* from East

Africa, cranial capacity is increased, and individual vault bones are robust.

Homo erectus as defined in this way is known from Indonesia, China, northwest Africa and the sub-Saharan region. It is my contention that *Homo erectus* is a real paleospecies rather than an arbitrary grade or stage in the evolution of a lineage. Acknowledging this discrete nature of paleospecies is important to the process of working out relationships. Species of early *Homo* in addition to *Homo habilis* as traditionally described may be present in Africa, as I have already pointed out. Taxa other than *Homo erectus* may have lived in Africa and/or Europe in the later Middle Pleistocene. Until all such groups are recognized, it will not be possible to reconstruct the phylogenetic history of the *Homo* clade.

Many anthropologists have assumed that at most three species of *Homo* succeeded one another in an unbroken linear sequence, ending with the appearance of *Homo sapiens*. This scenario invoking gradual change and continuity of populations in different geographic regions is now open to serious doubt. Some of the oldest fossils unearthed in Europe differ in important ways from *Homo erectus*. At the same time they do not closely resemble the Neanderthals or more recent Europeans. The crania and jaws from Petralona and Arago Cave are most similar to African specimens from Lake Ndutu, Broken Hill and Elandsfontein.

While they have usually been regarded as representing an archaic grade of *Homo sapiens*, Petralona and Broken Hill may better be placed in a separate species, as noted in Chapter 8. Presumably fossils such as Mauer and Bilzingsleben belong in this group also. Defining this species relative to the Neanderthals and recent *Homo sapiens* is difficult and will remain so until the record is improved. Nevertheless, such a rereading of the evidence suggests that *Homo erectus* was not transformed directly to our own species, in a gradual fashion. Perhaps we should look only toward Europe or Africa to find the ties of *Homo erectus* to other hominids. If the later Middle Pleistocene populations of these areas belong to a taxon descended from *Homo erectus* but still distinct from *Homo sapiens*, then the course of human evolution is more complex than we have supposed. Documenting this later history of *Homo* remains a challenge for the next decade.

REFERENCES

Andrews, P. 1984. An alternative interpretation of characters used to define *Homo erectus*. *Courier Forschungsinstitut Senckenberg*, **69**:167–75.

Arambourg, C. 1963. Le gisement de Ternifine, II. *L'Atlanthropus mauritanicus*. *Archives de l'Institut de Paléontologie Humaine*, Mémoire **32**:37–190.

Arambourg, C. & Hoffstetter, R. 1963. Le gisement de Ternifine, I. Historique et géologie. *Archives de l'Institut de Paléontologie Humaine*, Mémoire **32**:1–36.

Armelagos, G. J. & van Gerven, D. P. 1980. Sexual dimorphism and human evolution: an overview. *Journal of Human Evolution*, **9**:437–46.

Bartstra, G. -J. 1983. Comments and reply on: the fauna from Trinil, type locality of *Homo erectus*: a reinterpretation. Comment 1: The vertebrate-bearing deposits of Kedungbrubus and Trinil, Java, Indonesia. *Geologie en Mijnbouw*, **62**:329–36.

Bartstra, G. -J., Soegondho, S. & van der Wijk, A. 1988. Ngandong man: age and artifacts. *Journal of Human Evolution*, **17**:325–37.

Bilsborough, A. 1976. Patterns of evolution in Middle Pleistocene hominids. *Journal of Human Evolution*, **5**:423–39.

Bilsborough, A. & Wood, B. A. 1986. The nature, origin and fate of *Homo erectus*. In *Major Topics in Primate and Human Evolution*, eds. B. Wood, L. Martin & P. Andrews, pp. 295–316. Cambridge, Cambridge University Press.

Bonde, N. 1981. Problems of species concepts in palaeontology. In *Concept and Method in Paleontology*, ed. J. Martinelli, pp. 19–34. Barcelona, University of Barcelona.

Brain, C. K. 1985. Cultural and taphonomic comparisons of hominids from Swartkrans and Sterkfontein. In *Ancestors: The Hard Evidence*, ed. E. Delson, pp. 72–5. New York, Liss.

Broom, R. & Robinson, J. T. 1949. A new type of fossil man. *Nature*, **164**:322–3.

— 1950. Man contemporaneous with the Swartkrans ape-man. *American Journal of Physical Anthropology*, 8:151–6.

Brown, F. H. & Cerling, T. E. 1982. Stratigraphical significance of the Tulu Bor Tuff of the Koobi Fora Formation. *Nature*, 299:212–15.

Brown, F. H. & Feibel, C. S. 1985. Stratigraphical notes on the Okote Tuff Complex at Koobi Fora, Kenya. *Nature*, 316:794–7.

Brown, F. H., Harris, J., Leakey, R. E. & Walker, A. 1985. Early *Homo erectus* skeleton from West Lake Turkana, Kenya. *Nature*, 316:788–92.

Campbell, B. 1974. A new taxonomy of fossil man. *Yearbook of Physical Anthropology*, 17:194–201.

Cerling, T. E. & Brown, F. H. 1982. Tuffaceous marker horizons in the Koobi Fora region and the lower Omo Valley. *Nature*, 299:216–21.

Chiu, C. L., Ku, Y. M., Chang, Y. Y. & Chang, S. S. 1973. Peking man fossils and cultural remains newly discovered at Choukoutien. *Vertebrata Palasiatica*, 11:109–31.

Clarke, R. J. 1976. New cranium of *Homo erectus* from Lake Ndutu, Tanzania. *Nature*, 262:485–7.

— 1985. *Australopithecus* and early *Homo* in southern Africa. In *Ancestors: The Hard Evidence*, ed. E. Delson, pp. 171–7. New York, Liss.

Clarke, R. J. & Howell, F.C. 1972. Affinities of the Swartkrans 847 hominid cranium. *American Journal of Physical Anthropology*, 37:319–36.

Clarke, R. J., Howell, F. C. & Brain, C. K. 1970. More evidence of an advanced hominid at Swartkrans. *Nature*, 225:1219–22.

Cook, J., Stringer, C. B., Currant, A. P., Schwarcz, H. P. & Wintle, A. G. 1982. A review of the chronology of the European Middle Pleistocene hominid record. *Yearbook of Physical Anthropology*, 25:19–65.

Coon, C. S. 1962. *The Origin of Races*. New York, Knopf.

Cronin, J. E., Boaz, N. T., Stringer, C. B. & Rak, Y. 1981. Tempo and mode in hominid evolution. *Nature*, 292:113–22.

Dagley, P., Mussett, A. E. & Palmer, H. C. 1978. Preliminary observations on the paleomagnetic stratigraphy of the area west of Lake Baringo, Kenya. In *Geological Background to Fossil Man*, ed. W. W. Bishop, pp. 225–35. Edinburgh, Scottish Academic Press.

Day, M. H. 1971. Postcranial remains of *Homo erectus* from Bed IV, Olduvai Gorge, Tanzania. *Nature*, 232:383–7.

— 1976. Hominid postcranial remains from the East Rudolf succession. A review. In *Earliest Man and Environments in the Lake Rudolf Basin*, eds. Y. Coppens, F. C. Howell, G. Ll. Isaac & R. E. Leakey, pp. 507–21. Chicago, University of Chicago Press.

— 1984. The postcranial remains of *Homo erectus* from Africa, Asia and possibly Europe. *Courier Forschungsinstitut Senckenberg*, 69:113–21.

Day, M. H. & Leakey, R. E. 1973. New evidence for the genus *Homo* from East Rudolf, Kenya, I. *American Journal of Physical Anthropology*, 39: 341–54.

Day, M. H. & Molleson, T. I. 1973. The Trinil femora. In *Human Evolution*, ed. M. H. Day, pp. 127–54. London, Taylor and Francis.

Dean, M. C. & Wood, B. A. 1981. Metrical analysis of the basicranium of extant hominoids and *Australopithecus*. *American Journal of Physical Anthropology*, 54:63–71.

— 1982. Basicranial anatomy of Plio-Pleistocene hominids from East and South Africa. *American Journal of Physical Anthropology*, 59:157–74.

Debenath, A., Raynal, J. -P. & Texier, J. -P. 1982. Position stratigraphique des restes humains paléolithiques marocains sur la base des travaux récents. *Comptes Rendus de l'Academie des Sciences, Paris*, Série II, **294**: 1247–50.

De Bonis, L. & Melentis, J. K. 1982. L'Homme de Petralona: comparaisons avec l'homme de Tautavel. In *L'Homo erectus et la Place de l'Homme de Tautavel Parmi les Hominidés Fossiles*, ed. M. -A. de Lumley, pp. 847–69. Nice, CNRS.

Delson, E. 1981. Paleoanthropology: Pliocene and Pleistocene human evolution. *Paleobiology*, 7: 298–305.

Delson, E., Eldredge, N. & Tattersall, I. 1977. Reconstruction of hominid phylogeny: a testable framework based on cladistic analysis. *Journal of Human Evolution*, 6:263–78.

De Vos, J., Sartono, S., Hardja-Sasmita, S. & Sondaar, P. Y. 1982. The fauna from Trinil, type locality of *Homo erectus*: a reinterpretation. *Geologie en Mijnbouw*, 61:207–11.

Drake, R. E., Curtis, G. H., Cerling, T. E., Cerling, B. W. & Hampel, J. 1980. KBS Tuff dating and geochronology of tuffaceous sediments in the Koobi Fora and Shungura Formations, East Africa. *Nature*, 283:368–72.

Dubois, E. 1984. *Pithecanthropus erectus*, eine menschenähnliche Uebergangsform aus Java. Batavia.

— 1924. Figures of the calvarium and endocranial cast, a fragment of the mandible and three teeth of *Pithecanthropus erectus*. *Proceedings of the Koninklijke Nederlandse Akademie van Wetanschappen, Amsterdam*, **27**: 459–64.

Eldredge, N. & Tattersall, I. 1975. Evolutionary models, phylogenetic reconstruction and another look at hominid phylogeny. In *Approaches to Primate Paleobiology*, ed. F. S. Szalay, pp. 218–42. Basel, Karger.

—1982. *The Myths of Human Evolution*. New York, Columbia University Press.

Ennouchi, E. 1969. Découverte d'un pithécanthropien au Maroc. *Comptes Rendus de l'Academie des Sciences, Paris*, Série D, 269:763–5.

— 1972. Nouvelle découverte d'un archanthropien au Maroc. *Comptes Rendus de l'Academie des Sciences, Paris*, Série D, 274:3088–90.

— 1976. Le deuxième archanthropien à la carrière Thomas 3 (Maroc); étude préliminaire. *Bulletin du Museum National d'Histoire Naturelle, Paris*, Série 3, **56**:273–96.

Falk, D. 1987. Hominid paleoneurology. *Annual Review of Anthropology*, 16:13–30.

Feibel, C. S., Brown, F. H. & McDougall, I. 1989. Stratigraphic context of fossil hominids from the Omo Group deposits: northern Turkana basin, Kenya and Ethiopia. *American Journal of Physical Anthropology*, **78**: 595–622.

Franciscus, R. G. & Trinkaus, E. 1988. Nasal morphology and the emergence of *Homo erectus*. *American Journal of Physical Anthropology*, 75: 517–27.

Franzen, J. L. 1985a. What is '*Pithecanthropus dubius* Koenigswald 1950'? In *Ancestors: The Hard Evidence*, ed. E. Delson, pp. 221–6. New York, Liss.

— 1985b. Asian australopithecines? In *Hominid Evolution: Past, Present and Future*, ed. P. V. Tobias, pp. 255–63. New York, Liss.

Geraads, D. 1980. La faune des sites à '*Homo erectus*' des carrières Thomas (Casablanca, Maroc). *Quaternaria*, 22:65–94.

— 1981. Bovidae et Giraffidae (Artiodactyla, Mammalia) du Pléistocène de Ternifine (Algérie). *Bulletin du Museum National d'Histoire Naturelle, Paris*, Série 4, 3:47–86.

Geraads, D., Beriro, P. & Roche, H. 1980. La faune et l'industrie des sites à *Homo erectus* des carrières Thomas (Maroc). Précisions sur l'âge de ces Hominidés. *Comptes Rendus de l'Academie des Sciences, Paris*, Série D, 291:195–8.

Geraads, D., Hublin, J. -J., Jaeger, J. -J., Tong, H., Sen, S. & Toubeau, P. 1986. The Pleistocene hominid site of Ternifine, Algeria: new results on the environment, age and human industries. *Quaternary Research*, 25: 380–6.

Gingerich, P. D. 1979. The stratophenetic approach to phylogeny reconstruction in vertebrate paleontology. In *Phylogenetic Analysis and Paleontology*, eds. J. Cracraft & N. Eldredge, pp. 41–77. New York, Columbia University Press.

— 1985. Species in the fossil record: concepts, trends and transitions. *Paleobiology*, 11:27–41.

Godfrey, L. & Jacobs, K. H. 1981. Gradual, autocatalytic and punctuational models of hominid brain evolution: a cautionary tale. *Journal of Human Evolution*, 10:255–72.

Grine, F. 1984. Comparisons of the deciduous dentitions of African and Asian hominids. *Courier Forschungsinstitut Senckenberg*, 69:69–82.

Groves, C. P. & Mazák, V. 1975. An approach to the taxonomy of the Hominidae: gracile Villafranchian hominids of Africa. *Casopis pro Mineralogii a Geologii*, 20:225–46.

Hay, R. L. 1976. *Geology of the Olduvai Gorge. A Study of Sedimentation in a Semiarid Basin*. Berkeley, University of California Press.

Heberer, G. 1963. Uber einen neuen archanthropinen typus aus der Oldoway–Schlucht. *Zeitschrift für Morphologie und Anthropologie*, 53: 171–7.

Hennig, G. J., Herr, W., Weber, E. & Xirotiris, N. I. 1981. ESR-dating of the fossil hominid from Petralona Cave, Greece. *Nature*, 292:533–6.

Holloway, R. L. 1973. New endocranial values for the East African early hominids. *Nature*, 243:97–9.

— 1975. Early hominid endocasts: volumes, morphology and significance for hominid evolution. In *Primate Functional Morphology and Evolution*, ed. R. H. Tuttle, pp. 393–415. The Hague, Mouton.

— 1980. Indonesian 'Solo' (Ngandong) endocranial reconstructions: preliminary observations and comparisons with Neanderthal and *Homo erectus* groups. *American Journal of Physical Anthropology*, 53:285–95.

— 1981a. The Indonesian *Homo erectus* brain endocasts revisited. *American Journal of Physical Anthropology*, 55:503–21.

— 1981b. Volumetric and asymmetry determinations on recent hominid endocasts: Spy 1 and 2, Djebel Irhoud 1, and the Salé *Homo erectus* specimens, with some notes on Neanderthal brain size. *American Journal of Physical Anthropology*, 55:385–93.

— 1983. Human brain evolution: a search for units, models and synthesis. *Canadian Journal of Anthropology*, 3:215–30.

Holloway, R. L. & Post, D. G. 1982. The relativity of relative brain measures and hominid mosaic evolution. In *Primate Brain Evolution: Methods and Concepts*, eds. E. Armstrong & D. Falk, pp. 57–76. New York, Plenum.

Howell, F. C. 1960. European and northwest African Middle Pleistocene hominids. *Current Anthropology*, 1:195–232.

— 1978. Hominidae. In *Evolution of African Mammals*, eds. V. J. Maglio & H. B. S. Cooke, pp. 154–248. Cambridge, Massachusetts, Harvard University Press.

— 1986. Variabilité chez *Homo erectus*, et problème de la présence de cette espèce en Europe. *L'Anthropologie*, 90:447–81.

Howells, W. W. 1973. Cranial variation in man. A study by multivariate analysis of patterns of difference among recent human populations. *Papers of the Peabody Museum*, 67:1–259.

— 1975. Neanderthal man: facts and figures. In *Paleoanthropology. Morphology and Paleoecology*, ed. R. H. Tuttle, pp. 389–407. The Hague, Mouton.

— 1980. *Homo erectus* – who, when and where: a survey. *Yearbook of Physical Anthropology*, 23:1–23.

— 1982. Modern and Late Pleistocene cranial profiles. *Bulletin et Mémoires de la Societé d'Anthropologie de Paris*, Série 13, 9:333–7.

Hublin, J. -J. 1978a. Le torus occipital transverse et les structures associées: evolution dans le genre *Homo*. Thèse de Docteur du Troisième Cycle, Université de Paris VI.

— 1978b. Quelques charactères apomorphes de crâne néandertalien et leur interprétation phylogénique. *Comptes Rendus de l'Academie des Sciences, Paris*, Série D, 287:923–5.

— 1978c. Anatomie du centre de l'écaille de l'occipital. Le problème de l'inion. *Cahiers d'Anthropologie*, 1978:65–83.

— 1985. Human fossils from the north African Middle Pleistocene and the origin of *Homo sapiens*. In *Ancestors: The Hard Evidence*, ed. E. Delson, pp. 283–8. New York, Liss.

— 1986. Some comments on the diagnostic features of *Homo erectus*. *Anthropos* (Brno), 23:175–85.

Jacob, T. 1966. The sixth skull cap of *Pithecanthropus erectus*. *American Journal of Physical Anthropology*, 25:243–69.

— 1975. Morphology and paleoecology of early man in Java. In *Paleoanthropology. Morphology and Paleoecology*, ed. R. H. Tuttle, pp. 311–25. The Hague, Mouton.

— 1981. Solo man and Peking man. In *Homo erectus. Papers in Honor of Davidson Black*, eds. B. A. Sigmon & J. S. Cybulski, pp. 87–104. Toronto, University of Toronto Press.

Jaeger, J. -J. 1975. Découverte d'un crâne d'hominidé dans le Pléistocène moyen du Maroc. *Colloque International CNRS*, 218:897–902.

— 1981. Les hommes fossiles du Pléistocène moyen du Maghreb dans leur cadre géologique, chronologique, et paléoécologique. In *Homo erectus. Papers in Honor of Davidson Black*, eds. B. A. Sigmon & J. S. Cybulski, pp. 159–87. Toronto, University of Toronto Press.

Jelínek, J. 1980a. European *Homo erectus* and the origin of *Homo sapiens*. In *Current Argument on Early Man*, ed. L. -K. Königsson, pp. 137–44. Oxford, Pergamon.

— 1980b. Variability and geography. Contribution to our knowledge of European and North African Middle Pleistocene hominids. *Anthropologie* (Brno), 18:109–14.

— 1982. The East and Southeast Asian way of regional evolution. *Anthropos* (Brno), 21:195–212.

Johanson, D. C., Lovejoy, C. O., Kimbel, W. H., White, T. D., Ward, S. C., Bush, M. E., Latimer, B. M. & Coppens, Y. 1982. Morphology of the Pliocene partial hominid skeleton (A. L. 288–1) from the Hadar Formation, Ethiopia. *American Journal of Physical Anthropology*, 57:403–51.

Kennedy, G. E. 1983. A morphometric and taxonomic assessment of a hominine femur from the Lower Member, Koobi Fora, Lake Turkana. *American Journal of Physical Anthropology*, 61: 429–36.

Klein, R. G. 1973. Geological antiquity of Rhodesian man. *Nature*, 244:311–12.

Kraus, B. S., Jordan, R. E. & Abrams, L. 1969. *Dental Anatomy and Occlusion*. Baltimore, Williams and Wilkins.

Kurtén, B. & Poulianos, A. N. 1981. Fossil carnivora of Petralona Cave: status of 1980. *Anthropos* (Athens), 8:9–56.

Laitman, J. T. 1985. Evolution of the hominid upper respiratory tract: the fossil evidence. In *Hominid Evolution: Past, Present and Future*, ed. P. V. Tobias, pp. 281–6. New York, Liss.

Laitman, J. T., Heimbuch, R. C. & Crelin, E. S. 1979. The basicranium of fossil hominids as an indicator of their upper respiratory systems. *American Journal of Physical Anthopology*, 51:15–34.

Leakey, L. S. B, Tobias, P. V. & Napier, J. R. 1964. A new species of the genus *Homo* from Olduvai Gorge. *Nature*, 202:7–9.

Leakey, M., Tobias, P. V., Martyn, J. E. & Leakey, R. E. 1969. An Acheulean industry with prepared core technique and the discovery of a contemporary hominid at Lake Baringo, Kenya. *Proceedings of the Prehistoric Society*, 25:48–76.

Leakey, M. D. 1971a. *Olduvai Gorge, 3. Excavations in Beds I and II, 1960–1963*. Cambridge, Cambridge University Press.

— 1971b. Discovery of postcranial remains of *Homo erectus* and associated artifacts in Bed IV at Olduvai Gorge, Tanzania. *Nature*, 232:380–3.

Leakey, M. D. & Hay, R. L. 1982. The chronological position of the fossil hominids of Tanzania. In *L'Homo erectus et la Place de l'Homme de Tautavel Parmi les Hominidés Fossiles*, ed. M. -A. de Lumley, pp. 753–65. Nice, CNRS.

Leakey, M. G. & Leakey, R. E., eds. 1978. *Koobi Fora Research Project*, 1. *The Fossil Hominids and an Introduction to their Context, 1968–1974*. Oxford, Clarendon.

Leakey, R. E. & Walker, A. 1976. *Australopithecus, Homo erectus* and the single species hypothesis. *Nature*, 261:572–4.

— 1985. Further hominids from the Plio-Pleistocene of Koobi Fora, Kenya. *American Journal of Physical Anthropology*, 67:135–63.

Leakey, R. E. & Wood, B. A. 1973. New evidence of the genus *Homo* from East Rudolf, Kenya, II. *American Journal of Physical Anthropology*, 39: 355–63.

Le Gros Clark, W. E. 1964. *The Fossil Evidence for Human Evolution*. Chicago, University of Chicago Press.

Leinders, J. J. M., Aziz, F., Sondaar, P. Y. & de Vos, J. 1985. The age of the hominid-bearing deposits of Java: state of the art. *Geologie en Mijnbouw*, 64:167–73.

Lestrel, P. E. 1976. Hominid brain size versus time: revised regression estimates. *Journal of Human Evolution*, 5:207–12.

Liu, Z. 1985. Sequence of sediments at Locality 1 in Zhoukoudian and correlation with loess stratigraphy in northern China and with the chronology of deep-sea cores. *Quaternary Research*, 23:139–53.

Lovejoy, C. O. 1970. The taxonomic status of the '*Meganthropus*' mandibular fragments from the Djetis Beds of Java. *Man*, 5:228–36.

Macintosh, N. W. G. & Larnach, S. L. 1972. The persistence of *Homo erectus* traits in Australian aboriginal crania. *Archaeology and Physical Anthropology in Oceania*, 7:1–7.

Maier, W. & Nkini, A. 1984. Olduvai Hominid 9: new results of investigation. *Courier Forschungsinstitut Senckenberg*, 69:123–30.

Martin, R. 1928. *Lehrbuch der Anthropologie*. Jena, Gustav Fischer.

Martin, R. D. 1983. Human brain evolution in an ecological context. 52nd James Arthur Lecture on the Evolution of the Human Brain. New York, American Museum of Natural History.

Matsu'ura, S. 1982. A chronological framing for the Sangiran hominids: fundamental study by the fluorine dating method. *Bulletin of the National Science Museum, Tokyo*, 8:1–53.

McDougall, I. 1981. ^{40}Ar/^{39}Ar age spectra from the KBS Tuff, Koobi Fora Formation. *Nature*, 294:120–4.

— 1985. K–Ar and ^{40}Ar/^{39}Ar dating of the hominid-bearing Pliocene–Pleistocene sequence at Koobi Fora, Lake Turkana, northern Kenya. *Geological Society of America Bulletin*, 96:159–75.

McDougall, I., Davies, T., Maier, R. & Rudowski, R. 1985. Age of the Okote Tuff Complex at Koobi Fora, Kenya. *Nature*, 316:792–4.

McDougall, I., Maier, R., Sutherland-Hawkes, P. & Gleadow, A. J. W. 1980. K–Ar age estimate for the KBS Tuff, East Turkana, Kenya. *Nature*, 284:230–4.

Mturi, A. A. 1976. New hominid from Lake Ndutu, Tanzania. *Nature*, 262: 484–5.

Ninkovich, D. & Burckle, L. 1978. Absolute age of the hominid-bearing beds in eastern Java. *Nature*, 275:306–8.

Nishimura, S., Thio, K. & Hehuwat, F. 1980. Fission-track ages of the tuffs of the Pucangan and Kabuh formations, and the tektite at Sangiran, central Java. In *Physical Geology of Indonesian Island Arcs*, ed. S. Nishimura, pp. 72–80. Kyoto, Kyoto University Press.

Oakley, K. P., Campbell, B. G. & Molleson, T. I. 1975. *Catalogue of Fossil Hominids*. London, British Museum (Natural History).

Olson, T. R. 1978. Hominid phylogenetics and the existence of *Homo* in Member 1 of the Swartkrans Formation, South Africa. *Journal of Human Evolution*, 7:159–78.

Oppenoorth, W. F. F. 1932. Ein neuer diluvialer Urmensch von Java. *Natur und Museum* (Frankfurt), 62:269–79.

Pilbeam, D. R & Gould, S. J. 1974. Size and scaling in human evolution. *Science*, 186:892–901.

Pope, G. G. 1983. Evidence on the age of the Asian Hominidae. *Proceedings of the National Academy of Sciences*, 80:4988–92.

— 1988. Recent advances in Far Eastern paleoanthropology. *Annual Review of Anthropology*, 17:43–77.

Rightmire, G. P. 1975. New studies of post-Pleistocene human skeletal remains from the Rift Valley, Kenya. *American Journal of Physical Anthropology*, 42:351–69.

— 1976. Relationships of Middle and Upper Pleistocene hominids from sub-Saharan Africa. *Nature*, 260:238–40.

— 1979. Cranial remains of *Homo erectus* from Beds II and IV, Olduvai Gorge, Tanzania. *American Journal of Physical Anthropology*, 51:99–115.

— 1980. Middle Pleistocene hominids from Olduvai Gorge, northern Tanzania. *American Journal of Physical Anthropology*, 53:225–41.

— 1981. Patterns in the evolution of *Homo erectus*. *Paleobiology*, 7:241–6.

— 1983. The Lake Ndutu cranium and early *Homo sapiens* in Africa. *American Journal of Physical Anthropology*, 61:245–54.

— 1985. The tempo of change in the evolution of mid-Pleistocene *Homo*. In *Ancestors: The Hard Evidence*, ed. E. Delson, pp. 255–64. New York, Liss.

— 1986a. Body size and encephalization in *Homo erectus*. *Anthropos* (Brno), 23:139–50.

— 1986b. Species recognition and *Homo erectus*. *Journal of Human Evolution*, 15:823–6.

— 1986c. Stasis in *Homo erectus* defended. *Paleobiology*, 12:324–5.

Rose, M. D. 1984. A hominine hip bone, KNM-ER 3228, from east Lake Turkana, Kenya. *American Journal of Physical Anthropology*, 63:371–8.

Saban, R. 1977. The place of Rabat man (Kébibat, Morocco) in human evolution. *Current Anthropology*, **18**:518–24.

Santa Luca, A. P. 1978. A reexamination of presumed Neanderthal-like fossils. *Journal of Human Evolution*, **7**:619–36.

— 1980. *The Ngandong Fossil Hominids: A Comparative Study of a Far Eastern* Homo erectus *Group*. New Haven, Yale University, Department of Anthropology.

Sartono, S. 1975. Implications arising from *Pithecanthropus VIII*. In *Paleoanthropology. Morphology and Paleoecology*, ed. R. H. Tuttle, pp. 327–60. The Hague, Mouton.

Sausse, F. 1975. La mandibule atlanthropienne de la carrière Thomas I (Casablanca). *L'Anthropologie*, **79**:81–112.

Schaeffer, B., Hecht, M. K. & Eldredge, N. 1972. Paleontology and phylogeny. *Evolutionary Biology*, **6**:31–46.

Semah, F. 1982. Chronostratigraphie et paléomagnétisme du Plio-Pléistocène de Java. Application à l'age des sites à pithecanthropes. In *L'Homo erectus et la Place de l'Homme de Tautavel Parmi les Hominidés Fossiles*, ed. M. -A. de Lumley, pp. 542–58. Nice, CNRS.

— 1984. The Sangiran dome in the Javanese Plio-Pleistocene chronology. *Courier Forschungsinstitut Senckenberg*, **69**:245–52.

Shimizu, Y., Mubroto, B., Siagian, H. & Untung, M. 1985. A paleomagnetic study in the Sangiran area. In *Quaternary Geology of the Hominid Fossil Bearing Formations in Java*, eds. N. Watanabe & D. Kadar, pp. 275–307. Bandung, Geological Research and Development Centre.

Simpson, G. G. 1961. *Principles of Animal Taxonomy*. New York, Columbia University Press.

Smith, F. H. 1978. Evolutionary significance of the mandibular foramen area in Neanderthals. *American Journal of Physical Anthropology*, **48**:523–32.

Smith, R. J. 1983. The mandibular corpus of female primates: taxonomic, dietary, and allometric correlates of interspecific variations in size and shape. *American Journal of Physical Anthopology*, **61**:315–30.

Sondaar, P. Y. 1984. Faunal evolution and the mammalian biostratigraphy of Java. *Courier Forschungsinstitut Senckenberg*, **69**:219–35.

Stringer, C. B. 1981. The dating of European Middle Pleistocene hominids and the existence of *Homo erectus* in Europe. *Anthropologie* (Brno), **19**: 3–14.

— 1983. Some further notes on the morphology and dating of the Petralona hominid. *Journal of Human Evolution*, **12**:731–42.

— 1984. The definition of *Homo erectus* and the existence of the species in Africa and Europe. *Courier Forschungsinstitut Senckenberg*, **69**:131–43.

— 1985. Middle Pleistocene hominid variability and the origin of Late Pleistocene humans. In *Ancestors: The Hard Evidence*, ed. E. Delson, pp. 289–95.

— 1986a. The credibility of *Homo habilis*. In *Major Topics in Primate and Human Evolution*, eds. B. Wood, L. Martin & P. Andrews, pp. 266–94. Cambridge, Cambridge University Press.

— 1986b. An archaic character in the Broken Hill innominate E. 719. *American Journal of Physical Anthropology*, 71:115–20.

— 1987. A numerical cladistic analysis for the genus *Homo*. *Journal of Human Evolution*, 16:135–46.

Stringer, C. B., Howell, F. C. & Melentis, J. K. 1979. The significance of the fossil hominid skull from Petralona, Greece. *Journal of Archaeological Science*, 6:235–53.

Suzuki, M., Wikarno, Budisantoso, Saefudin, I. & Itihara, M. 1985. Fission track ages of pumice tuff, tuff layers and javites of hominid fossil bearing formations in Sangiran area, central Java. In *Quaternary Geology of the Hominid Fossil Bearing Formations in Java*, eds. N. Watanbe & D. Kadar, pp. 309–57. Bandung, Geological Research and Development Centre.

Tallon, P. W. J. 1978. Geological setting of the hominid fossils and Acheulian artifacts from the Kapthurin Formation, Baringo District, Kenya. In *Geological Background to Fossil Man*, ed. W. W. Bishop, pp. 361–73. Edinburgh, Scottish Academic Press.

Tattersall, I. 1986. Species recognition in human paleontology. *Journal of Human Evolution*, 15:165–76.

Thorne, A. & Wolpoff, M. H. 1981. Regional continuity in Australasian Pleistocene hominid evolution. *American Journal of Physical Anthropology*, 55:337–49.

Tobias, P. V. 1967. *Olduvai Gorge, 2. The Cranium and Maxillary Dentition of Australopithecus (Zinjanthropus) boisei*. Cambridge, Cambridge University Press.

— 1968. Middle and early Upper Pleistocene members of the genus *Homo* in Africa. In *Evolution und Hominisation*, ed. G. Kurth, pp. 176–94. Stuttgart, Gustav Fischer Verlag.

— 1971a. Human skeletal remains from the Cave of Hearths, Makapansgat, northern Transvaal. *American Journal of Physical Anthropology*, 34:335–67.

— 1971b. *The Brain in Hominid Evolution*. New York, Columbia University Press.

— 1975. Brain evolution in the Hominoidea. In *Primate Functional Morphology and Evolution*, ed. R. H. Tuttle, pp. 353–92. The Hague, Mouton.

— 1978. The earliest Transvaal members of the genus *Homo* with another look at some problems of hominid taxonomy and systematics. *Zeitschrift für Morphologie und Anthropologie*, 69:225–65.

— 1980. A survey and synthesis of the African hominids of the late Tertiary and early Quaternary periods. In *Current Argument on Early Man*, ed. L. -K. Königsson, pp. 86–113. Oxford, Pergamon.

— 1982. The antiquity of man: human evolution. In *Human Genetics*, A. *The Unfolding Genome*, eds. B. Bonné-Tamir, T. Cohen & R. M. Goodman, pp. 195–214. New York, Liss.

Tobias, P. V. & von Koenigswald, G. H. R. 1964. A comparison between the

Olduvai hominines and those of Java and some implications for hominid phylogeny. *Nature*, 204:515–18.

Trinkaus, E. 1984. Does KNM-ER 1481a establish *Homo erectus* at 2.0 myr BP? *American Journal of Physical Anthropology*, 64: 137–9.

Van Noten, F. 1983. News from Kenya. *Antiquity*, July:139–40.

von Koenigswald, G. H. R. 1934. Zur Stratigraphie des Javanischen Pleisto-cän. *De Ingenieur in Nederlandsch-Indie*, 1:185–201.

— 1935. Die fossilen Säugetierfaunen Javas. *Proceedings of the Koninklijke Nederlandse Akademie van Wetenschappen, Amsterdam*, 38:188–98.

— 1950. Fossil hominids from the Lower Pleistocene of Java. *International Geological Congress. Report of the Eighteenth Session, Great Britain*, 1948, Part IX, pp. 59–61.

— 1958. Der Solo-Mensch von Java: ein tropisher Neanderthaler. In *Hundert Jahre Neanderthaler*, ed. G. H. R. von Koenigswald, pp. 21–31. Utrecht, Kemink en Zoon.

— 1962. *The Evolution of Man*. Ann Arbor, University of Michigan Press.

Walker, A. 1981. The Koobi Fora hominids and their bearing on the origins of the genus *Homo*. In *Homo erectus. Papers in Honor of Davidson Black*, eds. B. A. Sigmon & J. S. Cybulski, pp. 193–215. Toronto, University of Toronto Press.

Walker, A. & Leakey, R. E. 1978. The hominids of East Turkana. *Scientific American*, 239:54–66.

Walker, A., Zimmerman, M. R. & Leakey, R. E. 1982. A possible case of hypervitaminosis A in *Homo erectus*. *Nature*, 296:248–50.

Weidenreich, F. 1936. The mandibles of *Sinanthropus pekinensis*: a comparative study. *Palaeontologia Sinica*, Series D, 7:1–162.

— 1937. The dentition of *Sinanthropus pekinensis*: a comparative odontography of the hominids. *Palaeontologia Sinica*, New Series D, 1:1–180.

— 1941. The extremity bones of *Sinanthropus pekinensis*. *Palaeontolgia Sinica*, New Series D, 5:1–150.

— 1943. The skull of *Sinanthropus pekinensis*: a comparative study of a primitive hominid skull. *Palaeontologia Sinica*, New Series D, 10:1–484.

— 1945. Giant early man from Java and South China. *Anthropological Papers of the American Museum of Natural History*, 40:1–134.

— 1951. Morphology of Solo man. *Anthropological Papers of the American Museum of Natural History*, 43:205–90.

White, T. D. 1977. The anterior mandibular corpus of early African Hominidae: functional significance of shape and size. Ph.D. thesis, University of Michigan, Ann Arbor.

White, T. D. & Harris, J. M. 1977. Suid evolution and correlation of African hominid localities. *Science*, 198:13–21.

White, T. D. & Johanson, D. C. 1982. Pliocene hominid mandibles from the Hadar Formation, Ethiopia: 1974–1977 collections. *American Journal of Physical Anthropology*, 57:501–44.

White, T. D., Johanson, D. C. & Kimbel, W. H. 1981. *Australopithecus africanus*. Its phyletic position reconsidered. *South African Journal of Science*, 77:445–70.

Wiley, E. O. 1978. The evolutionary species concept reconsidered. *Systematic Zoology*, 27:17–26.

Williamson, P. G. 1982. Molluscan biostratigraphy of the Koobi Fora hominid-bearing deposits. *Nature*, 295:140–2.

Wind, J. 1984. Computerized x-ray tomography of fossil hominid skulls. *American Journal of Physical Anthropology*, 63:265–82.

Wolpoff, M. H. 1980a. *Paleoanthropology*. New York, Knopf.

— 1980b. Cranial remains of Middle Pleistocene European hominids. *Journal of Human Evolution*, 9:339–58.

— 1982. The Arago dental sample in the context of hominid dental evolution. In *L'Homo erectus et la Place de l'Homme de Tautavel Parmi les Hominidés Fossiles*, ed. M. -A de Lumley, pp. 389–410. Nice, CNRS.

— 1984. Evolution in *Homo erectus*: the question of stasis. *Paleobiology*, 10: 389–406.

Wolpoff, M. H., Wu, X. Z. & Thorne, A. 1984. Modern *Homo sapiens* origins: a general theory of hominid evolution involving the fossil evidence from East Asia. In *The Origins of Modern Humans: A World Survey of the Fossil Evidence*, eds. F. Smith & F. Spencer, pp. 411–83. New York, Liss.

Woo, J. K. 1964. Mandibles of *Sinanthropus lantianensis*. *Current Anthropology*, 5:98–101.

— 1966. The skull of Lantian man. *Current Anthropology*, 7:83–6.

Woo, J. K. & Chao, T. K. 1959. New discovery of *Sinanthropus* mandible from Choukoutien. *Vertebrata Palasiatica*, 3:169–72.

Wood, B. A. 1976. Remains attributable to *Homo* in the East Rudolf succession. In *Earliest Man and Environments in the Lake Rudolf Basin*, eds. Y. Coppens, F. C. Howell, G. Ll. Isaac & R. E. Leakey, pp. 490–506. Chicago, University of Chicago Press.

— 1984. The origin of *Homo erectus*. *Courier Forschungsinstitut Senckenberg*, 69:99–111.

— 1985. Early *Homo* in Kenya, and its systematic relationships. In *Ancestors: The Hard Evidence*, ed. E. Delson, pp. 206–14. New York, Liss.

Wood, B. A. & Van Noten, F. L. 1986. Preliminary observations on the BK 8518 mandible from Baringo, Kenya. *American Journal of Physical Anthropology*, 69:117–27.

Wu, R. 1985. New Chinese *Homo erectus* and recent work at Zhoukoudian. In *Ancestors: The Hard Evidence*, ed. E. Delson, pp. 245–8. New York, Liss.

Wu, R. & Dong, X. 1982. Preliminary study of *Homo erectus* remains from Hexian, Anhui. *Acta Anthropologica Sinica*, 1:2–13.

Wu, R. & Lin, S. 1983. Peking man. *Scientific American*, 248:86–94.

AUTHOR INDEX

SUBJECT INDEX